KV-372-085

Global Sport-for-Development

Global Culture and Sport Series
Series Standing Order ISBN 978–0–230–57818–0 (**Hardback**) 978–0–230–57819–7
(**Paperback**)
(*outside North America only*)

You can receive future titles in this series as they are published by placing a standing order.
Please contact your bookseller or, in case of difficulty, write to us at the address below with
your name and address, the title of the series and one of the ISBNs quoted above.

Customer Services Department, Macmillan Distribution Ltd, Houndmills, Basingstoke,
Hampshire RG21 6XS, England

Global Sport-for-Development
Critical Perspectives

Edited by

Nico Schulenkorf
University of Technology, Sydney, Australia

and

Daryl Adair
University of Technology, Sydney, Australia

First published 2014 by
PALGRAVE MACMILLAN

Palgrave Macmillan in the UK is an imprint of Macmillan Publishers Limited,
registered in England, company number 785998, of Houndmills, Basingstoke,
Hampshire RG21 6XS.

Palgrave Macmillan in the US is a division of St Martin's Press LLC,
175 Fifth Avenue, New York, NY 10010.

Palgrave Macmillan is the global academic imprint of the above companies
and has companies and representatives throughout the world.

Palgrave® and Macmillan® are registered trademarks in the United States,
the United Kingdom, Europe and other countries

ISBN: 978–1–137–28962–9

This book is printed on paper suitable for recycling and made from fully
managed and sustained forest sources. Logging, pulping and manufacturing
processes are expected to conform to the environmental regulations of the
country of origin.

A catalogue record for this book is available from the British Library.

A catalog record for this book is available from the Library of Congress.

Contents

Part IV   Conclusions

List of Illustrations

Figures

Tables

Acknowledgements

This book was conceived with the assistance of several people. From within the global community of sport-for-development scholars, we received widespread encouragement and support for the book, with several colleagues engaged as contributors. The international expertise and practical experiences of these authors have provided profound insights into different sport-for-development programmes with specific social, cultural, psychological and health related foci. Thank you for sharing your wisdom and for taking time to write, edit and amend the chapters.

As editors, we were conscious of the need to make the material research driven, irrespective of whether the chapter was about theory or practice. Each of the contributing authors has honoured our intent; we thank them for their collegiality and enthusiasm in achieving that research goal. We also wanted to ensure the overall quality of the book and so subjected the chapters to strenuous editorial feedback. This approach has been important to ensure that the book has coherence and continuity in the development of the concepts and issues presented.

Colleagues at the University of Technology, Sydney, were also helpful by providing encouragement: Professor Tracy Taylor, Deputy Dean of the UTS Business School, and Associate Professor Antoine Hermens, Head of the Management Discipline Group, are great supporters of sport management research and sport-for-development scholarship within that sub-discipline.

We also wish to acknowledge the encouragement and professionalism of the Palgrave Macmillan editorial team: Philippa Grand (Head of Social Sciences), Andrew James (Assistant Editor) and Naomi Robinson (Editorial Assistant). Finally, and perhaps most importantly, thanks to Anja, Cheryl and Kane, who cheered from the sidelines as this book evolved.

Notes on Contributors

Daryl Adair is Associate Professor of Sport Management at UTS. His research focuses on sport and the challenges of, as well as the opportunities for, ethnocultural diversity. He has published on the intersection of sport with 'race', ethnicity, indigeneity, and masculinity. In recent years he has edited several special issues of journals around the theme of sport and diversity: *Australian Aboriginal Studies* (2009), *Sporting Traditions* (2009), *International Review for the Sociology of Sport* (2010), *Sport Management Review* (2010), *Cosmopolitan Civil Societies* (2010), *and Sport in Society* (2011). In recent years, Daryl has also edited a number of books on sport and diversity: *Sport, Race and Ethnicity: Narratives of Difference and Diversity* (2011); *Sport, Race, Ethnicity and Identity: Building Global Understanding* (with Taylor and Francis, 2012); *Managing the Olympic Games* (with Stephen Frawley, 2013); and *Embodied Masculinities in Global Sport* (with Jorge Knijnik, in press).

Gary Armstrong is Reader in the School of Sport and Education, Brunel University, UK. His research into sports-related matters has produced the following publications: *Football Hooligans*: *Knowing the Score* (1998), *Blade Runners: Lives in Football* (1999) and *Sheffield United FC: The Biography* (2007). He has co-edited with Richard Giulianotti, *Entering the Field, New Perspectives in World Football* (1997), *Football Cultures and Identities* (2000), *Fear and Loathing in World Football* (2001) and *Football in Africa: Conflict, Conciliation and Community* (2003). A 2009 book, co-authored with Jon Mitchell, titled *Local and Global Football* was followed in 2010 by the co-authored (with Alberto Testa) *Football, Fascism and Fandom: The UltraS of Italian Football*. His recent book published in February 2011 (co-authored with Pete Fussey, John Coaffee and Dick Hobbs) titled *Securing and Sustaining the 2012 Olympic City* examines the policing and security implications that surround London's hosting of the 2012 Olympic Games.

Fred Coalter is Professor of Sports Policy at Leeds Metropolitan University and was previously a Professor of Sports Policy at the University of Stirling. His research interests relate to sport's claimed contributions to various aspects of social policy. His published work includes *A Wider Social Role for Sport: Who's Keeping the Score?* (2007), *Sport-in-Development: A Monitoring and Evaluation Manual* (2006),

Sport-for-Development Impact Study (2010) – a major study based on fieldwork in Uganda, Tanzania, South Africa, Mumbai and Calcutta – and *Sport-for-Development: What Game Are We Playing?* (2013). Between 2004 and 2012 he was also responsible for compiling Sport England/UK Sport's on-line research-based *Value of Sport Monitor*. He is a member of the Scientific Advisory Board of the Swiss Academy Development, a board member of the Mathare Youth Sport Association's Leadership Academy, an M&E consultant to Magic Bus (India) and recently was a member of the UK-based Centre for Social Justice's working group on sport and social regeneration.

Simon C. Darnell a Lecturer in Sport in the School of Applied Social Sciences at Durham University, Durham, UK. Prior to this, he completed a post-doctoral research fellowship in the Department of International Development Studies at Dalhousie University, Canada. His recent research has focused on the social and political implications of mobilising sport to meet various international development goals. He is the author of *Sport for Development and Peace: A Critical Sociology* (2012). His work has also appeared in *Progress in Development Studies*, *Development in Practice*, the *Sociology of Sport Journal* and the *International Journal of Sport Policy and Politics*. He is currently researching the international development implications of Cuban sport policy (with Robert Huish) and exploring the connections between contemporary sport and various conceptualisations of 'global citizenship'.

Charlie Foster holds honorary academic posts at the Institutes of Human Sciences at the University of Oxford and University of Durham. He is Adjunct Professor at the University of Canberra and an Associate Researcher at the University of Newcastle, Australia. He joined the British Heart Foundation Health Promotion Research Group in October 1998 after working in health promotion for five years. He has extensive experience of lecturing, teaching and training principles and methods of evaluation, health behaviour change and health promotion. His research aims to improve the quality of the evidence base for basic epidemiology, measurement, correlates, interventions and policy for physical activity. He is passionate about sport-for-development and wants to improve the science and practice of this field. He is an academic board member for the *Journal of Sport for Development*.

Richard Giulianotti is Professor of Sociology at Loughborough University, and Visiting Professor at Telemark University College, Norway. His main research interests are in the fields of sport, development, peace, globalisation, crime and deviance, and research methods.

His books include *Football: A Sociology of the Global Game* (1999), *Sport: A Critical Sociology* (2005), *Ethics, Money and Sport* (2007; with Adrian J. Walsh) and *Globalization and Football* (2009; with Roland Robertson). He has recently acted as guest editor of special issues of the leading journals *Global Networks* (Vol. 7, No. 2, 2007), *Urban Studies* (Vol. 48, No. 15, 2011), and *British Journal of Sociology* (Vol. 63, No. 2, 2012). His recent and current research includes ESRC grant awards to investigate young people and sport-based interventions (with Laura Kelly), police and community relations at the London 2012 Olympics (with Gary Armstrong, Gavin Hales and Dick Hobbs), football and globalization (with Roland Robertson), European Commission funding for a project on sport and social inclusion (with various European partners), and European Union (FP7) funding to investigate football fandom and reflexivity (with Dino Numerato).

Lyndsay M.C. Hayhurst is a Social Sciences and Humanities Research Council (Canada) and Sport Canada postdoctoral fellow in the Institute of Women's Studies and School of Human Kinetics at the University of Ottawa, Canada. Her research interests include sport for development and peace; gender and development; cultural studies of girlhood; postcolonial feminist theory; indigenous feminism; global governance; corporate social responsibility and feminist physical cultural studies. Lyndsay's publications have appeared in *Third World Quarterly*, *Sociology of Sport Journal* and *Gender, Place and Culture*. Currently, she is conducting comparative research on corporate-funded, girl-focused Aboriginal sport, gender and development programmes in Canada and Australia.

Ruth Jeanes is Senior Lecturer in Sports Coaching and Community Development within the Faculty of Education at Monash University. Ruth is a social scientist whose research interests focus on the use of sport and recreation as a community development resource, particularly to address social exclusion amongst acutely marginalised groups. Recent publications include with T. Kay (2012) 'Conducting Research with Young People in the Global South', in K. te Reile and R. Brooks (eds) *Negotiating Ethical Challenges in Youth Research,* and with R. Spaaij (2012) 'Education for Social Change: A Freirean Critique of Sport for Development and Peace', *Physical Education and Sport Pedagogy.* She is currently working on a co-authored book with Ramon Spaaij and Jonathan Magee, *Sport and Social Exclusion in a Global Society* to be published in 2014.

Elizabeth Kath is a Vice Chancellor's Research Fellow with the School of Global, Urban and Social Studies at RMIT University, Co-Director of Global Reconciliation, and Honorary Research Fellow with the UN

Global Compact Cities Programme in relation to the programme's social inclusion project in Porto Alegre, Brazil. Her academic work is located within global studies and has been interdisciplinary, spanning political science, development and public health. This has included a major study of the social and political dimensions of Cuba's public health system, specifically its Maternal-Infant Health programme, for which she spent nine months conducting field research in Havana. She has a regional interest in Latin America and the Caribbean (particularly Cuba, Brazil and Mexico), including an emerging interest in Australia's relationship with the region. She teaches the course 'Culture and Politics in Latin America' at RMIT University. Her thematic areas of interest include reconciliation, social inclusion, health and wellbeing.

Zachary Kaufman is a PhD Candidate in Epidemiology at the London School of Hygiene and Tropical Medicine. He has four years of research/ evaluation experience in Southern Africa and the Caribbean, largely focused on sport-based HIV prevention. He has presented at eight international conferences and published articles in *AIDS Care* and *AIDS and Behavior*. Zak serves as the Editor of the *Journal of Sport for Development*, the Director of two randomised controlled trials in South Africa and Zimbabwe, and is the co-founder of Vera Solutions, a social enterprise dedicated to improving the data systems of social impact organisations. Zak holds an MSc in Epidemiology, graduated *Summa Cum Laude* from Dartmouth College, and has been honored as a Marshall Scholar, Truman Scholar and All-USA First Academic Team member.

John Lambert is Senior Lecturer in Physical Education and Sports Coaching at the University of Brighton. He is co-editor of *Values in Youth Sport and Physical Education* which is due to be published by in 2013. His research centres on the theory and practice of teaching values through sport and he is co-ordinator of coaching and coach education for Football for Peace. A UEFA A Licence coach and specialist in games teaching methodologies, he is an advocate of the TGFU pedagogical model. As Visiting Lecturer at the Deutsche Sporthochschule, Cologne, he contributes to their undergraduate games programme. He is also a member of the match analysis and talent identification department of a Premier League football club.

Jonathan Magee is Senior Lecturer in the School of Sport, Tourism and the Outdoors at the University of Central Lancashire, England, UK. He teaches across various sports-related courses and publishes on the socio-cultural study of sport with particular focus on sports labour migration, the football business, homelessness and disability. His most recent publications include '"Football's Coming Home": A Critical Evaluation of the Homeless World Cup as an Intervention to Combat Social Exclusion' (with R. Jeanes, 2013, *International Review for the Sociology of Sport*. Vol. 48, No. 1, pp. 3–19) and '"Can we play on the swings and roundabouts?": Creating inclusive play spaces for disabled young people and their families' (with R. Jeanes, 2012, *Leisure Studies*, Vol. 31, No. 2, pp. 193–210). Jonathan has also co-edited three books, including *The Bountiful Game: Football Identities and Finance* (2005).

Gabriela Moore graduated from the University of Virginia in May, 2013 with her undergraduate degree in Sociology and Latin American Studies. In July of 2013 she travelled to Joinville, Brazil, where she taught English to high school-aged students in the National Learning Service for Industry (SENAI) system as a Global Leaders Fellow. Previously she served as a Sport-for-Development intern at Partners of the Americas, where she worked on various projects with the Youth Sports Management Exchange and the "A Ganar" Youth Workforce Development programme during the summers of 2011–2013. Gabriela's future research and career interests include food and nutrition as they relate to international development and public policy.

Oscar Mwaanga is a Sport for Development and Peace social entrepreneur, academic and indigenous Sub-Saharan African activist. He has focused his work around sport as a tool for promoting HIV/AIDS education and empowerment of marginalised groups in Sub-Saharan Africa (SSA) and recently in the south of England. Oscar is recognised as one of the indigenous leaders of the Sub-Saharan African SDP movement of the last decade especially after founding EduSport Foundation and the international Kicking AIDS Out network. As an academic, Oscar is Senior Lecturer and course leader of the MA Sport and Development in the Faculty of Sport, Business and Enterprise at Southampton Solent University in the UK. His broad area of teaching and research expertise is the sociology of sport and development.

Kabanda Mwansa has considerable experience in teaching sport and Physical Education (PE). He has worked in this field for over 15 years in both the Global South and the Global North. He is an unsung expert in Sport for Development and Peace (SDP), particularly the use of sport and PE as a metaphor for the social development of young people in underserved communities. He is the co-founder of the EduSport Foundation and a vital backroom player in pioneering the renowned Kicking Aids Out! and the Go-Sisters Concepts. He is one of the few academics and practitioners from the Global South advocating to narrow the widening disparities between the Global North and the South at the core of SDP agenda, an activist of alternative discourse. Kabanda holds a master's in International Education and Development from Oslo University College and a bachelor's in Sports Science from the Norwegian School of Sport Science among other credentials.

Justin Richards completed his doctorate in Public Health at the University of Oxford in 2011. His research focused on the physical and mental health impacts of sport-for-development programmes in post-conflict settings. This included a case study in Northern Uganda where he was the Field Programme Manager for the Gum Marom Kids League. He is currently employed as a researcher leading a series of *Cochrane Reviews* that assess the effectiveness of different interventions for promoting physical activity. He is also the co-founder and deputy editor for the *Journal of Sport for Development*. His academic background includes a Bachelor of Physiotherapy at the University of Melbourne; in 2007 he completed an MSc in Science and Medicine of Athletic Performance at the University of Oxford. He has also enjoyed internships with the Global Strategy on Diet, Physical Activity and Health team at the WHO and the Physical Education and Sport Section of UNESCO.

Brooke Page Rosenbauer is the Senior Technical Coordinator for Sport-for-Development at Partners of the Americas where she coordinates the 'A Ganar' youth workforce development programme, which uses a sport-based employability curriculum to fight youth unemployment in Latin America and the Caribbean. Previously, she served as the Director of the Lose the Shoes campaign for Grassroot Soccer's HIV/AIDS awareness and prevention programme and has over ten years of youth coaching experience. Brooke is the 2008 Harry S. Truman Scholar for the state of Vermont and holds a Master of Science in International Health Policy and Management from the Heller School of Social Policy and Management at Brandeis University in Boston, Massachusetts. Brooke's main research and career interests include youth and health, specifically the use of sport and physical activity in preventing chronic disease.

Grant Schofield is the Director of the Human Potential Centre at AUT University in Auckland, New Zealand. His research and teaching interests are in chronic disease prevention especially reducing the risk and eventual mortality and morbidity from obesity, cardiovascular disease and diabetes. To complement his work in public health and physical health he is the chair of the Agencies for Nutrition Action Scientific Committee (ANA is the umbrella group who represents the NGOs in non-communicable diseases (NCD) prevention, the Cancer Society, Heart Foundation,

Diabetes NZ, Stroke Foundation) and he is a member of the Health Research Council's Public Health committee of New Zealand. Grant is a consultant to the World Health Organisation (South Pacific) completing several projects in non-communicable disease prevention in Vanuatu, Tuvalu, Tonga and Kiribati.

Nico Schulenkorf is Senior Lecturer for Sport Management at the University of Technology, Sydney (UTS). His research focuses on the social, cultural, psychological and health-related outcomes of sport and event projects. He is particularly interested in the role sport can play in contributing to social development within and between disadvantaged communities. For several years, Nico has been involved in sport-for-development programmes in countries such as Sri Lanka, Israel and the Pacific Islands. He has been working with local and international NGOs, government agencies, sport associations and ministries in developing capacities to design, implement, monitor and evaluate development projects. Nico has published his research in the leading sport management and sociology journals, including *Journal of Sport Management, Sport Management Review* and the *International Review for the Sociology of Sport*. He is Co-Founder and Deputy Editor of the *Journal of Sport for Development*.

Katja Siefken joined AUT University, Centre for Physical Activity and Nutrition, Auckland, New Zealand, in 2009 as a doctoral researcher and consultant for the World Health Organization South Pacific Office (WHO SP). Previous consultancy roles included work for the Fiji School of Medicine (FSM) and at WHO SP. Katja's research focuses on health promotion in low- and middle- income countries, seeking to prevent and reduce noncommunicable diseases through lifestyle interventions and policy development. Her most recent WHO funded projects investigate workplace health initiatives in Tuvalu, Kiribati, Tonga and Vanuatu. Katja completed her Doctoral Studies at AUT in 2013; previous academic qualifications include a Masters of Science degree in Health Promotion from the University of Kansas (USA) and an MA-equivalent in Physical Activity, Educational Sciences and Biology from the University of Hamburg (Germany). Sciences and Biology from Hamburg University (Germany).

John Sugden is Professor of the Sociology of Sport and Director of the Research and Graduate Centre in the University of Brighton's School of Sport and Service Management where he has been since 1996. He has researched and written widely around topics concerned with the politics and sociology of sport. He is also well known for his work on sport in divided societies, his studies of the world governing body for football, FIFA, and for his investigative research into football's underground economy. Professor Sugden is the Director of the University of Brighton's flagship international community relations and coexistence programme, Football for Peace International. He is author of *Sport and Peace Building in Divided Societies: Playing with the Enemy* (2013).

Nanko G. van Buuren is the founder and director of the Brazilian Institute for Innovations in Social Health (IBISS). Along with a team of IBISS staff, he has worked for over 20 years to build and support reconciliation processes and the building of urban peace in the deeply divided context of Rio de Janeiro. IBISS works in more than fifty of the city's most violent favelas (shantytowns) to develop long-term, community-engaged responses to social conflict, organised crime, poverty and the loss of hope. He has managed to establish working relationships with both the government and dozens of favela communities and to work simultaneously in territories controlled by cartels at war with one another. The ongoing work of IBISS includes social and psychological support, health education, informal education, vocational training, community organisation, conflict mediation and advocacy and the organisation has improved the lives of many Brazilians. IBISS uses sports and culture as tool for development. Overall the organisation's efforts strive towards establishing relationships between the favela communities and the broader society, and between communities divided from each other by conflict. Nanko was the recipient of the Desmond Tutu Reconciliation Award in 2011. He is also board member of the United Cultures for Development Network.

James Wallis is Senior Lecturer in the School of Sport and Service Management at the University of Brighton, England. He is course leader of the Sport Coaching degree and specialises in the teaching of physical education and sport pedagogy with a particular emphasis on different coaching methodologies and on psychological aspects of coaching practice. His current research interests are in learning theories with particular emphasis on the role played by emotion in learning and how practitioners can adapt their practice for greater impact. James was involved in the development and management of Football for Peace for eight years as coach educator and project leader. He co-edited the 2007 text *'Football for Peace? The Challenges of Using Sport for Co-Existence in Israel'*. Current applied work includes teacher and coach education in several European universities.

Part I

Global Sport-for-Development: Critical Perspectives

1
Sport-for-Development: The Emergence and Growth of a New Genre

Nico Schulenkorf and Daryl Adair

Over the last decade, the field of sport-for-development (S4D) has received significant attention from both practitioners and academics around the world. Where at the beginning of the 21st century it was difficult to find projects that used sport as a strategic vehicle for positive social, health and economic change, the number of S4D initiatives that aim to make a difference in disadvantaged communities has since grown substantially. One explanation for this escalation is the strong political support for a 'movement' that combines sport associations, aid agencies, development bodies, sponsoring organisations and non-governmental organisations (NGOs) under a single umbrella.

The creation of the United Nations Office for Sport for Development and Peace (UNOSDP) in 2001 was a significant step towards official recognition and legitimacy for S4D. Subsequent assertions, such as the Magglingen Declaration in 2003 and the United Nation's International Year of Sport and Physical Education in 2005, further raised awareness of S4D as a philosophy underpinning aspirations for positive change. Overall, the increased recognition of potential social, health and economic values of S4D quickly led to the establishment of thousands of local and international development projects supported and/or implemented by sport associations, aid agencies and funding bodies. Concurrently, a number of mainstream NGOs have incorporated sport as a vehicle through which to pursue their own development objectives.

Fundamentally, S4D aims to engage people from disadvantaged communities in physical activity projects that have an overarching aim of achieving various social, cultural, physical, economic or health-related outcomes. S4D therefore goes beyond traditional forms of sport development and sport participation for its own sake. From a S4D perspective, sport is a conduit rather than an end in itself. While publications on sport development (see, e.g. Bloyce and Smith, 2009; Collins, 2010; Girginov, 2008; Houlihan and White, 2002; Hylton and Bramham, 2008) have dwelt briefly on the S4D genre as part of the overall debate about community participation, engagement and inclusion in sport, S4D scholars instead focus on sport projects that are specifically designed to meet the needs of disadvantaged communities and/or development settings. For example, they have conducted studies into an array of pro-social programme areas including sport for socio-economic development (Kobayashi et al., in press), social change and identity building (Schulenkorf, 2010b; Vermeulen and Verweel, 2009), trauma relief (Gschwend and Selvaranju, 2007; Kunz, 2009), gender equality (Meier and Saavedra, 2009; Saavedra, 2009), health improvement (Banda et al., 2008; Webb, 2004), peace and reconciliation (Gasser and Levinsen, 2004; Schulenkorf, 2010a; Stidder and Haasner, 2007; Sugden, 2006) and local capacity building (Wright, 2009).

This flurry of activity has further extended to a number of books on the topic of S4D (Banda et al., 2008; Bennett an Gilbert, 2012; Coalter, 2007, 2013; Darnell, 2012; Hanrahan and Schinke, 2012). Of particular relevance for the present volume is the Levermore and Beacom-edited book *Sport and International Development*, published by Palgrave Macmillan in 2009. It was the first volume to explicitly offer conceptual discussions about both sport development and sport 'in' development at the outset, with associated case studies presented thereafter. The book intelligently addresses a range of challenges for the deployment of sport in international development contexts, taking in social justice issues like disability, gender and the rights of children. We trust that *Global Sport-for-Development* provides an ideal complement to this text, and extends the discussion to take on additional themes, environments and contexts, such as health issues in Pacific Island nations, drug-diversion programmes in Brazil and interfaith initiatives in the Middle East. However, there is such a vast array of S4D projects, programmes and approaches, that these two key Palgrave texts cannot possibly accommodate the whole field.

Overall, the depth and rigour of academic research into the efficacy and longevity of S4D programmes has improved over the past decade; one key reason is that policymakers and funding bodies are now keen to establish whether resources provided are actually bringing about promised S4D impacts and sustainable outcomes. This has its own challenges: many S4D programmes are too poorly funded to allow for adequate monitoring and evaluation (M&E), while some programme-funding bodies are so anxious for swift reporting of progress that the efficacy of S4D impacts are assessed prematurely. Albert Einstein[1] once opined that 'Not everything that can be counted counts, and not everything that counts can be counted.' The widespread insistence on measurement, especially in contexts where qualitative research is most often conducted, presents difficulties for both S4D scholars and practitioners, particularly in environments where there is limited infrastructure and meagre resources.

Background to Global Sport-for-Development

Some stakeholders within S4D, whether out of naivety or by design, are overly optimistic about the aims and efficacy of the programmes they either fund or deliver. Even a scant review of the Internet reveals organisations that triumphally profess to have made substantial differences to disadvantaged communities, yet their evangelical zeal does not seem to correlate with the actual impact of trumpeted programmes. They are, however, always on the lookout for donations and funding for such development projects. Importantly, such proponents of S4D often take the view that they know 'what is best' for disadvantaged communities and, because of that supposedly enlightened perspective, feel entitled and even compelled to 'come to the rescue' of those less fortunate. Whether well intentioned or misguided, such ethnocentric proponents of S4D are hardly equipped to facilitate changes that are meaningful to local communities. Rather than inept or cavalier exponents, S4D needs champions who drive programmes in concert with local stakeholders, and who seek to empower such people towards improved self-sufficiency (Coalter, 2010; Darnell, 2012; Schulenkorf, 2012).

In contrast to numerous NGO publications about S4D, many of which feature idealistic accounts of sport as a magic bullet to solve the ills of humanity, *Global Sport-for-Development* was conceived to encourage questioning of, and critical engagement with, the taken-for-granted assumptions and practices underlying this genre. In other words, while acknowledging the potential of S4D, the book emphasises its challenges, problems and limitations – particularly if programmes are not adequately planned, delivered or monitored. In this sense the book features both critical theory and reflective praxis, and is therefore intended to be useful to both academics and practitioners. It is also an effort to call into question what Fred Coalter has called the 'mythopoeic status' (Coalter, 2010: 296) of sport and the development genre that has evolved around it.

There are some definitional aspects to the field of S4D that warrant discussion and clarification in relation to this book. First, over the years a number of different descriptors and abbreviations have been used for the sport-for-development (and peace) sector, including SFD, S4D, SiD, S&D, SFDP and SDP. For us, the term sport-for-development (and its abbreviation S4D) encompasses all aspects of the genre, including sport programmes designed for particular social, cultural, educational, health, equity and economic purposes, *as well as* a contribution to reconciliation and peace. We see no reason for separating or highlighting 'peace' as an extra descriptor to the S4D term; for us, it forms an integral part of what S4D is all about. However, we ascertained that other authors had reasons for choosing one term and abbreviation over another; for example, some people engaged in projects that focus specifically on intergroup relations and reconciliation issues justifiably use 'sport for development and peace' in line with the previously mentioned UNOSDP. Therefore, we decided against standardising terminology in this book.

Similar definitional contention exists regarding places that have traditionally been described as 'developing countries'. While the World Bank and the World Health Organisation use the term 'low and middle income countries', others use the expression 'Majority World' or 'Third World' (see the academic journal *Third World Quarterly*). Again others categorise power in terms of 'Global North' and 'Global South' divides (see, e.g. Levermore and Beacom, 2009). While we are comfortable with either of the first two terms, we believe that the latter does not resonate well in a global context. In particular, the term 'Global South' may be more or less relevant when investigating projects in Africa or Latin America; however, its connotations do not apply to projects and research conducted in an Australian or New Zealand context. Readers will notice that, notwithstanding this overview of definitions, terms and characteristics of S4D, the authors in the chapters that follow have applied their own particular interpretations and nuances to the field.

Structure of *Global Sport-for-Development*

The book is divided into two separate but interdependent sections. First, the 'Framework' section – Chapters 2–5 – provides a critical conceptual background to S4D. These chapters are written by some of the most renowned scholars in the field of S4D, namely Fred Coalter, John Sugden, Richard Giulianotti, Gary Armstrong, Simon Darnell and Lindsay Hayhurst. Each of these authors has extensive academic influence and practical experience in this field; they provided scene-setting essays that are germinal to an understanding of the complexity of S4D. Second, Chapters 6–11 in the 'From the Field' section focus on practical initiatives, outcomes, challenges and limitations of local, governmental and corporate programmes in developing nation contexts. By doing so, the chapters also examine the crucial power dynamics that underpin interventions from agencies and programmes that are often conceived in the developed world.

Importantly, all contributors to this book have significant experience in S4D praxis and research in low- and middle-income countries. While some of them are local to the country and programme under investigation, others have an established track record of involvement with particular development organisations and/or projects. All authors were asked to critically reflect upon how, during the 21st century, in culturally and ethnically diverse societies, S4D projects might be better delivered through context-rich and flexible approaches to the diverse needs and well-being of disadvantaged communities. This typically involves alliances of stakeholders – external and internal – and an appreciation of the socio-cultural, economic and political nuances of localised S4D scenarios. However, as will be seen in the different contributions provided, the planning, implementation and evaluation stages of sport projects have provided practitioners and academics with a variety of challenges and limitations.

In this first chapter we have provided our rationale for compiling a book on critical perspectives on global sport-for-development and the impetus for undertaking this task. We have briefly surveyed the S4D field, evaluated its origins and evolution. We pinpointed key problems for the genre, both in terms of theory and praxis, and established how this book – and its constituent chapters – proposes to address these shortcomings. Our focus is on explaining the significance of critical theory informing practice, and of practice informing scholarship. In short, the first chapter highlights the value of conceptual rigour underlying S4D programme goals, planning and delivery, and the subsequent imperative for monitoring, evaluation and critical reflection thereafter. In this view, S4D is not a linear and abrupt process; instead, it requires reflexivity and the re-engagement of different stakeholders over time.

In Chapter 2, Richard Giulianotti and Gary Armstrong outline the benefits and challenges of critical and comparative research in S4D. They argue that social scientific analysis and understanding of the S4D sector needs to be underpinned by practical fieldwork as well as rigorous and reflexive analysis. Furthermore, their chapter provides an overview of the contemporary institutionalisation and cultural underpinnings of S4D.

The authors build on their extensive global fieldwork to discuss some of the key cultural, social, political, methodological and operational challenges that confront S4D projects and initiatives. In Chapter 3, Simon Darnell and Lyndsay Hayhurst remind us that the global S4D sector is inextricably linked to issues of power and the legacies of European colonisation. Building on feminist post-colonial theory, the authors highlight the need to understand neo-liberal power, informed resistance and knowledge production, each being critical to the prospect of a paradigm shift in S4D wherein locals have the opportunity to shape their own destinies.

In Chapter 4, Fred Coalter offers a critical perspective of S4D, summarising it acerbically as 'pessimism of the intellect, optimism of the will'. Coalter draws on his extensive experience in Africa and India to reveal what he describes as essentialist, mythical and neo-liberal assumptions underpinning the rhetoric of the genre. He then argues for a realist approach to understanding both context and process in S4D, a strategy that is intended to permit a more systematic approach to the meaning and purpose of 'development', as well as issues of displacement of scope – the relations between micro, meso and macro levels of 'development'. In Chapter 5, John Sugden compares 'rhetoric versus realism' in the discourse of S4D in fundamentally divided societies. He draws upon three decades of working in S4D environments, not just as a researcher and scholar but also as an activist. By bringing together his lived experiences in Northern Ireland, Israel/Palestine and South Africa, and combining this with critical 'sociological imagination', Sugden is both ethnographer and pragmatist. He argues that when carefully thought through – and when prevailing conditions permit – sport-centred and related civil society interventions can make a small, but nonetheless important contribution to the complex jigsaw of peace building in societies experiencing profound conflict.

Chapter 6 – the first in the 'From the Field' section – discusses the *Football for Peace* programme in Israel. James Wallis and John Lambert provide critical reflections about the management and delivery aspects of this co-existence project. Their chapter focuses on 'behind the scenes' challenges, including the differing motives and agendas of project partners. Building on a decade of personal experiences with *Football for Peace*, their chapter also makes a contribution to ongoing discussions about the potential impacts of S4D projects. The next chapters take us to the African continent. In Chapter 7, Oscar Mwaanga and Kabanda Mwansa provide an alternative post-colonial discourse about S4D by examining indigenous perspectives on community development. In particular, they discuss the case of the *EduSport Foundation* and its underpinning Sub-Saharan Ubuntu cultural philosophy, and they highlight the importance of local perspectives designed to shape S4D practice. In Chapter 8, Ruth Jeanes and Jonathan Magee explore local understandings of the role of sports within communities heavily affected by poverty. The authors present findings from a S4D project for young women in Zambia; they also highlight the complex power dynamics that shape women's experiences within and around externally funded S4D programmes. Next, in Chapter 9, Justin Richards and Charlie Foster provide a critique of a programme designed to improve mental and physical health indicators for adolescents in a post-war setting in Northern Uganda. Against the background of a newly designed theoretical framework, the authors discuss the disconnect between funders, implementers and evaluators, and highlight the detrimental effects the programme had on local communities. Importantly, recommendations for more effective, inclusive and locally relevant projects are provided.

In Chapter 10, Zak Kaufman, Brooke Rosenbauer and Gabriela Moore investigate the M&E aspects of S4D. They provide critical insights into different sport projects staged in six Caribbean nations. While previously few donors expected formal, independent evaluations of proposed development outcomes, there is now increasing demand for strategic and rigorous investigations. The authors analysed the organisational practices, successes and challenges pertaining to current M&E approaches, and they provide strategic recommendations for improved M&E systems in the Caribbean region. In Chapter 11, Elizabeth Kath and Nanko van Buuren give readers an insight into the work of The Brazilian Institute for Innovations in Social Health (IBISS). The chapter focuses on the *Soldados Nunca Mais* programme that attempts to (a) break down social prejudices in Rio de Janeiro and (b) encourage child soldiers to leave the drug trade. The authors reject the claim that sport in itself is able to achieve positive development; instead, they argue that the efforts of committed development workers and their ability to identify and innovate around informal social spaces allow for the prospect of positive change within and between communities. In Chapter 12, Katja Siefken, Grant Schofield and Nico Schulenkorf report on the challenges of designing, implementing, evaluating and sustaining a health promotion programme intended to increase physical activity and healthy lifestyles for women in an urban Pacific Island context. In particular, the chapter reports on programme logistics, limitations and success stories of a research-based lifestyle-change programme in Port Vila/Vanuatu. The reflective nature of the chapter is intended to aid future practitioners and/or researchers in programme design and management, and enhance collaboration with local personnel and authorities.

In Chapter 13, we as editors reflect on what the combination of essays in this book has revealed about the nuances of theory and praxis in S4D. This is done against a background where each of the chapters under 'Framework', while focused primarily on conceptual concerns, has drawn very much on previous field work. Similarly, each of the chapters under 'Field', while focused primarily on programme delivery issues, has fundamentally been informed by theoretical assumptions and conceptual goals. Therefore, the final chapter allows us to use comparisons from within sections and between cases across the whole book; it also highlights key challenges for the S4D genre and identifies emerging trends with respect to critical engagement and reforms to practice.

Note

1. See http://www.brainyquote.com/quotes/quotes/a/alberteins100201.html.

References

Banda, D., Lindsey, I., Jeanes, R. and Kay, T. (2008). *Partnerships Involving Sports-for-Development NGOs and the Fight against HIV/AIDS*. York: York St John University.
Bennett, W. and Gilbert, K. (eds). (2012). *Sport, Peace, and Development*. Champaign, IL: Common Ground Publishers.
Bloyce, D. an Smith, A. (2009). *Sport, Policy, and Development: An Introduction*. New York: Routledge.
Coalter, F. (2007). *A Wider Social Role for Sport: Who's Keeping the Score*. Abingdon, Oxon: Routledge.
Coalter, F. (2010). The Politics of Sport-for-Development: Limited Focus Programmes and Broad Gauge Problems? *International Review for the Sociology of Sport*, 45(3), 295–314. doi: 10.1177/1012690210366791.
Coalter, F. (2013). *Sport for Development: What Game Are We Playing?* London: Routledge.
Collins, M.F. (2010). *Examining Sports Development*. London: Routledge.
Darnell, S.C. (2012). *Sport for Development and Peace – A Critical Sociology*. London: Bloomsbury Academic.
Gasser, P.K. and Levinsen, A. (2004). Breaking Post-War Ice: Open Fun Football Schools in Bosnia and Herzegovina. *Sport in Society*, 7(3), 457–472.
Girginov, V. (ed.). (2008). *Management of Sports Development*. Burlington, MA: Elsevier.
Gschwend, A. and Selvaranju, U. (2007). *Psycho-Social Sport Programmes to Overcome Trauma in Post-Disaster Interventions*. Biel/Bienne: Swiss Academy for Development (SAD).
Hanrahan, S. and Schinke, R. (eds). (2012). *Sport for Development, Peace, and Social Justice*. Morgantown: Fitness Information Technology.

Houlihan, B. and White, A. (2002). *The Politics of Sports Development: Development of Sport or Development through Sport?* London: Routledge.

Hylton, K. and Bramham, P. (eds). (2008). *Sports Development: Policy, Process and Practice* (2nd edn). Abingdon, Oxon: Routledge.

Kobayashi, T., Nicholson, M. and Hoye, R.S. (2013). Football 'Wantok': Sport and Social Capital in Vanuatu. *International Review for the Sociology of Sport*, 48(1), 38–53. doi: 10.1177/1012690211423141.

Kunz, V. (2009). Sport as a post-disaster psychosocial intervention in Bam, Iran. *Sport in Society*, 12(9), 1147–1157.

Levermore, R. and Beacom, A. (eds). (2009). *Sport and International Development*. Basingstoke: Palgrave Macmillan.

Meier, M. and Saavedra, M. (2009). Esther Phiri and the Moutawakel Effect in Zambia: An Analysis of the Use of Female Role Models in Sport-for-Development. *Sport in Society*, 12(9), 1158–1176.

Saavedra, M. (2009). Dilemmas and Opportunities in Gender and Sport-in-Development. In R. Levermore and A. Beacom (eds), *Sport and International Development*, 124–155. Houndmills: Palgrave Macmillan.

Schulenkorf, N. (2010a). The Roles and Responsibilities of a Change Agent in Sport Event Development Projects. *Sport Management Review*, 13(2), 118–128. doi: 10.1016/j.smr.2009.05.001.

Schulenkorf, N. (2010b). Sport Events and Ethnic Reconciliation: Attempting to Create Social Change between Sinhalese, Tamil and Muslim Sportspeople in War-Torn Sri Lanka. *International Review for the Sociology of Sport*, 45(3), 273–294. doi: 10.1177/1012690210366789.

Schulenkorf, N. (2012). Sustainable Community Development through Sport and Events: A Conceptual Framework for Sport-for-Development Projects. *Sport Management Review*, 15(1), 1–12. doi: 10.1016/j.smr.2011.06.001.

Stidder, G. and Haasner, A. (2007). Developing Outdoor and Adventurous Activities for Co-Existence and Reconciliation in Israel: An Anglo-German Approach. *Journal of Adventure Education and Outdoor Learning*, 7(2), 131–140.

Sugden, J. (2006). Teaching and Playing Sport for Conflict Resolution and Co-Existence in Israel. *International Review for the Sociology of Sport*, 41(2), 221–240.

Vermeulen, J. and Verweel, P. (2009). Participation in Sport: Bonding and Bridging as Identity Work. *Sport in Society*, 12(9), 1206–1219.

Webb, D. (2004). Legitimate Actors? The Future Roles for NGOs against HIV/AIDS in Sub-Saharan Africa. In N. Poku and A. Whiteside (eds), *The Political Economy of AIDS in Africa*. Aldershot: Ashgate, 19–32.

Wright, R.W. (2009). *Understanding the Role of Sport for Development in Community Capacity Building in a Refugee Camp in Tanzania*. MSc, University of Saskatchewan, Saskatoon.

Part II
Framework

2
The Sport for Development and Peace Sector: A Critical Sociological Analysis

Richard Giulianotti and Gary Armstrong

In recent years, there has been considerable interest at political and public levels in the contribution that sport might make to advancing what is commonly referred to as social development, as well as peace and conflict resolution in divided and conflict-damaged societies. As a consequence, the 'Sport for Development and Peace' (hereon, SDP) sector emerged to promote a wide variety of personal, social and community developments. Within that genre, critical roles are played by a host of institutions, including governments, inter-governmental organisations (IGOs), non-governmental organisations (NGOs), sport governing bodies, and private agencies and corporations. Out of this an observer can evidence SDP work delivered globally, but particularly in developing nations or the global South (Darnell, 2012; Levermore, 2008; Lindsey, 2008).

The SDP sector has emerged steadily since the early 1990s, albeit for much of this time the role of sport in development work was distinctly marginal. However, a key role in the expansion and wider legitimation of the SDP sector has been played by the United Nations (UN). Most significantly, the United Nations established its own Office of Sport for Development and Peace (UNOSDP) in 2001, and marked 2005 as its International Year of Sport and Physical Education (see UN General Assembly, 2006). Since that point, sport-focused development work has gained more credibility within the broader development sector (Armstrong and Collison, 2009). Concomitantly, social scientific studies of SDP activities have mushroomed in recent years, and this field has been approached from a diversity of methodological and epistemological standpoints (see, e.g. Armstrong, 2004, 2007; Calloway, 2004; Coalter,

2007, 2010; Darnell, 2008, 2012; Gasser and Levinsen, 2004; Giulianotti, 2004, 2011a, 2011b, 2011c; Giulianotti and Armstrong, 2011; Hartmann and Kwauk, 2011; Höglund and Sundberg, 2008; Hognestad and Tollisen, 2004; Kidd, 2008; Lea-Howarth, 2006; Schulenkorf, 2010; Whitfield, 2006; Willis, 2000). Now, there is much debate within the SDP sector as to what might constitute best practise and the processes of monitoring and evaluation. These will not abate; nor should they.

In what follows, we seek to draw together some of the main analyses and findings generated through research into SDP. The focus here is less on the everyday projects of SDP organisations or their effectiveness; rather, the concern is more with the ways in which the SDP sector is structured and orientated. First, we set out a brief conceptual framework with reference to two main theories: global civil society and glocalisation. Second, we consider briefly the range and diversity of sport-related activities that, in our view, constitute the SDP sector. Third, we set out a model of four categorical types of SDP agency or organisation. Fourth, we set out a three-fold model of the different types of SDP projects that are undertaken by various organisations. Our discussion here is substantially underpinned by fieldwork into the broad development and peace aspects and possibilities of sport, which has been under way since the late 1990s. The research has been undertaken in diverse locations, including Africa (Liberia, Nigeria and Zimbabwe), Europe (Bosnia-Herzegovina), the Middle East (Jordan) and south Asia (Sri Lanka). For reasons of brevity, we are unable to enter into a full discussion of this fieldwork. Further research has been undertaken at the many national and international conferences and conventions on SDP that we have attended since the late 1990s. Our observations at these events have significantly underpinned our understandings of how the SDP sector is played out, particularly with regard to the types of partnership that emerge between different types of agency therein.

We offer a critical approach not only in terms of opening-up SDP to analysis, revealing power relations between individuals, social groups and institutions, but also with the goal of pointing to future possibilities of how the sector might be established and organised. We adopt a social scientific approach towards both SDP and the broader social impact of sport. That is, we avoid 'sport evangelism' – or indeed, what might also be termed the 'sport pentecostalism' – that pervades some parts of the sector, as we have discussed previously (Giulianotti, 2004). Such approaches tend to essentialise 'the power of sport' by assuming that sport has an innate capability to effect social change. Rather, as social scientists, we recognise that sport is socially constructed, that it is context specific, and that its social meanings and impacts are shaped by the interplay between social structural and cultural processes. To illustrate the point, consider the case of sport in the Balkan region of Europe: while SDP agencies may utilise sport to promote peace building in the region, we should also note that sport has also been used there for other ends, such as to express and to intensify forms of virulent and violent nationalism, and indeed as one catalyst for the outbreak of the Yugoslavian civil war (Vrcan and Lalic 1998). Likewise, we find that the meanings on any aspect of sport – as expressed, for example, through political and public discourses on sport spectators – can change significantly over time (Giulianotti, 1994). If we bear in mind the very different ways in which sport has been played out in diverse contexts, then we are in a better position to advance a constructive, critical, sociological analysis of the current condition and future possibilities of sport.

Global civil society and glocalisation: power and culture in SDP

Turning to consider how the SDP sector may be theorised, we suggest that two particular theories are particularly useful. These relate to theories of *global civil society* and *glocalisation*. Global civil society is helpful mainly in enabling a critical exploration of the power relations between and within the SDP sector. Glocalisation theory enables us to examine the cultural aspects of SDP projects and organisations, particularly in the extent to which local communities are able to shape the implementation of SDP projects. Both theories may be understood as deriving from the broader field of globalisation theory.

First, we understand the SDP sector as embedded within global civil society. The concept of global civil society is widely contested by social scientists, and is understood in a variety of descriptive, strategically political and normative ways (Keane, 2003). The idea of global civil society in recent years has been utilised particularly to examine the political and social arrangements surrounding globalisation, with respect to the way in which issues of human development, transnational interdependency, peace, environmental sustainability, and social justice are to be debated and resolved. We draw particularly on the work of Kaldor (2003a, 2003b) to examine global civil society as a strongly contested idea and political platform, in which various social groups argue over and contest 'the arrangements that shape global developments' (Kaldor 2003b: 591). Adopting this approach, we argue that global civil society should be understood as a competitive 'field', in Bourdieu's (1984) sense of the term. In this way, the field is constituted by different institutional and political forces within the SDP sector, such as nation-states, IGOs, NGOs, new social movements and transnational corporations. The field is a site of struggle. Consequently, diverse institutional and political forces endeavour to shape it, in line with their distinctive interests and ideologies (cf. Anheier et al., 2007; Kaldor 2003a, 2003b). For example, IGOs like the United Nations favour a global civil society in which highly pragmatic NGOs compete among themselves to win contracts in order to carry out development work. Such an arrangement may be said to be neo-liberal in the sense that it produces a marketplace among NGOs, enabling more powerful agencies to set the SDP agenda, which usually involves pursuing projects that are mainly focused on meeting basic human needs (e.g. alleviating hunger, preventing conflicts), while not addressing the more fundamental causes of such problems (e.g. social injustices, exploitation). In substantial contrast, new social movements favour a more politically active global civil society that is committed to policies which pursue social justice, such as human rights, gender equality, and fair industrial relations in developing nations. One important point that needs to be made here is that, while these types of organisation or institution are within a competitive field, there are inevitably significant levels of *cooperation* between them, particularly where they hold relatively similar visions and strategies on SDP or the global civil society more broadly. Overall, the SDP sector is one element of a wider global civil society. We shall consider in later sections the different participants within this competitive field.

Second, glocalisation theory is particularly useful in exploring different forms of social and cultural agency with regard to global phenomena and processes. Robertson (1992, 1995) played the key role in developing and applying glocalisation theory in social science, particularly as a way of examining how individuals and social groups relocate and recontextualise global processes with regard to local cultures. Robertson argues that glocalisation captures the intensified interpenetration of the local and the global, and the societal co-presence of sameness and difference. Glocalisation theory has been used extensively in the context of sport through collaborative work with Robertson (see, e.g. Giulianotti and Robertson, 2004, 2007, 2009). In broad terms, glocalisation theory serves to register the complex interplay between local and global processes in the making of SDP organisations and initiatives.

We see local processes being played out at a number of levels within the SDP sector. In general terms, SDP appears as a global movement that is driven by major global or transnational organisations (e.g. United Nations and its agencies, international NGOs, international donors to SDP projects such as Nike or Adidas); also this movement appears in different cultural contexts, such as through national or local agencies that implement SDP projects on the ground. A key question that is rooted in glocalisation theory here is: to what extent, and in what ways, are these local projects able to adapt or to shape the global SDP movement according to local needs?

Typically, there is some kind of balance that is struck at local levels between sameness and difference, between convergence and divergence with the 'global' movement or model. Thus, for example, on one hand, facilitating global sameness, we find that international NGOs make available online various 'toolkits' or manuals that show how SDP projects can be implemented using specific sport activities in any location across the world. On the other hand, promoting difference, at local levels, the more creative NGOs will use these toolkits or manuals in a selective and critical fashion, adapting their contents in line with local needs and local contexts. In broader terms, we also find that, while SDP agencies may share the same basic goals and objectives (such as in promoting peace in conflict zones) at international level, the everyday cultures of these organisations may vary markedly as they reflect local cultural values, practices and needs.

One benefit of glocalisation theory here is that it serves to place power relations in cultural context, and to register the forms of cultural agency, creativity, and autonomy that individuals, groups and institutions may exercise within the SDP sector at everyday level. These issues are particularly relevant in the later sections when we consider the types of SDP project that are at play across the sector.

Glocalisation theory and global civil society theory provide the analytical basis for examining the SDP sector with regard to its projects and agencies, to which we now turn.

SDP projects and initiatives

Here, we begin by noting the wide range of projects and initiatives that are commonly identified with the SDP sector. Perhaps the best-known types of activities and problems include those that promote:

- *Peace and conflict resolution*: In divided and violent communities, such as in the Balkans, West Africa, Middle East or south Asia. Sport in this context is used to try to bring these divided communities together, or at least to facilitate positive social interaction between the opposing sides (Armstrong, 2004, 2007; Armstrong and Vest, 2012; Giulianotti, 2011b, 2011c; Giulianotti and Armstrong, 2011; Schulenkorf, 2010).

- *Health*: Sport here is used to promote health education, including measures to reduce risky personal behaviours – particularly in the context of major health crises or pandemics, such as with HIV/AIDS in sub-Saharan Africa (Maro et al., 2009).
- *Social inclusion of marginalised and disempowered groups and communities*: Sport here provides an enjoyable recreational space in which groups may build a stronger public presence and social role, enjoy healthy and playful exercise, and improve substantially their self-esteem and confidence (Coalter, 2005; Tacon, 2007).
- *Poverty reduction*: Sport here may be used to draw the most marginalised groups into contact with key social services (e.g. offering basic accommodation or health and education provisions), and also to promote international awareness of poverty (Walseth and Fasting, 2004).

Many of these types of projects are closely in line with the United Nations' Millennium Development Goals (MDGs). To summarise, the MDGs are intended to meet universal targets by 2015 in eight fundamental areas: eradicating poverty and hunger; universal primary education; promoting gender equality; reducing child poverty; improving maternal health; combating HIV, malaria and other such diseases; ensuring environmental sustainability; and building global partnerships for development. The focus of the MDGs, and of much SDP activity, is on seeking to meet these fundamental needs, with a particular concentration on the global South or developing nations and regions, including Africa, south and south-east Asia, and Central and South America.

We now turn to consider these observations with respect to our key theories of global civil society and glocalisation, as set out earlier. On glocalisation, we contend that the effectiveness of such broad projects will depend to a significant degree on the extent to which they are adapted and shaped relative to context. On global civil society, one observation is that the range of projects set out earlier is indicative of the influence and status of supporting institutions, such as the UN, within the SDP sector. But we also recognise that the SDP sector – as a competitive field, in line with thinking about global civil society – does actually contain a wider range of activities and initiatives than those listed thus far. We note, for example, that in its broad sense global civil society also includes initiatives that promote human rights, civil rights and social justice. Thus, we can consider how these issues play out in sport, and consider that the SDP sector also includes:

- *Human rights campaigns and initiatives*: These might focus, for example, on political rights, freedom of expression and civil rights. Sport is often used as a public platform for advancing campaigns. For instance, at the Olympic Games, we have witnessed: 1968 Mexico City, the African-American civil rights demonstrations; 2000 Sydney, the Aboriginal rights demonstrations; and around 2008 Beijing, freedom of speech demonstrations (Timms, 2012).
- *Industrial rights campaigns*: Such campaigns focus on promoting the rights of workers in developing nations who are employed in sports-related production. The obvious example here relates to campaigns against sport apparel companies, such as Adidas or Nike, whose production plants in developing nations have been criticised for poverty wages and abusive industrial practices. While these types of campaign also fall under the wider category of human rights, they may be waged at a continuous, everyday level and involve a different set of power dynamics between major sport institutions and marginalised or oppressed social groups (Pillay and Bass, 2008).
- *Sport-related development work in developed nations*: Such campaigns and programmes might focus on a whole host of areas for sport interventionist work. The inclusion of developed nations here reflects the scale of sport-based social interventions in these settings, and also recognises that issues such as human rights, civil rights and social justice remain contested in the global North. The relevant projects here typically include those that use sport as a hook or interventionist tool in order to reduce crime, violence or drug use; and, to promote education, training, health and social integration. Illustrations here would include the Midnight Basketball programmes in the United States, or the Street League programmes in the United Kingdom that use football to draw marginalised young people into education, employment or training (Salis et al., 1998; Hartmann, 2001; Hartmann and Depro, 2006).

Again, these categories of SDP initiative or campaign are perhaps at their strongest when they are 'glocalised', thereby being effectively adapted to the particular sociological contours of the local context.

One final point we make here in passing relates to the potential wider scale impacts of SDP projects. In other words, if an SDP project is focused on working with a particular social group or community, its effects may also be experienced by a wider range of social groups. For example, if a project works to promote AIDS awareness among 20–30 young people in a village, it is most likely that project workers will look to encourage the knowledge and new behaviours among this group to be extended to a much wider social circle. This point serves to illustrate the *ripple effect* of SDP work, as projects may have impacts that reverberate across wider communities, beyond the immediate participants (for more detail, refer to Chapter 5 in this book). The concept of 'ripple effect' has an extensive history in social science. It has been applied by Gavriel Salomon (2011) to examine the potential impacts of Israeli-Arab peace education programmes on wider communities. Salomon's colleague Baha Zoubi (2011) has employed the concept in his study of bi-national (Israeli and Arab) participation in football clubs in Israel.

The SDP sector: four categories of active institution

We turn now to consider the types of agency or institution that are active within the SDP sector. These organisations differ significantly with respect to their location, size or scale, ideologies, policies and objectives. In our view, these organisations may be separated into four broad categories, which reflect their respective positions within the SDP field. As this is an ideal-type model, inevitably some of these agencies may fit into more than one category; however, our classification is made on the basis of each agency's main characteristics and the nature of its relationships with other institutions within the sector.

Non-governmental, non-profit organisations

Our first category relates to the *non-governmental, non-profit organisations (NGOs)* which in large part are committed to facilitating or implementing SDP projects. These organisations vary in size, and thus may be distinguished according to scale, in terms of international, national and local/grassroots levels. The largest such organisations operate at international level, and tend to play a networking and coordinating role, such as in generating and pooling funding and other resources, which is then distributed to local SDP agencies. Often, national-level partners are identified to work with these international agencies, as the former are established within the nation and are ideally well-placed to identify the particular needs within each setting. International NGOs that are focused on SDP work include *Right to Play, streetfootballworld, Football Against Racism in Europe* and *Open Fun Football Schools*. Some of these organisations have their own agencies at local and national level. At the national and local levels, organisations such as the *Sarvodaya* movement in Sri Lanka are also utilised to implement SDP projects. It is worth noting that NGOs doing sport work may also be differentiated into two categories: those that are explicitly focused on sport-related work, as discussed; and the wider pool of NGOs that engage in development work, and have engaged at times in sport work in order to fulfill these wider missions. This latter category includes, for example, *Action Aid* and *Care*.

Inter-governmental and governmental organisations

Our second category features the *IGOs* and *governmental organisations* whose main activities include overseeing and facilitating SDP projects. These organisations also contribute to the implementation of SDP programmes. As noted earlier, the United Nations has acquired a critical role in undertaking such work, notably under the auspices of the UNOSDP; in addition, many of the UN's associate agencies undertake SDP work, and these include the United Nations Development Programme (UNDP), UNESCO, and UNICEF. Other IGOs that promote SDP work include the Commonwealth Secretariat, which represents the 54 independent states that are members of the UK-based Commonwealth. At a national level, many governments feature international development departments and agencies that undertake SDP work include, for example, the British Council, NORAD (Norway) and Canadian Heritage. In the United Kingdom, the government-funded UK Sport agency also undertakes substantial SDP work, and contributes to the networking and knowledge-transfer of SDP-related institutions.

In our view, this category should include national and international sport governing bodies that contribute to SDP work. In theory, these institutions might fit into other categories, such as the NGO sector, or the private sector (given their increasingly commercial orientation). However, we locate these bodies among the IGOs and governmental organisations as their main purpose is to function as governmental institutions while also seeking to advance the interests of their particular sports. We have in mind here governing bodies such as the Fédération Internationale de Football Association (FIFA), the International Olympic Committee (IOC) and the International Cricket Council (ICC); and, at a national level, there are various national governing bodies that control sports, as well as the National Olympic Committees (NOCs) that perform the same role for Olympic sports. These governing bodies are increasingly involved in SDP work, and in some instances such work has been around for a long time. For example, FIFA has been a partner of the SOS

Children's Villages charity since 1995, and later established a large international Football for Hope initiative to run until 2015. The Union of European Football Associations (UEFA), European football's governing body, also has a significant 'Social Responsibility' platform.

Private sector

That we simply call the *private sector* can include a variety of different types of organisation or contributor. At an individual level there are private donors, philanthropic individuals who provide support for the SDP work of NGOs and other agencies. At an institutional level, the largest private SDP supporters are transnational corporations such as Nike, Adidas, Vodafone, Daimler or Mercedes-Benz. They help to finance SDP programmes by, for example, contributing to organisations like the Laureus Foundation that undertake SDP activities. The SDP-related interests of these private companies can also include, where applicable, the introduction of reporting mechanisms to address issues related to their manufacture of sport products, such as shoes and apparel. A strong example here is Nike, which since the late 20th century has replied to anti-sweatshop campaigns and claims of similarly poor labour practices in their production plants by publishing self-reports of the industrial conditions and treatment of their workforces in developing countries.

Corporate social responsibility (CSR) programmes are central to the SDP engagement of many private donors. CSR plays strongly to a credo of private philanthropy, to a choice-based policy philosophy that advocates the voluntary self-regulation of corporations in terms of their commercial, political and social activities. This free-market philosophy stands in direct contrast or opposition to alternative, more interventionist social and economic models, which, for example, advocate greater legal regulation of business and a much more substantial, social democratic type of welfare state (Babiak and Wolf, 2006; Becker-Olsen et al., 2006; Godfrey, 2009). Many corporations explain their CSR programmes in strongly commercial terms, as good for productivity and profitability. Thus, SDP involvement has the corporate benefit of improving public profile, being associated with positive humanitarian themes and goals, possibly connecting with future consumers in the targeted nations and regions, and providing the company with new and potentially profitable understandings of international settings – and all of this was achieved at very low cost relative to turnover or annual profit (Savery and Gilbert, 2011).

Radical NGOs and social movements

Our final category is provided by *radical NGOs and social movements,* which typically focus on sport-related campaigns, and which thus display more politicised approaches towards SDP and are more focused on promoting social justice and human and civil rights, as noted earlier. Illustrations of these types of SDP activity might include campaigns by Amnesty International or Human Rights Watch, which sought to focus on human rights violations in mainland China or Tibet when Beijing was hosting the 2008 Olympics. These initiatives have also included various campaigns by social movements and radical NGO, such as with protests against specific sponsors of the 2012 London Olympics. For example, the War on Want campaigning movement targeted Adidas, accusing the Olympics corporate partner of 'making millions out of the exploitation of workers who make its clothes'.

[1]Meanwhile, the 'Greenwash Gold' campaign run by a network of social movements targeted Olympic corporate partners – Dow Chemical, Rio Tinto and BP – for their alleged impacts on the environment and local communities.[2] Historically, these campaigns have played a key role in the emergence of the SDP sector, such as with regard to protests against child labour in the use of football manufacturing in Pakistan in the 1990s and early 2000s.[3]

SDP partnerships and interrelations

Three further points should be made in regard to these different categories of social actor. First, while the four-fold categorisation has a real value in clarifying the full range of SDP agencies and their underlying approaches, we also found that some organisations have multiple or ambiguous characteristics and qualities, which feature more than one set of SDP policies or strategies. For example, sport governing bodies such as FIFA and the IOC are in effect with the world governing organisations within their fields of sport; they also may be classified as NGOs, and as multi-billion-dollar transnational enterprises having a major private sector focus. Similarly, the Peace and Sport organisation based in Monaco may fall into several categories: it acts as an NGO by supporting SDP initiatives; and, it resembles a national governmental organisation in being backed by Prince Albert, the head of state of Monaco, and in the extensive work that it undertakes in promoting networking and knowledge-transfer across the SDP sector.

Second, the SDP sector is largely structured and played out through the large volume of cooperative activity that occurs between different types of organisation. Here, we should emphasise that the first three categories – NGOs, governmental organisations and private donors – are by far the most active. We see this collaborative activity occurring at major conferences and symposia, which may be run or convened by governmental organisations while enabling NGOs and private donors in particular to meet, engage in knowledge-transfer and other discussions, and of course to enable further partnerships to be established. The collaborative work that occurs is often orientated towards planning, financing and implementing SDP projects. For example, we might see an IGO agency such as the UNDP highlighting a particular major problem, such as a health crisis; then an international NGO and local NGO may combine to establish a sports project with support from the UN agency; and finally, a TNC and a sport federation may provide funding and other resources (such as sports equipment) to support the project. One example is provided by the SDP initiative in which one of us is working. The project is financed by the European Commission with the objective of empowering European football supporters to promote anti-discrimination messages and practices. The project partners include several international NGOs in sport, several national football associations, the international football players' union and a group of academics.[4]

It is worth noting that different types of partnership or work arise depending on how the project is funded. Some of the most progressive NGOs reported to us that private individual donors were often the best to work with when the projects were innovative and unusual, with potentially uncertain results; in a sense, they were more willing to examine the distinctive, glocal aspects of such project work, in being carefully and creatively adapted to the local setting. In contrast, larger donors tended to look for measurable or demonstrable returns on their outlay. Some NGOs also reported that, when the project was funded by governmental organisations, there would be a routine for engagement in terms of attending a round of meetings and submitting interim and final reports. Relations with large corporate donors were often different, with these organisations seeking to take a more hands-on role in planning and implementing projects, preferring to engage in direct contact where possible, and exploring how these initiatives might improve the corporation's practices and outlook.

Third, as implied earlier, the campaigning NGOs and social movements tend to be on the outside of the SDP sector, with relatively low participation in building social capital, such as through invitations to attendance conferences. Part of this is explained by the nature of some of these organisations, in using sport as a platform for promoting a particular cause to a wider audience. Examples of this include the afore-mentioned *War on Want* campaign against the industrial practices of Adidas, or the '*Greenwash Gold*' campaigns against energy and mining companies that sponsor the Olympics. However, these organisations are also likely to come into conflict with many other types of SDP agency – for example, in the anti-Nike campaigns run by some social movements, or in the human rights protests against the 2008 Beijing Olympics. In this sense, these campaigning organisations are rather marginalised within this area of the global civil society.

In the final section, we briefly consider three categories or ideal types of SDP project. These categories refer to projects that focus on SDP development work, rather than the campaigning approaches and strategies associated with radical NGOs and new social movements. However, these three categories are relevant to our theorisation of global civil society with regard to SDP, as well as to glocalisation theory.

Types of SDP project: technical/practical/critical

We differentiate SDP projects into three broad categories. These categories are 'ideal types' which ideally capture how these agencies understand their main objectives, roles, methods and relations with client groups and other agencies. Such ideal types have heuristic and analytical value in allowing us to model the SDP sector, and to identify how close the actual SDP agencies and organisations are to each category. The three categories we examine here are the 'technical', the 'practical' and the 'critical'; these categories were set out in previous papers that focused on peace building projects (see Giulianotti, 2011a). We now look at these more closely.

First, *technical* projects tend to adopt a relatively hierarchical or 'top-down' approach to SDP work. In such instances the agency will tend to view itself as having an expert position with regard to relations with potential user groups. The role of the project is to contribute towards 'problem-solving', with the agency assuming that it has the advantage of being able to see or understand the identified problem in a clearer way than the user groups. Thus, dialogical relations with user groups are relatively circumscribed. The project tends to be organised through the delivery of scheduled interventions such as at specific 'clinics'. The outcomes of these activities are understood as being measurable, particularly through the use of positivist methodologies.

Second, we have *practical* or *dialogical* projects that tend to pursue new social relations in the contexts in which these initiatives are implemented.

By definition, such projects adopt a more dialogical approach in relations with user groups, but ultimately project officials will assume the roles of leaders, arbiters and instructors to ensure that core aims and objectives are secured. One method for conducting these projects is the 'training the trainers' approach, which conveys training to local people who then train groups of other locals to implement programmes.

Third, there are *critical* projects that pursue substantial forms of social transformation. The social relations between project officials and user groups are relatively horizontal; thus, user groups are in a position to actively influence and to shape the aims, strategies and techniques within the project. At the same time, project officials are alive to the processual aspects of their work, recognizing the scope for them to learn and to improve or transform their own practices. Projects here would tend to have deeper forms of engagement or immersion with their user groups and the local communities, and thereby use a diversity of working methods according to context.

Overall, we might identify some connections between these categories and the different types of SDP agency discussed earlier. The technical model is more likely to be located among the most pragmatic TNCs, particular corporate donors and other pro-market organisations. The practical or dialogical model is more associated with relatively embedded IGOs, as well as networking NGOs. The critical model is more evident among small-scale, innovative NGOs, while its strong engagement with local communities is in line with the campaigning approach taken by new social movements. The critical project, and to a lesser extent the practical project, have a strong 'glocal' ethic in terms of adapting project structure, organisation and methods according to the local setting and negotiated needs.

Of course, SDP projects tend to exhibit different mixtures of these ideal-type models (especially the technical and practical/dialogical). The more prominent technical aspects, for example, include problem-solving objectives, strong interventionist approaches and positivistic techniques for measuring impacts. Prominent practical/dialogical features include 'training the trainers' methods and adopting a mixed communicator/leader role. The critical approach is less apparent, but some evident features may include strong engagement with local community needs and views regarding the project delivery.

There is a significant and direct relationship of these categories to the playing out of the SDP sector as an aspect of global civil society. The extent to which any of these categories is more or less apparent in actual SDP projects is determined in large part by how the SDP sector is shaped out of the competitive and/or collaborative relationships between different SDP agencies and institutions. Historically, the more technical and practical/dialogical approaches towards SDP projects have tended to be more prevalent. This confirms observations presented earlier in this chapter about how the SDP field is loaded more towards the collaborative relationships between established NGOs, IGOs, governmental organisations and private or corporate donors.

Conclusion

What precedes has endeavoured to map out the main structure and organisation of the SDP sector. Drawing on theories of global civil society and glocalisation, we have developed two main analytical models: first, through a four-fold model of the main organisational categories within the SDP sector; second, through a three-fold ideal-type model of different SDP projects. Crucially, we argue that the SDP sector is a broader field than it is often perceived to be. Our analysis is sympathetic to those features of the SDP sector that advocate human/civil rights and social justice, and which enable 'critical' SDP projects to be undertaken. If we consider the SDP sector as an aspect of global civil society, these progressive features would be best secured through radical NGOs and social movements finding a more influential presence. These features are also more associated with culturally creative, glocal practices, where local cultures and grassroots SDP agencies are empowered to engage selectively and innovatively with the more transnational features of the SDP movement. There is, we argue, a sense in which the SDP sector has become rather routinised and short of invention. The contribution of these other groups would help to move the SDP sector forward in terms of pursuing more critical or 'glocal' projects, more creative partnerships, and more democratic relationships with their user communities.

Acknowledgements

The authors would like to thank the editors for their constructive and insightful comments on an earlier version of this chapter. The research for this paper was funded in part by a research grant from the Nuffield Foundation.

Notes

1. See http://www.waronwant.org/news/press-releases/17617-olympic-projection-spotlights-adidas-factories-exploitation.

2. See http://www.greenwashgold.org.
3. See for example http://www.cleanclothes.org/resources/national-ccc/1131-sialkot-pakistan-the-football-industry-from-child-lab.
4. See www.prosupporters.net.

References

Anheier, H.K., Kaldor, M. and Glasius, M. (eds) (2007). *Global Civil Society Yearbook 2005/6*, London: Sage.

Armstrong, G. (2004). The Lords of Misrule: Football and the Rights of the Child in Liberia, West Africa. *Sport in Society*, 7(3), 473–502.

Armstrong, G. (2007). The Global Footballer and the Local War-Zone: George Weah and Transnational Networks in Liberia, West Africa. *Global Networks*, 7(2), 230–247.

Armstrong, G. and Collison, H. (2009). The United Nations and the Millenium Goals: Implications for Sport and Development. In A. Robias, E. Stamatakis and K. Black (eds), *Design for Sport*. Aldershot: Gower, London.

Armstrong, G. and Vest, E. (2012). Defending and the Faith: Reflections on Football in Post-Conflict Bosnia-Herzegovina. In K. Gilbert and W. Bennett (eds), *Sport, Peace and Development*. Champaign, Ill: Common Ground Publishing.

Babiak, K. and Wolfe, R. (2006). More than Just a Game? Corporate Social Responsibility and Super Bowl XL. *Sport Marketing Quarterly*, 15, 214–222.

Becker-Olsen, K.L., Cudmore, A., and Hill, R.P. (2006). The Impact of Perceived Corporate Social Responsibility on Consumer Behavior. *Journal of Business Research*, 59(1), 46–53.

Bourdieu, P. (1984) *Distinction*. London: Routledge.

Calloway, J. (2004) Leave No Child Behind: Recreation and Sports – Instruments for World Peace. *Youth Studies Australia*, 23(1), 35–41.

Coalter, F. (2005). Sport, Social Inclusion and Crime Reduction. In G. Faulkner and A. Taylor (eds), *Exercises Health and Mental Health*. London: Routledge.

Coalter, F. (2007). *A Wider Social Role for Sport: Who's keeping the score?* London: Routledge.

Coalter, F. (2010). The Politics of Sport-for-Development: Limited Focus Programmes and Broad Gauge Problems? *International Review for the Sociology of Sport*, 45(3), 295–314.

Darnell, S. (2008). *Changing the World Through Sport and Play: A Post-Colonial Analysis of Canadian Volunteers Within the 'Sport for Development and Peace' Movement*, unpublished PhD thesis, University of Toronto.

Darnell, S. (2012). *Sport for Development and Peace*. London: A and C Black.

Gasser, P.K. and Levinsen, A. (2004). Breaking Post-War Ice: Open Fun Football Schools in Bosnia and Herzegovina. *Sport in Society*, 7(3), 457–472.

Giulianotti, R. (1994). Social Identity and Public Order: Political and Academic Discourses on Football Violence. In R. Giulianotti, N. Bonney and M. Hepworth (eds), *Football Violence and Social Identity*. London: Routledge.

Giulianotti, R. (2004). Human Rights, Globalization and Sentimental Education: The Case of Sport. *Sport in Society*, 7(3), 355–369.

Giulianotti, R. (2011a). Sport, Peacemaking and Conflict Resolution: A Contextual Analysis and Modeling of the Sport, Development and Peace Sector. *Ethnic and Racial Studies*, 34(2), 207–228.

Giulianotti, R. (2011b). Sport, Transnational Peace-Making and the Global Civil Society: Exploring the Reflective Discourses of 'Sport, Development and Peace' Project Officials. *Journal of Sport and Social Issues*, 35(1), 50–71.

Giulianotti, R. (2011c). The Sport, Development and Peace Sector: A Model of Four Social Policy Domains. *Journal of Social Policy*, 40(4), 757–776.

Giulianotti, R. and Armstrong, G. (2011). Sport, the Military and Peacemaking. *Third World Quarterly*, 32(3), 379–394.

Giulianotti, R. and Robertson, R. (2004). The Globalization of Football: A Study in the Glocalization of the 'Serious Life'. *British Journal of Sociology*, 55(4), 545–568.

Giulianotti, R. and Robertson, R. (2007). Globalization and Sport: Transnational Dimensions. *Global Networks*, 7(2), 166–186.

Giulianotti, R. and Robertson, R. (2009). *Globalization and Football*. London: Sage.

Godfrey, P. (2009). Corporate Social Responsibility in Sport: An Overview and Key Issues. *Journal of Sport Management*, 23, 698–716.

Hartmann, D. and Kwauk, C. (2011). Sport and Development: An Overview, Critique, and Reconstruction. *Journal of Sport and Social Issues*, 35(3), 284–305.

Hartmann, D. (2001). Notes on Midnight Basketball and the Cultural Politics of Recreation, Race, and At-Risk Urban Youth. *Journal of Sport and Social Issues*, 25, 339–371.

Hartmann, D. and Depro, B. (2006). Rethinking Sports-based Community Crime Prevention. A Preliminary Analysis of the Relationship between Midnight Basketball and Urban Crime Rates. *Journal of Sport & Social Issues*, 30(2), 180–196.

Höglund, K. and R. Sundberg (2008). Reconciliation through Sports? The Case of South Africa. *Third World Quarterly*, 29(4), 805–818.

Hognestad, H. and Tollisen, A. (2004). Playing against Deprivation: Football and Development in Nairobi, Kenya. In G. Armstrong and R. Giulianotti (eds), *Football in Africa*. Basingstoke: Palgrave.

Kaldor, M. (2003a). *Global Civil Society*. Cambridge: Polity.

Kaldor, M. (2003b). The Idea of Global Civil Society. *International Affairs*, 79(3), 583–593.

Keane, J. (2003). *Global Civil Society?* Cambridge: Cambridge University Press.

Kidd, B. (2008). A New Social Movement: Sport for Development and Peace. *Sport in Society*, 11(4), 370–380.

Lea-Howarth, J. (2006). *Sport and Conflict: Is Football An Appropriate Tool to Utilise in Conflict Resolution, Reconciliation and Reconstruction?*, MA Dissertation, University of Sussex, accessed at: http://archive.sportanddev.org/data/document/document/238.pdf.

Levermore, R. (2008). Sport: A New Engine of Development. *Progress in Development Studies*, 8(2), 183–190.

Lindsey, I. (2008). Conceptualising Sustainability in Sports Development. *Leisure Studies*, 27(3), 279–294.

Maro, C.N., Roberts, G.C., and Sorensen, M. (2009). Using Sport to Promote HIV/AIDS Education for At-Risk Youths: An Intervention Using Peer Coaches in Football. *Scandinavian Journal of Medicine & Science in Sports*, 19, 129–141.

Pillay, U., and Bass, O. (2008). Mega-events as a Response to Poverty Reduction: The 2012 FIFA World Cup and its Urban Development Implications. *Urban Forum*, 19(3), 329–346.

Robertson, R. (1992). *Globalization: Social Theory and Global Culture.* London: Sage.

Robertson, R. (1995). Glocalization: Time-space and Homogeneity-Heterogeneity. In M. Featherstone, S. Lash and R. Robertson (eds), *Global Modernities.* London: Sage.

Salis, J.F., Bauman, A., and Pratt, M. (1998). Environmental and Policy Interventions to Promote Physical activity. *American Journal of Preventative Medicine*, 15, 379–397.

Salomon, G. (2011). Four Major Challenges Facing Peace Education in Regions of Intractable Conflict. *Peace and Conflict*, 17, 46–59.

Savery, J., and Gilbert, K. (eds) (2011). *Sustainability and Sport.* Champaign, IL: Common Ground.

Schulenkorf, N. (2010). Sport Events and Ethnic Reconciliation: Attempting to Create Social Change in War-Torn Sri Lanka. *International Review for the Sociology of Sport*, 43(3): 273–294.

Tacon, R. (2007). Football and Social Inclusion: Evaluating Social Policy. *Managing Leisure*, 12(1), 1–23.

Timms, J. (2012). The Olympics as a Platform for Protest: A Case Study of the London 2012 'Ethical' Games and the Play Fair Campaign for Workers' rights. *Leisure Studies*, 31(3), 355–372.

UN General Assembly (2006). *Sport for Development and Peace: The Way Forward*, Report of the Secretary-General, A/61/73, New York: United Nations.

Vrcan, S. and D. Lalic (1998). From Ends to Trenches and Back: Football in the Former Yugoslavia. In G. Armstrong and R. Giulianotti (eds), *Football Cultures and Identities*, Basingstoke: Macmillan.

Walseth, K., and Fasting, K. (2004). Sport as a Means of Integrating Minority Women. *Sport in Society*, 7(1), 109–129.

Whitfield, G. (2006). *Amity in the Middle East: How the World Sport Peace Project and the Passion for Football Brought Together Arab and Jewish Youngsters.* London: Alpha Press.

Willis, O. (2000). Sport and Development: The Significance of Mathare Youth Sports Association. *Canadian Journal of Development Studies*, 21, 825–849.

Zoubi, B. (2011). *The Direct and Indirect Influence of Jewish and Arab Participation in Bi-National Soccer Clubs on the Attitudes and Perceptions of Their Family Members and Friends toward the Other Side*, unpublished PhD thesis, University of Haifa.

3
De-Colonising the Politics and Practice of Sport-for-Development: Critical Insights from Post-Colonial Feminist Theory and Methods

Simon C. Darnell and Lyndsay M.C. Hayhurst

Introduction

There is now significant global recognition of, and support for, the role of sport in helping to achieve international development goals and peaceful co-existence. This can be seen in the institutionalisation and professionalisation of the 'Sport for Development and Peace' (SDP) sector, and the work of numerous non-governmental organisations (NGOs) that now plan and implement SDP programmes around the world.[1] The establishment of the SDP sector is also evident through the work of the United Nations Office on Sport for Development and Peace (UNOSDP), which acts as an advocate and organiser. In its recent report (2011), the UNOSDP described its mandate as working:

> to promote sport as an innovative and efficient tool in advancing the United Nations' goals, missions and values. Through advocacy, partnership facilitation, policy work, project support and diplomacy, UNOSDP strives to maximize the contribution of sport and physical activity to help create a safer, more secure, more sustainable, more equitable future.

The report goes on to state that the UNOSDP has recently assumed a more direct-action approach to SDP, particularly through its financial and organisational support of programme implementation. For example, it took a leadership role in mobilising one million Euros of funding from the Union of European Football Associations (UEFA) – known as the 'Monaco Charity Award' – and then identifying five programmes to receive a share of the funding. One recipient was the Gatumba Youth Centre in Bujumbura, Burundi, a programme that organises sport in order to promote HIV/AIDS awareness, citizenship education and social and cultural reconciliation, particularly given the history of ethnic violence in that country. As the UNOSDP stated, the centre will '... provide a social and cultural point of gathering for 7,000 young women and men in the commune of Mutimbuzi and at the cross-borders of Gatumba, and thus promote better social cohesion between Burundi, the Democratic Republic of Congo and Rwanda youth' (un.org, 2012).

While the UNOSDP's mandate to organise and mobilise sport to make a positive contribution to equitable and sustainable development in countries like Burundi is laudable,[2] what is rarely acknowledged within SDP discourse, rhetoric and policy is the fact that many current programmes – such as the Gatumba Youth Centre – operate within a social, political and geographic context directly and indelibly marked by the history of colonisation. Indeed, implementing a SDP project to redress issues of underdevelopment and violence, such as ethnic conflict in Burundi, can be understood as the mobilisation of sport to overcome current social and political inequalities that have roots in the European colonial project and are implicated in processes of neo-colonialism.[3]

Given this criticism, our central argument in this chapter is that the implementation of SDP programmes and policies, particularly those organised and supported by international organisations like the UNOSDP and its 'partners' in places like Bujumbura, Burundi, calls for an accompanying understanding of (a) the history of colonialism, (b) the connections of this history to contemporary practices and structures of imperialism and/or neo-colonialism, and, (c) theories and methodologies of decolonisation. From this critical perspective, a post-colonial feminist approach is particularly useful for foregrounding, situating and deconstructing the ways that cross-cultural and/or global relations of power, domination and resistance are deeply enmeshed in the locales of SDP activity and even in SDP policy and programming itself. Post-colonial feminist theory is principally concerned with resisting and transforming the traditional production and circulation of global power, knowledge and resources in order to destabilise assumptions that perpetuate colonialism in both material and discursive forms. In addition, the *feminist* orientation of post-colonial theory reminds us that gender hierarchies – produced and constrained by structures of race, ethnicity, class and sexuality – were organising principles of the traditional colonial project, and that women and girls have borne the brunt of global poverty and exploitation, and continue to do so. Post-colonial feminism therefore promotes a praxis of resistance that strives to unsettle Eurocentric, ahistorical understandings of women, men and the classed, racialised body particularly within modern political-economic forces of neo-liberal globalisation[4] (Peterson and Runyan, 2010).

In turn, this theoretical approach draws attention to the vulnerabilities experienced by gendered and ethno-racialised subjects and bodies and considers these exposures in relation to agency, resistance and collective action. Thus, we argue that post-colonial feminism is useful for the purposes of our chapter as it questions presumptions about the 'beneficiaries' of development programmes (see Agathangelou and Ling, 2009; Rankin, 2010), an issue particularly relevant in the case of the Gatumba Youth Centre. For example, according to Seckinelgin et al. (2010), a lack of attention paid to gender hierarchies in understanding HIV/AIDS in Burundi has served to solidify the notion that the pandemic is a matter first and foremost of national security and that women living with the virus, such as those working in the sex trade, are a threat thereto. This type of analysis should lead scholars to think critically about the dominant logic put forth within the SDP sector that often conceptualises sport as a tool by which to 'empower' women and girls (see Chawansky, 2011; Hayhurst, in press) and/or to build social capital among youth (see Coalter, 2010), but tends to do so through a rationalised, input-output model that may secure current colonising hierarchies (see Kay, 2009). We therefore suggest that a post-colonial feminist framework helps to think of gendered, racialised bodies as more than instrumentalised and passive targets of SDP programmes, and to consider how multiple femininities (and masculinities) may be produced and constrained by the historical implications of colonialism and current structures of inequality.

Indeed, and as we argue in this chapter, when post-colonial feminist perspectives take up a participatory action research (PAR) approach, there is potential to move away from traditional, and potentially colonising flows of development as stewardship and aid and towards more socially just and collaborative efforts that challenge normative structures of dialogue and programme implementation within SDP. Post-colonial feminism provides a useful theoretical approach to community based PAR, enabling academics to explore how their scholarship may foster more ethical, transformational actions and tangible social change (see Reid et al., 2012).[5] Scholars utilising this approach will not only confront colonising tendencies within SDP policy, practice and research, but also 'relinquish some of [our] power within the research process ... to facilitate community control' (Reid et al., 2012: 191). Doing research in this way can be messy, uncomfortable and ethically challenging. However, SDP researchers have called recently for theoretically informed analyses of the processes by which long-term, sustainable and equitable development and peace outcomes for marginalised peoples may (or may not) be achieved (see Coalter, 2007, 2010; Kay, 2009; Schnitzer et al., 2013). In response to this, a post-colonial feminist, PAR-infused approach to SDP is timely, one that focuses on deconstructing neo-colonialism, particularly by privileging local knowledge, political agency and struggle within structures of inequality.

In this way, a post-colonial feminist praxis encourages scholars of SDP to acknowledge in material terms the history of colonisation within which sport-for-development programmes now operate, but also to engage with practices of knowledge production aimed at unravelling traditional hierarchies and binaries built along lines of race, class, gender and sexuality (see Darnell, 2012). With both of these goals in mind, this chapter offers a framework for understanding colonialism (both post- and neo-) within the spaces of SDP, and then offers insights from post-colonial feminist theory that provide theoretical and methodological tools to scholars and practitioners interested in de-colonising the practice of sport-for-development (S4D). We pay specific attention to (a) material relations, (b) representation and knowledge and (c) ethical encounters with those involved in our research and SDP programming more broadly. The chapter is not based on our empirical work directly, but the themes discussed have been developed from insights we have drawn from post-colonial feminism and found useful and challenging in the study of SDP. We are not suggesting that SDP practices are essentially neo-colonialist;[6] rather we draw attention to the history that underpins development inequality, the potential complicity between SDP and contemporary forms of colonising knowledge and policy, and the need to activate a politically explicit, socially engaged approach to researching and practicing SDP. Overall, our aim is to contribute to destabilising 'colonial continuities' in international development initiatives (Heron, 2007), particularly those focused on sport.

Post-colonialism and development (through sport)

The term 'colonialism' most often refers to the European colonial project (historical in its origins, but also contemporary in its effects and even practices) during which European people and nations colonised, controlled and dominated large swathes of the world after the Renaissance (Ashgate et al., 1998).[7] According to Loomba (2005), by the 1930s, 84 per cent of the land surface of the Earth was a colony or ex-colony. Burundi, of particular interest in this chapter, was controlled by Germany from 1897 to 1916 as part of the colony of Ruanda-Urundi and then, after Germany's defeat in World War I, came under control of the Belgian empire from 1916 to 1962 (Curtis, 2013; Daley, 2006).[8]

The inequalities and violence rooted in this history of colonialism underpin many of the current development and peace efforts of SDP. Traditional European colonial practices mobilised racism in tandem with patriarchy, social class and normative sexuality to support the spatial and economic dominance of European subjects (Stoler, 1995), with often devastating effects for the colonised. One result was the complex formation of strict ethnic identities out of a pre-colonial tradition of hybridity in the south of Africa (Berman, 2010). In Burundi, the ethnic conflicts between Hutus and Tutsis in the twentieth century, during which an estimated 200,000 people were killed in 1972 and 20,000 in 1988 (Daley, 2008) can be traced back to colonialist practices of social engineering and economic exploitation that took existing (though complex and fluid) identities among Burundian people and supported their transformation into rigid ethnicities. In this sense, 'violence in Burundi is the product of historic processes tied to colonialism and state formation' (Curtis, 2013: 79). According to Daley (2006: 664):

> In Burundi, colonialism transformed the political culture and destroyed the national consensus. Colonial social and administrative policies created and supported a new racial and ethnic hierarchy through the introduction of racist ideology and its application to pre-existing patterns of social differentiation.

Given that the legacy of ethnic conflict in Burundi is inseparable from the legacy of colonial intervention and stewardship, at the very least knowledge and understanding about these legacies should inform the politics, purposes and design of current development programmes and policies in that country, including those focused on and utilising sport.

Of course, formal processes of global decolonisation did occur in the 1950s and 1960s. Burundi became a sovereign nation in 1962, and many other countries in Africa and the 'developing world' also asserted independence during this era. As a result, the term 'decolonisation' is now often used to refer to 'a process by which colonial powers left, whether voluntarily or by force, from their overseas possessions in various areas of Africa and Asia' (Le Sueur, 2003: 2). From this perspective, it is possible to use the prefix 'post' in post-colonial as a means to designate the end of the formal period of European colonisation.

However, suggesting that the era of decolonisation brought to an end the effects of colonialism, and using 'post-colonial' as a term to designate the end of the colonial project, can be misleading because the concept of 'colonialism' also connects to contemporary inequalities and the current global and transnational machinations of power and authority. Specifically, it is reasonable to argue that the social, political and economic order established through the European colonial project remains largely in place within the current economic global order of the One-Third/Two-Thirds worlds.[9] In fact, many scholars argue that *re-colonisation* of the Two-Thirds world occurred through global capitalism and neo-liberal globalisation (Li, 2007; Saul, 2008). The quintessential example here is the policy of structural adjustment introduced by the International Monetary Fund and the World Bank in the second half of the twentieth century that made political reforms a condition of financial lending to poor countries. Promoted as a means of reducing corruption, improving efficiency and trade, and bringing post-colonial polities in line with the preferred global system of governance, structural adjustment programmes (SAPs) instead devastated public services, reduced public confidence in the state, and encouraged government officials to bolster their own authority (see Adekanye, 1995). In Burundi, a country that saw its national debt increase by 479 per cent in the 1980s, the social and economic destabilisation supported by SAPs fomented militarisation and conflict, particularly along ethnic lines (Adekanye, 1995). SAPs were, in effect, modern day practices of re- or neo-colonialism; as such, we advocate for *post-colonialism* to refer not to the end of colonialism but as a theory, method and praxis that attends to, and attempts to unpack, the effects of colonisation on people and cultures (Ashgate et al., 1998). This perspective requires understanding the *conditions* of the post-colonial as ' … the political, cultural and economic realities of societies living with the legacies and in the aftermath of colonialism' (McEwan, 2009: 21), supported by a de-colonising praxis that deconstructs the marginalisation and inequalities that follow from these legacies (Smith, 1999).

In this sense, even without the physical occupation and direct rule characteristic of traditional colonialism, many of its effects continue. For example, even though the World Bank began to move away from SAPs in the 1990s, due in part to sustained criticism of its effects, it replaced such policies with Performance Based Allocations (PBAs) that directed loans towards regions and states deemed by donors to have suitable geo-political environments for investment and growth (Van Waeyenberge, 2010). This new approach promoted a greater 'pedagogical' role for the World Bank and donor community based on its self-identification as a knowledge hub for international development (Van Waeyenberge, 2010: 96), and suggested an on-going colonising relationship with low-income countries and the Two-Thirds World.[10] Within these shifting structures of global neo-liberal policy and politics, it is the poor, people of colour and women who not only disproportionately suffer but also are most likely to be rendered to subaltern status. The context, then, within which SDP programmes most regularly occur can be thought of as one in which to apply a de-colonising framework (see Darnell and Hayhurst, 2011).

Crucially for the study of SDP, these colonial histories and their contemporary effects also connect to the prevalence, popularity and intelligibility of global sports like football/soccer. According to Darby (2003: 359), it 'is undeniable ... that football in Africa is a legacy of European colonialism.' This allows Darby to argue that the implementation of the conditions necessary for the popularisation of the game on the African continent during the late 19th and early 20th centuries occurred within the same social and political milieu that facilitated the exploitation of African people and their impoverishment under European rule. The universality of sports such as football, upon which much SDP discourse and practice rests, should therefore be recognised as largely inseparable from colonial histories (see Saavedra, 2009) and a de-colonising toolkit can be highlighted as a logical response.

In turn, bringing a post-colonial feminist perspective to bear on SDP is important given the regularity of critical research that demonstrates colonising tendencies within the sector (also see Giles and Lynch, in press). Indeed, in our previous work (see Darnell and Hayhurst, 2011), we cited several studies of SDP that offered evidence of colonising tendencies. Since the writing of that article, more research has demonstrated such proclivities. Nicholls et al. (2011) argued recently that the on-going call for evidence to 'prove' the effectiveness of SDP programmes in the Global South perpetuates a colonising relationship between the expertise of northern financial donors and policy-makers, versus local knowledge of S4D that is often subjugated within structures of monitoring and evaluation. In order for knowledge and policy to be co-produced, rather than imposed within SDP, they call for donors and researchers to ' ... systematically examine and try to dismantle colonial power relations that still pervade this field' (Nicholls et al., 2011: 261).

Similarly, Chawansky (2011) has called attention to gender within the post-colonial spaces of SDP, arguing that dominant approaches to S4D tend to provide for girls' participation in mixed-gender environments, or facilitate female empowerment through the overcoming of obstacles, but rarely argue for the deconstruction of dominant gender hierarchies that lead to the oppression of girls and women in the first place, hierarchies that can actually be perpetuated in the normative culture of sport itself.[11] This is a familiar refrain for critical scholars of sport. As Hargreaves argued nearly a decade ago (2004: 197), there is 'a tendency to view sport development for Third World women as essentially beneficial and a way of addressing their underdevelopment and bringing them into the modern world.' This aligns with Connor and McEwen's (2011) recent examination of development efforts led by the International Association of Athletics Federations (IAAF) which, through its Regional Development Centres, claims to support the development of athletics in the Two-Thirds World, but does so through top-down programmes and policies that benefit its marketing and media exposure but do not translate into the development of the sport at a local level. Men and women, particularly those of colour, are often marginalised and exploited in this type of structure and critical responses thereto are called for. At the same time, post-colonial theory also reminds us of the importance of analysing ostensibly progressive forms of feminism that can actually re-inscribe colonial relations. As Hargreaves has suggested (2004: 197):

> women from the West and neo-colonial elites are characterized as benefactors arguing for sports resources on behalf of the dispossessed – a position that silences the voices and desires of women in poor communities who are struggling for autonomy in sport on their own terms.

When taken together, the movement of athletic labour out of Africa and the Caribbean via traditionally colonial geographic and social vectors, combined with attempts to modernise and 'develop' women through sport, makes clear the neo-colonial potential of international sport. Given that international sport organisations have clear ties to the SDP sector,[12] the need for a post-colonial feminist commitment to policies and practices of SDP is evident.

Before highlighting some key dimensions of a post-colonial feminist approach to practicing and researching SDP, it is important to recognise the criticisms of post-colonial theorising, and to learn from its limitations. There remains a compelling argument that post-colonial theorising, particularly in its focus on literature and culture, has tended to overlook or even reject history as a discipline implicated in the production of imperial power (see Kennedy, 2003).[13] Similar arguments have suggested that critiques of colonialism and colonising practices afford undue attention to people in power and, in doing so, perpetuate the centrality and importance of the colonising subject. While sympathetic to such critiques of Western-led knowledge production and preoccupation with the experiences of the privileged, we are here, following Mohanty (2003), calling for analysis of *specific and particular* histories and their effects in contemporary post-colonial spaces.[14] This scholarly effort should not only focus on the experiences and contexts of marginalised people, but also actively resist knowledge of and about post-colonial people that proffers neutrality or benevolence yet permits colonising histories, discourses and knowledge production to remain intact (also see Smith, 1999). Mohanty's theorising impels us to recognise that despite a burgeoning field of critical SDP research, it remains rare for scholars or practitioners to seek out, learn of, and deconstruct the specific political, social and economic factors that led to the development inequalities to which sport and SDP now attend. Nor do many SDP researchers or advocates deconstruct their own complicity in the histories and structures that have established and maintained global hierarchies. In response, we have identified three ways in which to conceptualise SDP as a post-colonial space and through which to pursue a deconstructionist methodology in an ethically accountable fashion.

Post-colonial feminist approaches to SDP: theory and practice

SDP is implicated in post- and neo-colonialism in multiple ways. First, as mentioned earlier, SDP is implicated in colonial histories to the extent that the problems of violence and underdevelopment that the sector regularly seeks to solve often have historical and colonial underpinnings, and that, second, global sport itself has a colonial history. Third, SDP is associated with a contemporary global order of neo-liberal globalisation and hyper-capitalist patriarchy. This global order prioritises a universal, neo-liberal, market-based system that tends to exacerbate social and structural inequalities along lines of race, class and gender, yet continues to be normalised as the solution to all social problems.[15] In turn, and fourth, belief in the benevolent power of sport as a tool for development and peace increases the possibility that SDP programmes and policies might overlook the history of colonialism and the current need for decolonisation. Finally, there is always the possibility for SDP to contribute to colonising knowledge by aligning with, rather than exposing, critiquing or organising against the dominant logic of neo-liberal globalisation (see Darnell, 2010a; Hayhurst, 2013).

Given these challenges, we advocate expanding the concept of post-colonialism and decolonisation in the study of SDP in order to include and be used to embrace 'the process of revealing and dismantling colonialist power in all its forms' (Ashgate et al, 1998: 63). Here we offer some suggestions – and highlight some struggles and personal experiences – that may be helpful for researchers who are interested in bringing postcolonial feminism to bear on SDP. Several specific frameworks of theory/method exist through which to mobilise post-colonial feminism in and through SDP, but given the scope of this chapter we focus on three that we feel best illustrate the varied significance, importance and application of this praxis: Material Relations; Representation and Knowledge; and Ethical Encounters.

Issue 1 – material relations

By material relations, we refer to the fact that the actual conditions and experiences of life in the Two-Thirds World – such as poverty, lack of resources and even violence – that serve as the foci of so many international development inequalities have colonial histories and can be considered to be the effects of neo-colonialist practice.[16] Yet, given the lack of a sustained post-colonial approach to SDP, these relations are also often over-looked or even (mis)understood as fundamental failings or lacks on the part of the inhabitants of the Two-Thirds World. For example, returning to the case of Burundi, while ethnic cleavages between Hutus and Tutsis have undoubtedly been implicated in the violence and underdevelopment experienced in that country, it has become an attractive, and even dominant, discourse to reduce the conflict in Burundi to something of an 'age-old enmity' between rival tribes (Daley, 2006: 658). This type of knowledge serves to simplify the roots of conflict in Burundi to essentialised ethnicities and ethnic characteristics rather than recognise that the construction of ethnicity has always been connected to struggles for economic and political control within the country. When considering SDP programming in Burundi, rather than applying sport in order to transcend longstanding conflicts, what is needed in research and practice is an:

understanding of the complexities of identity politics in the context of the postcolonial state, and their relationship to the historical processes and structural forces that have continued to ensure the impoverishment of African communities and the persistence of non-representative politics (Daley, 2006: 659).

From this perspective, post-colonial feminism can be supported through critical pedagogy and the embracing of development (and SDP) as a form of political activism.[17] In the case of SDP, this might mean that in addition to, or even instead of, drawing on the popularity or convening power of sport to promote individual behaviour change, security, or social capital, sport could be organised to draw explicit attention to the history of colonialism in Burundi, and to move towards peace by supporting the political struggles and courage of local people as they build their own communities. This could also involve connecting the popularity of sport, and particular sports events, to meetings, hearings or commissions in the social and political tradition of truth and reconciliation. In all of these cases, SDP advocates, particularly those who travel from the One-Third World to work in the SDP sector internationally, both require and deserve educational support and training that goes beyond 'cultural sensitivity' and embraces critiques of neo-liberalism and the political contestability of traditional development practices. Perhaps more importantly, though, this approach could also mean that powerful SDP organisations – like the UNOSDP or IOC – might move away from perpetuating notions of sport's political transcendence, or promoting and securing flows of charitable aid, and move towards linking the popularity of sport to organised calls for international debt relief, fair trade practices and distributive justice. While we do not expect to see global sport organisations like the IOC embrace such a de-colonising approach to SDP in the near future, particularly given their complicity in global flows of exploitation, the need for this type of critical analysis of SDP remains (see Maguire, 2011).

   Approaching the material conditions of post-colonialism in this way is also useful for responding to the criticism that post-colonial theory tends to facilitate analysis of cultural difference but oftentimes does so at the expense of analysing economic exploitation (see Loomba, 2005). A thorough de-colonising framework should acknowledge and – where appropriate – challenge structural forces of exploitation. In Burundi, a country living with the effects of SAPs, neo-liberal peace proposals in the 1990s and early 2000s reduced state power in an effort to displace ethnic elites. However, this approach had the effect of stripping health and welfare programmes at the time they were most desperately needed (Daley, 2007). For SDP programmes and policies, committing to decolonisation would mean organising SDP and sport-for-peace in ways that not only bring people together but also encourage protest and resistance against the material and social hierarchies and structures induced by neo-liberal policy that perpetuate inequality and impoverishment and lead to violence and desperation. These factors may often be external to sport, though, as Connor and McEwen (2011) have shown, sport organisations and structures may actually perpetuate them as well. In either case, where athletes in previous formations of SDP were motivated to raise money to support international aid efforts (Kidd, 2008), a move towards decolonisation of SDP suggests a very different model. It underscores instead the need for SDP activist struggles that work to expose the effects of neo-liberal capital and policy in countries like Burundi, and in turn seek to support local communities in working towards self-sustainment and independence.

Such an approach to SDP is clearly no small chore, given that, like development more broadly, SDP programming has been shown to be borne out of, and therefore susceptible to, the logic of neo-liberalism (Darnell, 2010a; Hartmann and Kwauk, 2011; Hayhurst, 2009). That is, SDP programming can actually reproduce the hegemony of neo-liberalism by striving to 'teach' inhabitants of the Two-Thirds World to participate better in competitive capitalism (and therefore to secure and sustain it) rather than to challenge structures underlying their exploitation and division (see Darnell, 2010a; Hartmann and Kwauk, 2011). In places like Burundi, such logic is particularly noticeable, and may be particularly attractive to those working in SDP, given that neo-liberalism has regularly underpinned efforts to broker and promote peaceful co-existence (Daley, 2007). Rather than positioning peace negotiations as an opportunity to attend to both the history of colonial oppression and current structures of social injustice in Burundi, ethnic conflict has been pitched as a struggle between combatants for access to, and representation within, political authority, state institutions and economic structures (see Curtis, 2013). International donors and diplomats have therefore tended to construct peacebuilding in Burundi as a process of improving the sharing of power among civil society actors or reducing the grip of particular ethnic elites; however, in doing so the peacebuilding process has rarely questioned the dominant logic of private ownership, reduced state sovereignty, and international dependence that sustains inequality and exacerbates violence (Daley, 2007). As Berman (2010: 30) argues, ethnic conflicts over claims to land and group purity in African states – violence that is regularly interpreted in the One-Third World as an essential feature of African culture – are underpinned by the differential access to wealth and power characteristic of neo-liberal globalisation. The 'scientific' application of democracy to African states since formal decolonisation has therefore seen states differentially recognise groups and allocate resources in ways that secure exclusive and competitive group identities (Berman, 2010). It is reasonable to argue that SDP's preferred response to such endemic issues of violence and discord has been to mobilise sport as a tool for cross-ethnic understanding, the promotion and education of individual capital, and the building of skills necessary to survive within such structures of violence. In contrast, a post-colonial feminist approach to SDP would call for collective mobilisation against the Eurocentric, gendered, ethno-racialised and often externally induced processes that secure private interests in the name of competition.

Again, we do recognise the extent of the challenge involved in successfully encouraging the SDP sector to actively and effectively resist neo-liberal policies that contribute to global inequalities and local suffering. While this is a daunting task, a starting point is for progressive SDP stakeholders to recognise and acknowledge that economic underdevelopment and violence in Burundi is a result, at least in part, of the complexities of colonisation and contemporary policies and politics, rather than the essential character and failings of the Burundian people. This could then lead to policy reform that works *with* local people to support their resistance to neo-liberalism rather than 'teaching' them the skills to survive within competitive capitalism. From this perspective, the representation and knowledge of development inequalities and social actors in places like Burundi takes on significant importance and we discuss this topic next.

Issue 2 – representation and knowledge

A second, but no less important reason for committing to a post-colonial feminist approach to SDP is that without such a perspective, colonising myths and stereotypes tend to continue, and even prevail. At issue here is the politics of representation, and the types of knowledge that various representations can and do produce, a topic that constitutes a major point of discussion within post-colonial feminist theory, critical development studies and de-colonising methodologies. As Spivak (1988) has contended, the post-colonial critic has to confront a 'dark vision' of 'Otherness', which can detract from the ability of the 'subaltern to speak' as they are denied full political representation. At the same time, concerns with representation and knowledge are often 'perceived as too far removed from the exigencies of the lived experiences of millions of impoverished people' (Jackson, 1997, as cited in McEwan, 2009: 112). Issues of representation and knowledge may fail to connect with the material realities and local conditions of everyday life experienced by subalterns.[18] In response, what is called for is the deconstruction of systems of representation that produce claims to truth and reality in SDP in ways that sustain unjust hierarchies of knowledge production and privilege northern understandings of the success or failure of SDP. In order to underline this point, we use the example of technologies of aid evaluation as they relate to representation and knowledge in SDP.

By calling attention to the rigidity of technologies of aid evaluation in SDP, we highlight the fact that particular methodologies, such as quantitative donor monitoring and evaluation reports, tend to dominate analyses of SDP effectiveness using Westernised notions of 'success' and 'evidence' (see Nicholls et al., 2011). In turn, such reporting can silence targeted beneficiaries and represent 'outputs,' such as women's empowerment, healthy living and other outcomes of SDP programmes in homogenising ways; these often fail to address the agency, contexts and nuanced lives of those on the 'receiving end' of such initiatives (Kay, 2009). All too frequently, the stories, experiences, 'truths' – and indeed, the 'pain' – of those involved in SDP are simply quantified, photographed or written about for the purposes of monitoring and evaluation, publications and other uses (sometimes without informed consent).

For example, when donors (and even researchers) visit SDP programmes, they may take photos, record the number of participants, document the stories of programme participants, and then use these images and texts in order to solicit donations, report back to other funders in the One-Third World, or claim to have proven that the programme 'works' by meeting certain outputs. In many ways, these actions are a form of re-colonisation through neo-liberal systems of aid, and illustrate the ways that race, ethnicity, gender, and even neoliberalism intersect to create and represent 'knowable Others' through governmental strategies. The discursive formations of aid effectiveness tend to use evaluative language that conceal and misconstrue the lived realities of what 'success' actually means on the ground in a specific cultural context (Campbell and Teghtsoonian, 2010; Mosse, 2004). Aid effectiveness, then, can construct forms of SDP as universal or apolitical, when in fact the indices of development and/or peacebuilding success that are often inserted by ruling entities (i.e. donors) into local practices tend to privilege neo-liberal politics and policies (Darnell, 2010a).[19] Such processes can serve to establish a regulatory framework aimed at the 'targeted beneficiaries' of development programming and policy (Campbell and Teghtsoonian, 2010) that instead reflects the needs, desires, experiences and politics of donors more than participants.

This is not to say that targeted beneficiaries have no agency or ability to resist, change or challenge the ways they participate and are represented in SDP programmes (see Darnell and Hayhurst, 2012; Lindsey and Grattan, 2012). Indeed, those working 'on the ground' in SDP – whether as participants or as local sport-for-development programmers – are often able to exert agency and strategically assert their voices, opinions and perspectives through, for example, the power of visual representation and online testimonials presented on their websites. As one interviewee (a staff member from a Ugandan NGO doing work on girls' empowerment through martial arts) from Hayhurst's (2011) study noted:

> In the PR [public relations] department [of the NGO] I have also been taking [the girls'] videos and photos, and what they have been so much interested in is the way they look at their photos on how they have participated in karate. They like it so much because they feel that they are being exposed to the outside world.

In this way, sport can offer a medium in and through which to assert identity and forms of agency, and actors in post-colonial spaces are increasingly using the Internet and new media to disseminate visual images and texts that *they have created*, so that the local is privileged, and resistance to stewardship is (potentially) mobilised.[20] As Prabhu (2003, as cited by McEwan, 2009) has argued, 'the use of testimonials, novels, art, images, films and photography is potentially useful to development researchers in the context of postcolonial critiques and the urgency of moving away from purely economic analyses' (Prabhu, 2003: 273).

At the same time, the imperative remains to consider such forms of representation against the hegemonic development practices of donors that may exploit partners in the Two-Thirds World and leave minimal space for the resistance of people and groups working on their *own* SDP initiatives. Photography played an influential role in colonialism by 'representing' the 'exotic Other' to 'audiences back home' (Gallagher and Kim, 2008: 104). In the face of these opportunities and challenges, SDP research from a post-colonial feminist perspective should investigate how different knowledge, meanings and representations of S4D are constructed in dissimilar post-colonial contexts. This must include an understanding of practices that potentially challenge and contest the dominant discursive formations of SDP as circulated by donors, celebrity NGO ambassadors and UN officials.

Issue 3 – ethical encounters

How do we connect inquiry with a commitment to feminist politics? How do we represent lives and sensibilities from a space of otherness and render them intimate and with the dignity they deserve? Hedge (2009: 279)

These questions from Hedge illuminate the types of ethical struggles incurred when taking on a post-colonial feminist, de-colonising approach to studying SDP. From our perspective, ethical research that challenges colonising relations and knowledge would begin by questioning the politics of traditional, modernist attitudes and valuing diversity over universality (Battiste, 2008). In recognition of this, we maintain that it is necessary to acknowledge and account for the embodiment, positionality, social location and biography of the researcher. Indeed, in post-colonial feminist research, as with other research fields, 'positionality has become a critical concept and practice to address questions of voice and authority' (Benson and Nagar, 2006: 583). In this way, it is important to question how and whether we can acknowledge the voices of subalterns and speak against colonising tendencies through research when, unavoidably, our voices as White, middle-class, non-local, one-third world researchers become 'the authority' in our studies as we write on behalf of the 'subaltern subject.' That is, (how) is it possible to ethically explore or explain the experience of others while respecting their full subjectivity?

This is an on-going challenge. Kapoor (2004) has contended that Spivak's work on subaltern agency instigated a plethora of hyper-self-reflexive research on development in the Two-Thirds World, where researchers must now be 'unscrupulously vigilant ... about our complicities' (Kapoor, 2004: 641). The hope is that 'Hyper-self-reflexive' research in the Two-Thirds World 'contextualize(s) our claims, reduces the risk of personal arrogance or geoinstitutional imperialism, and moves one toward a non-hierarchical encounter with the Third World/subaltern' (Kapoor, 2004: 641). And yet, the micro-local elements of hyper-reflexivity often fail to engage with the realities of carrying out institutional, macro-global research, particularly the type of project outlined in many studies that explore SDP programmes in multiple countries (e.g. Giulianotti, 2011; Kay, 2009). For example, how is it possible for researchers exploring 'global SDP' to ensure a compassionate, ethical, respectful face-to-face encounter with subalterns that is attentive to their local contexts? As Kapoor (2004: 643) enquired: 'is an intimate relationship with the subaltern even compatible with institutional processes, let alone on a large scale?' On this point, we concur with Rankin's (2010) submission that the challenge for those conducting critical development research is in fostering a reflexive praxis that nurtures – in accountable, historical, contextual, ethical and respectful ways – issues of difference as well as local, micro-level relations with Two-Thirds World inhabitants.[21]

Further, while striving for mutual respect and hyper-self-reflexivity is important, we are not convinced that simply rehearsing and confessing power differences that recognise our social and spatial locations does enough to disentangle the colonial residue and the complexity of methodological and ethical issues that arise through carrying out qualitative research in SDP, a topic that we have both reflected on in our recent research (e.g. Darnell, 2012; Hayhurst, 2011). Bhavnani (2007: 642), for example, is critical of researchers who simply note their racial/ethnic identity, sex/gender, age, class and ability and then proceed to discuss their research 'as if objectivity is possible as a transcendent vision'. Therefore, we suggest that it is crucial to go beyond mere reflexivity and to strive to ensure that SDP research disseminates truth that holds meaning for the individuals, communities and institutions under examination (see Benson and Nagar, 2006; Kirkham and Anderson, 2002; Racine, 2003).

A specific example of this is the issue of language – where 'lin-guicide' has worked to erase diversity (see Swadener and Kagendo, 2008). Hall (1997) has shown how language creates representation, resulting in meaning, and that examining meaning in terms of processes of translation is fruitful in order to 'facilitate cultural communication', while recognising interlocking systems of power and difference between speakers (Hall, 1997). In the context of cross-cultural communication, notions of difference often become 'softened' through the political act of the translator, as local people's agency over their own dialect, priorities, knowledge and understanding is increasingly lost (West, 2005). Palmary (2011: 102) warns of such assimilating tendencies given that 'translation is first and foremost a process of acculturation, which aims to make the speech familiar in the target language so that the listener may recognise her own culture in a cultural other'. This reminds us that the English language has been, and continues to be, a practice of colonisation, and we concur with Swadener and Kagendo (2008: 39), who warn that translating the experiences of all local interviewees into English works to re-affirm 'lin-guicide' as a hegemonic vernacular in social sciences research:

> Lin-guicide has become a powerful force, with the hegemony of the English and other 'globalized' languages threatening indigenous languages and the language rights of those who speak such 'endangered' languages or feel pressures to write in English when many indigenous concepts do not accurately translate – if they translate at all – into English or other European languages.

These ethical concerns have surfaced as we have conducted interviews with non-English speakers, and with participants for whom English was a second language. And yet, cross-cultural research in SDP need not focus solely on the inevitabilities of barriers to communication and misinterpretation. Rather, we prefer Maclean's (2007: 789) understandings of translation as 'an act of creation and a dynamic, ongoing process.' The work of Maclean (2007) and Palmary (2011) therefore suggests that translation may provide an opportunity to promote and facilitate cross-cultural dialogue and ethical encounters with research participants.

These issues link to an ethical framework that we suggest to be particularly useful for guiding SDP research, captured in the acronym OCAP: Ownership, Control, Access and Possession (see Lavallée and Howard, 2011). In short, upholding these elements of research and practice means that we must prioritise the community, sovereignty, capacity, authority and leadership of local people when it comes to SDP programming and practice (Kay et al., 2012). These OCAP principles also tend to be embedded and operationalised in PAR approaches that seek meaningful dialogue and community engagement *before* a study is conducted (Reid and Frisby, 2008). This may involve organising workshops, community meetings and seminars that bring relevant stakeholders to the table before a research programme begins in order to ensure a collaborative approach, and that a range of questions and perspectives will recognised.

To date, examples of PAR approaches in the SDP context remain scarce. However, two recent studies draw upon, and indeed demonstrate, the ways that ethical, and even socially transformative research agendas might enhance SDP. These studies have the potential to: (a) connect research to the material lived realities of the post-colonial world and (b) facilitate perspectives beyond those of academics sympathetic to the neo-liberal paradigm, or those who are located within neo-liberal academies in the One-Third World. First, recent research by Sara Forde (2008) usefully engages with the lived realities of a SDP programme known as *Moving the Goalposts* (*MTG*), an initiative that uses football (among other 'tools') to try to improve the lives of young women residing in Kilfili, Kenya. Forde – a White, middle-class woman born in England who resides in Kilfili with her family – founded MTG in 2002. Through her research with young women participating in MTG's programmes, Forde uses her proficiency in Kiswahili (the local language), combined with her experiences as a journalist and her interest in activism, football and SDP, to engage MTG participants to share their stories of football and the life challenges they face as young women growing up in Kenya. We contend that Forde's work offers refreshing insights and perspectives into how reflexive, place-focused, community-driven and ethical research in SDP might be advanced (also see Holte-McKenzie et al., 2006 for further research on MTG's participatory approaches to monitoring and evaluation).[22]

Second, recent work by a group of African scholars studying gender as it intersects with sport and development provides auspicious examples of research by academics in Two-Thirds World countries that help to describe, critique and question the dominant logic of SDP and to do so from the perspective and context of the post-colonial subject (Shehu, 2010). *Gender, Sport and Development in Africa* presents findings that contextualise the sporting landscape for women and girls in Sub-Saharan Africa. For example, in distinction to the presumption of sport as an inherent form of gender empowerment, Shehu shows how, in many Sub-Saharan countries, women are viewed as a threat to the male system of power relations in sport, and that females subsequently 'become targets of toxic myths, stigmas, and harassment in sport spaces to perpetuate the domination of these spaces by heterosexual, masculine males' (Shehu, 2010: x). Similarly, in Zimbabwe, Daimon (2010) describes how by entering the soccer stadium, female spectators are often the more susceptible targets of soccer violence, increasingly subjected to sexual harassment, gender-based violence and insulting remarks and ridicule supported by the public, which inevitably makes women feel as though they 'ask for harassment' by going to the stadium in the first place. Norms of femininity in Zimbabwe (e.g. passivity and submissiveness) mean that women are not expected to attend soccer matches alone or to enter the 'public sphere' without a male escort. Women and girls who choose to enter such spaces are deemed to do so at their own risk, and are therefore subjected to various forms of violence and ridicule (Daimon, 2010). Besides Zimbabwe, the text also provides case studies from academics based in countries across Sub-Saharan Africa, such as

Malawi and Nigeria. Notably, the book is published by the Council for the Development of Social Science Research in Africa (CODESRIA), 'an independent organisation whose principal objectives are to facilitate research, promote research-based publishing and create multiple forums geared towards the exchange of views and information among African scholars' (Shehu, 2010: vii).

Overall, this edited collection serves as a signpost for a potential move towards de-colonising, cross-cultural and ethical research in SDP; its arguments and findings are therefore pertinent for various stakeholders in SDP, including policy-makers, NGOs, volunteers, government officials and academics. At the same time, vigilance is required in analysing how such accounts are taken up in SDP practice and policy and whether these align with – or challenge – neo-liberal hierarchies and dominance. There is always the possibility that the sport-based narratives of Shehu, Daimon and others might be used problematically as evidence of the enlightenment of Western subjects deemed to be the arbiters and pedagogues of freedom, peace and development. This then could be used to justify practices of stewardship through SDP in ways that effectively continue the logic and practice of colonialism. As Darnell (2010b) has argued, the experiences of SDP stakeholders, such as volunteers from the One-Third World, suggest that the intersections of race and gender hierarchies may render intelligible the passivity of Others and validate the privilege and authority of Whiteness in post-colonial spaces. For this reason, a vigilant post-colonial feminist critique of encounters in SDP remains called for.

Conclusion

Throughout this chapter, we have attempted to demonstrate the importance of a sustained and critical engagement with post-colonial feminist theory and three dimensions of SDP research that it may enhance: prioritising of material relations, considerations of representation and knowledge, and ethical encounters. We strongly advocate a post-colonial feminist approach to SDP because it presents an opportunity to bring not only a more ethical – but also a more informed, effective and socially transformative – approach to SDP. Returning to the work of Patricia Daley (2006, 2007), approaches to development and peacebuilding in post-colonial spaces like Burundi are unlikely to succeed without recognising and deconstructing presumed knowledge of Burundian culture that is often 'obvious' to Western eyes but clearly (neo) colonial in its construction, utility and effect. With that said, much work remains to be done to explore the processes by which actual interventions into current SDP policy and practice could be made in order to reform the sector along the lines called for in this chapter. At the least, however, the on-going struggle for peace in Burundi, and the involvement of the international donor and diplomat community, remains an instructive example of the need to consider both structures of injustice and practices of resistance by people who live in that country. Curtis (2013) reminds us that despite their colonial bedrock, neo-liberal peacekeeping policies based on power sharing and increased security – but not on social justice – were not simply imposed on an unsuspecting political class in Burundi. Rather, these policies and politics were re-appropriated by Burundian leaders in ways that secured their own interests while also sustaining low-level violence. Similarly, while SDP programmes may be susceptible to neo-liberal logic, they are not imposed on passive recipients either, and are likely to be re-imagined and re-interpreted by beneficiaries (Guest, 2009). What Curtis's (2013) analysis does show is that new rhetoric in the twenty-first century about a move to inclusive donor practices and diplomacy in pursuit of peace in Burundi has not yet led to a break in longstanding political patterns that tend to benefit elite interests, internationally and domestically. This reminds scholars and advocates of SDP that the simple application of sport programmes to this type of political context is unlikely to solve such problems; an alternative is to bring a critical perspective to the ways in which colonising practices keep such patterns intact and to organise SDP away from facilitating conformity amidst neo-liberalism and towards resistance and independence from its exploitative features.

In sum, we respectfully suggest that given the history of colonialism, SDP researchers would be remiss not to consider employing a post-colonial feminist research ethic that acknowledges and openly engages with the geo-political, material and historical divides between SDP programmers, 'targeted beneficiaries' and academics, while also trying to locate common ground and shared mutuality (see Rankin, 2010). As Marchand (2009: 931) contends,

> Postcolonial feminist thought, with its emphasis on decolonisation theory and discourse, provides us with a set of concepts to counter (and decolonise) the present 'culture war' informed by the 'clash of civilisations' thesis. Such decolonising needs to occur through discourses and practices of differences and not 'othering' or representation.

Our hope is that prioritising mutuality and dialogue around practices of differences through feminist participatory action-driven research can lead to the establishment of an ethical, collaborative and ultimately responsible paradigm for SDP research and practice.

Notes

1. Many of these organisations are catalogued on the International Platform on Sport and Development, sportanddev.org
2. It is worth remembering that the roots of SDP are in athlete-led efforts and organising to make a social contribution through sport, particularly in response to criticisms that dominant sporting forms and institutions have often failed to live up to reasonable standards of governance and/or contribute to the social good (see Kidd, 2008).
3. We make specific reference to Burundi throughout this chapter as it offers a timely and accessible example of a post-colonial context in which SDP programmes, supported by organisations like the UNOSDP, take place. In doing so, we rely on the work of critical scholars like Patricia Daley (2006, 2007, 2008), Devon Curtis (2013) and Seckinelgin et al. (2010) whose writings on Burundi offer examples of the type of scholarship that we advocate bringing to the study of SDP.
4. Here, we understand the neo-liberal perspective as one that 'envisions a world ordered according to market principles. It assumes that markets generate and distribute wealth most efficiently. Thus, while few neo-liberals are explicitly opposed to equity, they believe that a single-minded focus on markets is the best approach to improving the lives of most people' (Smith, 2008: 6). Neo-liberals tend to advocate for reduced state intervention, mobile capital, and private interests. The critical rejoinder to this is that neo-liberalism as a means of governance has largely served to secure wealth, power and privilege at the top of a global pyramid and to justify the marginalisation of swathes of people as a lack of ingenuity, competitiveness or effort (see Harvey, 2005).Despite the role of the 2008 global financial crisis in exposing the fallibility of neo-liberalism, it has proved resilient as both a political ideology and a policy model (see Clarke, 2010; Crouch, 2011).
5. In an international development context, Angeles (2011: 41) argues that PAR research should have the following elements: (1) the participation in the research and ensuing action by community members as co-investigators; (2) the research exercise as an opportunity for consciousness raising and education of participants and facilitators; (3) the inclusion of popular, local, or indigenous knowledge, particularly that of the poor in general, poor women, ethnic minorities, and other disadvantaged groups; and (4) the inclusion of political action, participatory planning, and decision making (or empowerment) based on a process of mutual learning and analysis, as well as continuous action and reflection.
6. While the UNOSDP's support for the Gatumba Youth Centre propelled us, for the purposes of this chapter, to use Burundi as an example of a post-colonial context, this does not mean that the Gatumba Youth Centre constitutes an essentially colonising organisation or practice. Rather, we suggest that the process of

mobilising sport-for-development in places like Bujumbura, particularly with support from the UNOSDP, calls for attention to be paid to the material and discursive effects of colonialism in that region and for the people who live there.

7. Many scholars have noted that practices of colonialism has been evident throughout human history, but here we follow Loomba (2005: xiii) in arguing that 'Modern European colonialism was distinctive and by far the most extensive of the different kinds of colonial contact.'

8. This does not mean that colonial authorities constructed the state of Burundi because, unlike several African states, it existed prior to colonisation; however colonialism did lead to the redefining of its boundaries (Daley, 2006: 662).

9. Though there are many terms used for distinguishing the (messy) geographical divisions between North/South, we concur with Mohanty (2006: 226–227, drawing on Esteva and Prakash, 1998) that 'One-Third World' (to refer to the Global North) and 'Two-Thirds World' (to refer to the Global South) usefully highlight the fluidity and nuances of power, agency and global forces that continue to position people as the social, economic and political minorities and majorities in both the 'North' and 'South'. Furthermore, these terms attempt to remove ideological and geographical binaries as found in other terms (e.g. North/ South). At the same time, Mohanty (2006: 227) argues that these terms potentially ignore 'a history of colonisation that the terms Western/Third World draw attention to'. Still, we feel that these terms are useful given the issues we seek to address in this chapter.

10. Of course, it remains '...to be seen whether, and if so, to what extent the current financial and economic crisis will alter the neoliberal imperatives that the World Bank pursues, especially in those countries where it maintains significant leverage' (Van Waeyenberge, 2010: 107).

11. For example, such hierarchies were evident in Hayhurst's (2011) research on a SDP programme in Uganda that used martial arts programmes to 'empower' young women targeted by domestic violence. Though the programme was mandated to challenge gender norms through the participation of young women and girls in martial arts programming (a sport perceived as 'masculine' in Uganda), many of the young women involved experienced verbal abuse from boys and men, and were ridiculed for taking part in a sport deemed 'unfeminine'. Indeed, members of the local community suggested that the young women's reproductive organs would be damaged by 'kicking their legs high' and contended that girls wearing trousers while practicing was culturally inappropriate. We suggest this is an important example of how gender hierarchies in sport continue to play out in SDP.

12. http://www.olympic.org/development-through-sport

13. Preeminent post-colonial theorist Edward Said, for example, has been criticised for promoting the *importance* of history while simultaneously rejecting the *practice* of history as an exercise of dominance (Kennedy, 2003).

14. Mohanty's 1984 essay 'Under Western Eyes: Feminist Scholarship and Colonial Discourses' in which she challenged the colonial practices and racist knowledge production of Western, liberal feminism, remains a foundational text in post-colonial studies. Importantly, in her 2003 follow up 'Under Western Eyes Revisited: Feminist Solidarity through Anticapitalist Struggles', Mohanty rejected the notion that her initial essay simply offered a basis for the uncritical support of multiple feminisms and histories. Rather, she asserted that it was

a call to seek out the truth of history that is anti-colonial in its approach and praxis. We follow this assertion in our approach used here.

15. The concept of hypercapitalism illustrates how patriarchy, modernism and colonialist assumptions interlock when global challenges to human suffering are approached through 'solutions' of capital, resources and markets (Cannella and Viruru, 2004: 117). According to Perez and Cannella (2011: 49–50), patriarchal and colonial undertones of hypercapitalism are evident through: (1) the political uses of modernist universalisms that tend to ignore inequalities based on racial, socioeconomic, or gender privilege, (2) the proffering of solutions that intensify economic inequalities between the privileged and the oppressed and (3) the continuing assertion on a global scale that societies and social services (like education and health care) can only function under a capitalist, market-based system.

16. We also reference material relations to remind readers that post-colonial theory has never been focused only on representation in literature or cultural forms, but has also been concerned with the implications of colonialism for people's everyday lives.

17. In our previous chapter, we discussed how ' ... the "activist" element of decolonizing research continues to be over-looked and under-theorized' (Darnell and Hayhurst, 2011: 187).

18. It is important to assert that, in the tradition of Spivak, the term 'subaltern' ' ... signifies very specifically a group of people whose voices cannot be heard or that are wilfully ignored in dominant modes of narrative production' (McEwan, 2009: 16).

19. Guest's critical ethnography of SDP in the early 2000s showed that Olympic Aid, a northern NGO and the precursor to Right to Play, drew upon universal humanism as a basis for their initiatives in Angola but that such programmes were re-interpreted by local people in culturally specific ways. While sporting forms were invoked and organised within the development context by Olympic Aid in an effort to facilitate life skills of self-esteem and teamwork, such an approach was at cultural odds with local priorities of employment and tangible, economic competencies.

20. Various studies have explored the use of photography in post-colonial contexts to consider issues of representation, resistance and agency. Those such as Sherazade contend that photography has the potential to 'blur the lines between the subject and the object of the gaze' (as cited in Eileraas, 2003: 807), while others contend that, through photography, it is possible to 'construct a sense of self that both assumes and subverts the other's gaze' (Eileraas, 2003: 807). These debates aside, we are using the example from Hayhurst's (2011) study to underline the importance of challenging the dominant representations of 'targeted beneficiaries' in SDP projects. Indeed, even if these forms of resistance and agency are subsumed (and potentially even exploited) by the neo-liberal, competitive (SDP) NGO climate, we suggest that these instances of autonomy – for example, by the Ugandan NGO staff member deciding how to portray her SDP organisation on their website – are pertinent moments worthy of documenting, understanding and examining in future studies.

21. We have touched on what such an approach might look like in Darnell and Hayhurst (2011).

22. Forde's work is a good example of the application of OCAP principles in SDP. Through her unique position as founder and researcher of MTG, Forde makes a concerted effort to promote power sharing and mutual ownership throughout the organisation. As mentioned, MTG also co-creates and collaboratively conducts their monitoring and evaluation and are focused on the importance of 'accountability from below.' In our previous chapter (Darnell and Hayhurst, 2011) we cited Forde's research as an example of PAR in SDP; as we write this chapter, we have yet to find many further examples of FPAR-focused, de-colonising approaches to SDP research – perspectives we hope to continue pursuing in our own work.

References

Adekanye, J. (1995). Structural Adjustment, Democratization and Rising Ethnic Tensions in Africa. *Development and Change*, 26(2), 355–374.

Agathangelou, A.M, and Ling, L.H.M. (2009). *Transforming World Politics: From Empire to Multiple Worlds*. Routledge.

Angeles, L.C. (2011). Feminist Demands, Dilemmas, and Dreams in Introducing Participatory Action Research in a Canada-Vietnam, Capacity Building Project. In G. Creese and W. Frisby (eds), *Feminist Community Research: Case Studies and Methodologies*. Vancouver: University of British Columbia Press, 37–58.

Ashgate, B., Griffiths, G. and Tiffin, H. (1998). *Key Concepts in Post-Colonial Studies*. London: Routledge.

Battiste, M. (2008). Research Ethics for Protecting Indigenous Knowledge and Heritage: Institutional and Researcher Responsibilities. In N.K. Denzin, Y.S. Lincoln, and L.T. Smith (eds), *Handbook of Critical and Indigenous Methodologies*. Thousand Oaks, CA: Sage, 497–511.

Bhavnani, K.-K. (2007). Interconnections and Configurations: Toward a Global Feminist Ethnography. In S. Nagy Hesse-Biber (ed.), *Handbook of Feminist Research: Theory and Praxis*. London, UK: Sage, 639–650.

Benson, K. and Nagar, R. (2006). Collaboration as Resistance? Reconsidering the Processes, and Possibilities of Feminist Oral History and Ethnography. *Gender, Place and Culture*, 13(5), 581–592.

Berman, B.J. (2010). *Ethnicity and Democracy in Africa*. JICA-RI Working Paper, Japan International Cooperation Agency Research Institute.

Campbell, M.L., and Teghtsoonian, K. (2010). Aid Effectiveness and Women's Empowerment: Practices of Governance in the Funding of International Development. *Signs*, 36(1), 177–202.

Cannella, G.S., and Viruru, R. (2004). *Childhood and Postcolonization: Power, Education, and Contemporary Practice*. New York: Routledge Falmer.

Katrina New Orleans. *International Critical Childhood Policy Studies*, 4(1), 47–68.

Chawansky, M. (2011). New Social Movements, Old Gender Games?: Locating Girls in the Sport for Development and Peace Movement. *Research in Social Movements, Conflicts and Change*, 32, 121–134.

Clarke, J. (2010). After Neo-Liberalism? *Cultural studies*, 24(3), 375–394.

Coalter, F. (2007). *A Wider Social Role for Sport: Who's Keeping the Score?* Abingdon, Oxon: Routledge.

Coalter, F. (2010). The Politics of Sport-for-Development: Limited Focus Programmes and Broad Gauge Problems? *International Review for the Sociology of Sport*, 45(3), 295–314.

Connor, J. and McEwen, M. (2011). International Development or White Man's Burden? the IAAF's Regional Development Centres and Regional Sporting Assistance. *Sport in Society*, 14(6), 805–817.

Crouch, C. (2011). *The Strange Non-Death of Neoliberalism*. Cambridge, MA: Polity Press.

Curtis, D. (2013). The International Peacebuilding Paradox: Power Sharing and Post-Conflict Governance in Burundi. *African Affairs*, 112(446), 72–91.

Daimon, A. (2010). The Most Beautiful Game, or the Most Gender Violent Sport? Exploring the Interface between Soccer, Gender and Violence in Zimbabwe. In J. Shehu (ed.), *Gender, Sport and Development in Africa: Cross-Cultural Perspectives on Patterns of Representations and Marginalization*. Dakar, Senegal: Council for the Development of Social Science Research in Africa, 1–11.

Daley, P. (2006). Ethnicity and Political Violence in Africa: The Challenge to the Burundi State. *Political Geography*, 25(6), 657–679.

Daley, P. (2007). The Burundi Peace Negotiations: An African Experience of Peace–Making. *Review of African Political Economy*, 34(112), 333–352.

Daley, P.O. (2008). *Gender & Genocide in Burundi: the Search for Spaces of Peace in the Great Lakes Region*. Bloomington, Indiana: Indiana University Press.

Darby, P. (2003). Football, Colonial Doctrine, and Indigenous Resistance: Mapping the Political Persona of FIFA's African Constituency. In J. Le Sueur (ed.), *The Decolonization Reader*. New York: Routledge, 358–373.

Darnell, S.C. (2010a). Power, Politics and 'Sport for Development and Peace': Investigating the Utility of Sport for International Development. *Sociology of Sport Journal*, 27(1), 54–75.

Darnell, S.C. (2010b). Sport, Race, and Bio-Politics: Encounters with Difference in 'Sport for Development and Peace' Internships. *Journal of Sport & Social Issues*, 34(4), 396–417.

Darnell, S.C. (2012). *Sport for Development and Peace: A Critical Sociology*. London: Bloomsbury Academic Press.

Darnell, S.C. and Hayhurst, L.M.C. (2011). Sport for Decolonization: Exploring a New Praxis of Sport for Development. *Progress in Development Studies*, 11(3), 183–196.

Darnell, S.C. and Hayhurst, L. (2012). Hegemony, Postcolonialism and Sport-for-Development: A Response to Lindsey and Grattan. *International Journal of Sport Policy and Politics*, 4(1), 111–124.

Eileraas, K. (2003). Reframing the Colonial Gaze: Photography, Ownership and Feminist Resistance. *Modern Language Notes*, 118(4), 807–840.

Esteva, G. and Prakash, M. S. (1998). *Grassroots Post-Modernism: Remaking the Soil of Cultures*. London: Zed Books.

Forde, S. (2008). *Playing by their Rules: Coastal Teenage Girls in Kenya on Life, Love and Football*. Moving the Goalposts. Charleston, U.S. Create Space.

Gallagher, K. and Kim, I. (2008). Moving towards Postcolonial, Digital Methods in Qualitative Research. in K. Gallagher (ed.), *The Methodological Dilemma: Critical, Creative, and Post-Positivist Approaches to Qualitative Research*. New York: Taylor and Francis, 103.

Giles, A.R. and Lynch, M. (In Press). Postcolonial and Feminist Critiques of Sport for Development. In R. Schinke (ed.), *Development through Sport*. Morgantown, WV: Fitness Information Technology.

Giulianotti, R. (2011). Sport, Transnational Peacemaking, and Global Civil Society: Exploring the Reflective Discourses of 'Sport, Development, and Peace' Project Officials. *Journal of Sport & Social Issues*, 35(1), 50–71.

Guest, A.M. (2009). The Diffusion of Development-through-sport: Analysing the History and Practice of the Olympic Movement's Grassroots Outreach to Africa. *Sport in Society: Cultures, Commerce, Media, Politics*, 12(10), 1336–1352.

Hall, S. (1997). The Spectacle of the Other. In S. Hall (ed.), *Representation: Cultural Representations and Signifying Practices*. London, UK: Sage, 225–277.

Hargreaves, J. (2004). Querying Sport Feminism: Personal or Political? In R. Giulianotti (ed.), *Sport and Modern Social Theorists*. New York: Palgrave MacMillan, 187–205.

Hartmann, D. and Kwauk, C. (2011). Sport and Development: An Overview, Critique and Reconstruction. *Journal of Sport & Social Issues*, 35(3), 284–305.

Harvey, D. (2005) *A Brief History of Neoliberalism*. Oxford: Oxford University Press.

Hayhurst, L.M.C. (2009). The Power to Shape Policy: Charting Sport for Development Policy Discourses. *International Journal of Sport Policy*, 1(2), 203–227.

Hayhurst, L.M.C. (2011). *'Governing' the 'Girl Effect' through Sport and Development: Postcolonial Girlhoods, Corporate Social Responsibility and Constellations of Aid*. Unpublished Doctoral Dissertation. Faculty of Physical Education and Health, University of Toronto.

Hayhurst, L.M.C. (2013). The 'Girl Effect' and Martial Arts: Social Entrepreneurship and Sport, Gender and Development in Uganda. *Gender, Place and Culture*. Online first: doi: 10.1080/0966369X.2013.802674.

Hedge, R.S. (2009). Fragments and Interruptions: Sensory Regimes of Violence and the Limits of Feminist Ethnography. *Qualitative Inquiry*, 15(2), 276–296.

Heron, B. (2007). *Desire for Development: Whiteness, Gender, and the Helping Imperative*. Waterloo, Ontario: Wilfrid Laurier University Press.

Holte-McKenzie, M., Forde, S. and Theobald, S. (2006). Development of a Participatory Monitoring and Evaluation Strategy. *Evaluation & Program Planning*, 29, 365–376.

Jackson, C. (1997). Post Poverty, Gender and Development? *IDS Bulletin*, 28(3), 145–155.

Kapoor, I. (2004). Hyper-Self-Reflexive Development? Spivak on Representing the Third World 'Other'. *Third World Quarterly*, 25(4), 627–647.

Kay, T., Hayhurst, L.M.C. and Dudfield, O. (2012). *The State of Play: Emerging Issues in the Contribution of Sport to Development. A Position Paper for the Commonwealth Secretariat*. London, UK: Commonwealth Secretariat.

Kay, T. (2009). Developing through Sport: Evidencing Sport Impacts on Young People. *Sport in Society*, 12(9), 1177–1191.

Kennedy, D. (2003). Imperial History and Post-Colonial Theory. In J. Le Sueur (ed.), *The Decolonization Reader*. New York: Routledge, 10–22.

Kidd, B. (2008). A New Social Movement: Sport for Development and Peace. *Sport in Society*, 11(4), 370–380.

Kirkham, S. R. and Anderson, J. M. (2002). Postcolonial Nursing Scholarship: From Epistemology to Method. *Advances in Nursing Science*, 25(1), 1–17.

Lavallée, L.F. and Howard, H.A. (2011). *Urban Aboriginal Diabetes Research Project Report*. Toronto, ON: Anishnawbe Health Toronto.

Le Sueur, J. (2003). *The Decolonization Reader*. New York: Routledge.

Li, T. (2007). *The Will to Improve: Governmentality, Development, and the Practice of Politics*. Durham: Duke University Press.

Lindsey, I. and Grattan, A. (2012). An 'International Movement'? Decentring Sport-for-Development within Zambian Communities. *International Journal of Sport Policy and Politics*, 4(1), 91–110.

Loomba, A. (2005). *Colonialism/Postcolonialism* (2nd edn). London; New York: Routledge.

Maclean, K. (2007). Translation in Cross-Cultural Research: An Example from Bolivia. *Development in Practice*, 17(6), 784–790.

Maguire, J.A. (2011). Development through Sport and the Sports–Industrial Complex: The Case for Human Development in Sports and Exercise Sciences. *Sport in Society*, 14(7–8), 937–949.

Marchand, M. (2009). The Future of Gender and Development after 9/11: Insights from Postcolonial Feminism and Transnationalism. *Third World Quarterly*, 30(5), 921–935.

McEwan, C. (2009). *Postcolonialism and Development*. London: Routledge.

Mohanty, C.T. (1984). Under Western Eyes: Feminist Scholarship and Colonial Discourses. *boundary 2*, 12, 333–358.

Mohanty, C.T. (2003). 'Under Western Eyes' Revisited: Feminist Solidarity through Anticapitalist Struggles. *Signs*, 28(2), 499–535.

Mohanty, C.T. (2006). *Feminism without Borders: Decolonizing Theory, Practicing Solidarity*. Durham; London: Duke University Press.

Mosse, D. (2004). Is Good Policy Unimplementable? Reflections on the Ethnography of Aid Policy and Practice. *Development and Change*, 35(4), 639–671.

Nicholls, S., Giles, A.R. and Sethna, C. (2011). Perpetuating the 'Lack of Evidence' Discourse in Sport for Development: Privileged Voices, Unheard Stories and Subjugated Knowledge. *International Review for the Sociology of Sport*, 46(3), 249–264.

Palmary, I. (2011). 'In Your Experience': Research as Gendered Cultural Translation. *Gender, Place and Culture*, 18(1), 99–113.

Perez, M.S. and Cannella, G.S. (2011). Disaster Capitalism as Neoliberal Instrument for the Construction of Early Childhood Education/Care Policy: Charter Schools in Post-Katrina New Orleans. *International Critical Childhood Policy Studies Journal*, 4(1), 47–68.

Peterson, V. and Runyan, A.S. (2010). *Global Gender Issues in the New Millennium*: Westview.

Prabhu, A. (2003). Mariama Ba's So Longa Letter: Women, Culture and Development from a Francophone/Postcolonial Perspective. In K. K. Bhavnani, J. Foran and P. Kurian (eds), *Feminist Futures: Re-Imagining Women, Culture and Development*. London: Zed Books, 239–255.

Racine, L. (2003). Implementing a Postcolonial Feminist Perspective in Nursing Research Related to Non-Western Populations. *Nursing Inquiry*, 10(2), 91–102.

Rankin, K. (2010). Reflexivity and Post-Colonial Critique: Toward an Ethics of Accountability in Planning Praxis. *Planning Theory*, 9(3), 181–199.

Reid, C. and Frisby, W. (2008). Continuing the Journey: Articulating Dimensions of Feminist Participatory Action Research. In P. Reason and H. Bradbury (eds), *Handbook of Action Research: Participative Inquiry and Practice* (2nd edn). London: Sage, 93–105.

Reid, C., Ponic, P., Hara, L., Ledrew, R., Kaweesi, C. and Newman, V. (2012). Living an Ethical Agreement: Negotiating Confidentiality and Harm in Feminist Participatory Action Research. In G. Creese and W. Frisby (eds), *Feminist Community Research: Case Studies and Methodologies*. Vancouver: University of British Columbia Press, 189–210.

Saavedra, M. (2009). Dilemmas and Opportunities in Gender and Sport-in-Development. In R. Levermore and A. Beacom (eds), *Sport and International Development*. Basingstoke: Palgrave MacMillan, 124–155.

Saul, J. (2008). *Decolonization and Empire: Contesting the Rhetoric and Practice of Resubordination in Southern Africa and Beyond*. London: Routledge.

Schnitzer, M., Stephenson Jr, M., Zanotti, L. and Stivachtis, Y. (2013). Theorizing the Role of Sport for Development and Peacebuilding. *Sport in Society*, 16(5), 595–610.

Seckinelgin, H., Bigirumwami, J. and Morris, J. (2010). Securitization of HIV /AIDS in Context: Gendered Vulnerability in Burundi. *Security Dialogue*, 41(5), 515–535.

Shehu, J. (ed.) (2010). *Gender, Sport and Development in Africa: Cross-Cultural Perspectives on Patterns of Representations and Marginalization*. Dakar, Senegal: Council for the Development of Social Science Research in Africa.

Spivak, G. (1988). Can the Subaltern Speak? In C. Nelson and L. Grossberg (eds), *Marxism and the Interpretation of Culture*. London: Macmillan, 271–313.

Smith, J. (2008) *Social Movements for Global Democracy*. Baltimore, MD: The Johns Hopkins University Press.

Smith, L.T. (1999). *Decolonizing Methodologies: Research and Indigenous Peoples*. London, Dunedin: Zed; University of Otago Press.

Stoler, A.L. (1995). *Race and the Education of Desire: Foucault's History of Sexuality and the Colonial Order of Things*. London and Durham: Duke University Press.

Swadener, B.B., and Kagendo, M. (2008). Decolonizing Performances: Deconstructing the Global Postcolonial. In N. Denzin, Y. Lincoln, and L.T. Smith (eds), *Handbook of Critical and Indigenous Methodologies*. London: Sage, 31–43.

United Nations. (2011). *UNOSDP Annual Report – Ten Years of Action*. Geneva.

United Nations. (2011). UN-Supported Youth Centre in Burundi Welcomes Special Adviser on Sport. Retrieved 19 September 2012, from http://www.un.org/wcm/content/site/sport/home/unplayers/fundsprogrammesagencies/undp/template/news_item.jsp?cid=32720.

Van Waeyenberge, E. (2010). Tightening the Web: The World Bank and Enforced Policy Reform. In K. Birch and V. Mykhnenko (eds), *The Rise and Fall of Neo-liberalism: The Collapse of an Economic World Order?* London: Zed Books, 94–111.

West, P. (2005). Translation, Value and Space: Theorizing an Ethnographic and Engaged Environmental Anthropology. *American Anthropologist*, 107(4), 632–642.

4
Sport-for-Development: Pessimism of the Intellect, Optimism of the Will

Fred Coalter

Introduction

The sub-title of this chapter is a paraphrase of Gramsci's advice to radicals. He argued that the challenge of modernity was to live without illusions and without becoming disillusioned. In that context he stated that 'I'm a pessimist because of intelligence, but an optimist because of will' (Letter from Prison, 19 December 1929). This represents a succinct summary of the conflicts I have faced undertaking research in sport-for-development in nine African countries, India and Brazil, and working very closely with some sport-for-development organisations.

As the issues underpinning my pessimism form the basis of most of this chapter, I will begin by explaining the reference to optimism of the will. Kruse (2006: 8), rather critically, refers to the widespread existence in sport-for-development of strong beliefs 'based on an intuitive certainty and experience that there is a positive link between sport and development'. Such faith provides impressive motivation – an optimism of the will – for many practitioners who deliver such programmes. In this regard, I have been privileged to meet and learn from some of the most committed, selfless, innovative and optimistic people that I have ever met, working in unimaginably difficult circumstances with limited resources. My reactions are succinctly summarised by Black (2010: 121) who states that,

> there is much to admire about the enthusiasm, idealism and 'can-do' zeal of many of those caught up in it. Their preoccupation with development practice – with the imperative of 'making a difference' in the lives of poor, marginalized and often conflict-affected communities globally – is also both admirable and inevitable ... development as

a field of study indissolubly links theoretical reflection on issues of justice, equity and social change with the imperative of action.

Further, I continue to work closely with Magic Bus – the biggest sport-for-development programme in India (probably in the world) and the Mathare Youth Sport Association (MYSA) in Nairobi – the oldest sport-for-development organisation, established in 1987, and the largest in Africa.

Despite this I have strong reservations about many of the assertions and claims made by the various sports evangelists and conceptual entrepreneurs (Coalter, 2013; Hewitt, 1998) who dominate the rhetoric and politics of sport-for-development. My pessimism – or at least a strong scepticism – derives in reaction to this self-interested rhetoric purporting to represent the public interest, but more importantly from associated material and intellectual concerns.

Descending into hell

The material concerns can be best be expressed by two brief quotations from a report I wrote to the funders of a sport-for-development monitoring and evaluation manual, produced via fieldwork with three organisations in Africa and one in India (Coalter, 2006). On my first visit to Magic Bus I was taken to Dharavi, the Mumbai slum that subsequently featured in the film Slumdog Millionaire. My report stated:

> My expression when we visited Dharavi was that we had 'descended into hell'– it was like the last stages of the journey up the river in the film Apocalypse Now. The people live in indescribable conditions, with an average household of 5 in 15-20 square metres, they are packed extremely close together with very narrow pathways providing access. These pathways are so close there is little light and no privacy, or space for children to play. It is estimated that 25 to 35 per cent of children work 6-7 hours per day in zari factories/garbage picking/selling utensils.

The day before I had visited an illegal settlement called Bombay Port Trust (BPT). I reported that,

> it is almost impossible to describe the conditions in these areas – the closest I can get is that BPT is like a post-holocaust environment, dominated by metal salvaging, metal dust and extremely polluted

water, in which children swim. It has few public health and educational facilities and it is estimated that about 20 per cent of the children work 5–8 hours per day in leather factories, garages and stealing iron/steel/scrap materials from disused factories and old ships, sometimes being killed in the process. There is little open space and the children mostly 'play' in narrow lanes between a dense collection of tiny huts, made of a mixture of cardboard, corrugated iron, tarpaulin and plastic. The lanes are not wide enough for two people to pass easily and the huts are so close together there is very little light – the images of Dickensian England appear luxurious compared to this.

These experiences and others in a camp for internally displaced people in Northern Uganda, the Kamwokya slum in Kampala with very high levels of HIV infection, a post-conflict sports programme in Liberia, a programme in rural Senegal, a programme for street children in Malawi, and an organisation working with railway children in Kolkata, all served to make my concerns with finding ways to measure the impact on individuals of participation in sport-for-development programmes seem utterly trivial. Perhaps it was a failure of my imagination, but I was unable to understand how participation in such programmes would lead to what was vaguely referred to as 'development'. The complexity and depth of the social, cultural and economic problems that characterised these communities were not only beyond simple summary – certainly beyond my ability to describe accurately to someone who has not experienced them – but also seemingly beyond any solution.

'Says who?'

These material concerns were, and continue to be, confounded by a number of intellectual concerns. At its most fundamental, it is the duty of an academic to bring a degree of informed scepticism to the claims made for sport-for-development – or any self-interested lobby. For example, Portes (2000: 4) has referred to the 'trained skepticism' of sociologists and argued that 'gaps between received theory and actual reality have been so consistent as to institutionalize a disciplinary skepticism in sociology against sweeping statements, no matter from what ideological quarter they come'. Berger (1971) – whose interest in the sociology of religion is oddly relevant to sport-for-development – argued that,

the sociological perspective, with its irritating interjection of the question '*says who?*' ... introduces an element of sober scepticism that has an immediate utility in giving some protection at least against converting too readily … [and] makes us a little less likely to be trapped by every missionary band we encounter on the way.

Consequently, despite any desire to 'make a difference', the academic imperative is to begin with a degree of scepticism. Not only is this an academic imperative, but I would suggest that it is also a moral obligation to the poor and deprived who seem to be promised so much – 'development' – via the obtuse rhetoric of the sports evangelists. However, as we will see, there are a number of factors that serve to modify such scepticism.

The political benefits of studied vagueness

I have written elsewhere about the pre-scientific, 'mythopoeic', nature of sport (Coalter, 2007) and how this serves well the rhetoric of sport-for-development. Mythopoeic concepts are those whose demarcation criteria are not specific and are based on popular and idealistic ideas that are produced outside sociological analysis (Glasner, 1977). Such myths contain elements of truth – tales of individual conversion – which become reified and distorted. They are used to 'represent' rather than reflect reality, standing for supposed, but largely unexamined, impacts and processes.

The problems associated with such vague and generalised rhetoric about 'sport' are compounded when combined with the amorphous notion of 'development'. For example, Black (2010: 122) refers to 'the inherently contentious and contested character of this ubiquitous concept', while Hartmann and Kwauk (2011: 286) describe it as 'deeply complicated and poly-vocal'. Kruse (2006: 8) has commented on the fact that the term 'sport-for-development is intriguingly vague and open for several interpretations'.

Such 'studied ambiguity' is attractive for the sports evangelists and conceptual entrepreneurs because of certain aspects of the policy and resource-bargaining process. The formulation of ambitious, wide-ranging, vague and ill-defined claims is in part a function of the processes of lobbying, persuasion, negotiation, alliance-building and pragmatic opportunism that are central to all policy processes. Weiss (1993: 96) has emphasised the political nature of much policy formulation, resource bidding and programme development, arguing that:

Because of the political processes of persuasion and negotiation that are required to get a program enacted, inflated promises are made in the guise of program goals. Furthermore, the goals often lack the clarity and intellectual coherence that evaluation criteria should have. ... Holders of diverse values and different interests have to be won over, and in the process a host of realistic and unrealistic goal commitments are made.

However, Weiss (1993) has contended that inflated promises are most likely to occur in marginal policy areas that suffer from status anxiety and seek to gain legitimacy and funding from mainstream agencies – a reasonable description of the position of sport-for-development (Levermore, 2008; Black, 2010; Kidd, 2008). In such circumstances, the studied vagueness of sports evangelism and the use of the populist, mythopoeic view of sport with its 'ability to evoke vague and generalised images' (Glasner, 1977: 1) as contributing to a range of policy areas is an obvious advantage. It is not wholly clear whether this is the function of a belief system – sports evangelism – or a conscious and pragmatic strategy. Whatever the reason, the practical implication of this for monitoring and evaluating the effectiveness of sport-for-development programmes is that 'intermediate objectives are missing [thus not] providing targets for how much and when results were expected' and 'indicators are used in the application for funds, but not for actual monitoring and reporting', with the absence of clear targets 'making it difficult to assess performance' (Kruse, 2006: 27).

Cognitive, affective and normative theorising

However, while a lack of precision in the rhetoric of policy and politics can be understood, its reflection in academic discourse is more difficult to understand. Many academics seem to have an ambivalent relationship with sport-for-development. For example, even the stern critics of certain so-called neo-colonialist policies and top-down management practices retain a type of neo-functionalist belief in the inherent, but rarely defined, developmental potential of 'bottom-up' sport (Kay, 2011; Lindsey and Grattan, 2012; Nicholls, 2008; Nicholls et al., 2001), and frequently work with funding organisations whom they accuse of exploitative practices.

One consequence is that 'in its contemporary manifestation, the SDP [Sport-for-Development-and-Peace] emphasis on practice has come, for the most part, at the expense of critical and theoretically-informed reflection' (Black, 2010: 122). Coakley (2011: 307) refers to 'unquestioned beliefs grounded in wishful thinking', while Hartmann and Kwauk (2011: 286) refer to the use of evidence that is often little more than testimonies and 'heartfelt narratives, evocative images, and quotable sound bites'. In fact, attempts to define and measure impacts and outcomes are often summarily rejected as the dreaded 'positivism'. Via processes of epistemological and ideological over-reach, this is turn is viewed as being unavoidably part of neo-colonialist hegemonic repression and contributing to the reproduction of unequal power relations (Darnell and Hayhurst, 2012; Kay, 2009; Lindsey and Grattan, 2012; Nicholls et al., 2011).

One way of seeking to understand this is to consider Craib's (1984) argument that social theory has three dimensions and that theorists are doing three different things simultaneously, with varying balances between them. The *cognitive dimension* seeks to establish objective knowledge about the social world. The *affective dimension* is one in which elements of the theories embody the experience and feeling of the theorist, which means that any debate involves more than rational argument. The third dimension is *normative* – any theory of the way that the world is, is also based on assumptions about the way that the world ought to be and what sort of actions are possible or desirable. It could be argued that, because of a desire to be on the side of the oppressed, the cognitive element is too often compromised in sport-for-development.

In this regard, Hartmann and Kwauk (2011: 289) refer to the functionalist view of sport, which underpins much sport-for-development, as being based on 'the normative vision of social life, social change, and the status quo embedded in this dominant vision'. They also suggest that 'given its history and ideology, sport is easily understood by the dominant class as a socially beneficial and culturally normative character builder' (Hartmann and Kwauk, 2011: 292). Coakley (2011: 309) refers to the fact that commitment to neo-liberal ideas 'runs deep in ... the global social problems industry funded primarily by North Americans and Northern Europeans', and that:

> When organized into interpretive perspectives, these ideas constitute widely shared visions of how social worlds could and should be organized – much like other interpretive frameworks inspired by ideology more than research and theory. When combined with similarly shared emotions, identities, and dominant narratives, they tend to resist change, even when evidence contradicts them (Coakley, 2011: 309).

Although tensions between normative, affective and cognitive perspectives are inevitable, within sport-for-development they are often sub-optimally confused among those whose imperative is 'to make a difference'.

Displacement of scope

The combination of a mythopoeic approach to sport, a failure to address systematically the precise meaning of the 'development' facilitated by sport, the sub-optimal mixture of cognitive, affective and normative theorising, a continuing commitment to what might be termed a 'neo-functionalist' perspective, and an associated failure to specify precise performance indicators, leads to a fundamental issue of displacement of scope (Wagner, 1964).

This refers to the process of wrongly generalising micro-level effects to the macro. In part this relates to old debates within social science about the relationship between structure and action, between the individual and the social, or even between values, attitudes and behaviour. It is worth noting that Wagner (1964: 582) has suggested that,

> the problem of differentiated scope is inherent in the tremendous range of sociological subject matter itself. In other words, it imposes not only theoretical but also methodological tasks upon sociologists who are concerned with the micro-macro-sociological continuum as a whole.

This can be regarded as analogous to seeking to deal with the vast range of issues encapsulated in the summative term 'development', but rarely articulated. Like the term 'sport', 'development' conceals much more than it reveals, and contains mostly unanswered questions about the nature and extent of relations between the micro-level (e.g. the *possible* impacts on the individual of participating in a sport-for-development programme and any *possible* changes in behaviour); the meso level of communities, organisations, institutions and governance that might facilitate certain behaviours and development processes and the macro level of economy, government and a globalised world. The rhetoric of sport-for-development is replete with claims about everything from individual self-confidence, changed sexual behaviour, increased community cohesion, the development of social capital, to peace and reconciliation.

However, at its core, sport-for-development seems to be based on a neo-liberal, individualistic perspective – often symbolised, reinforced and promoted by elite sporting ambassadors and 'celebrity diplomats'

(Black, 2010: 126) who 'imbibed the developmental rhetoric of sport throughout their lives and saw themselves as living testimonials' (Kidd, 2008: 374). This is often complemented by theoretically loose talk about 'role models' (Bandura, 1962; Coalter, 2013). However, Kidd (2008: 377) comments that 'the single-minded purpose and confidence that sport instils in champions, a commendable attribute when transferred to many other settings', may be ill-suited to the uncertain landscape of development. Such a perspective brings to mind Weiss's (1993: 105) concern with a 'blame the victim' approach in which:

> We mount limited-focus programs to cope with broad-gauge problems. We devote limited resources to long-standing and stubborn problems. Above all we concentrate attention on changing the attitudes and behaviour of target groups without concomitant attention to the institutional structures and social arrangements that tend to keep them 'target groups'.

We can explore such issues – and the current practical and intellectual limitations of sport-for-development – by slightly adjusting Wagner's (1964) notion of displacement of scope to address a logical sequence of questions.

In what ways are the participants in need of 'development'?

It seems legitimate to assume that a core assumption of, and rationale for, sport-for-development programmes is a deficit model in which poor communities automatically produce deficient people, who can be 'developed' through sport. Such an assumption seems to be an essential rationale, although experience suggests that there is little systematic analysis of prior values, attitudes, knowledge and behaviour. In this regard, the survey data from my work with four programmes in three African countries and two in India (Coalter, 2013; Coalter and Taylor, 2010), raise some legitimate questions about such assumptions. The young people in these programmes were not homogeneous groups and had a range of self-evaluations, with many expressing quite strong self-belief in their own perceived self-efficacy and most were within an accepted 'normal' range of self-esteem. It is a reasonable assumption that living in such deprivation means that many have to develop certain levels of *perceived* self-efficacy and sense of self-worth in order to remain positive and to survive. I would not claim that the data are representative of the so-called Global South/Majority World/low income countries (Kay, 2009; Lindsey and Grattan, 2012;

Woodcock et al., 2012) – politically correct terms that are wholly inappropriate to issues of empirical research. However, at the very least, the data raise questions about the extent to which participants can be regarded as relatively normal young people living in often dreadful circumstances.

Further, such data raise questions about overly-generalised deficit models that ignore the fact that the nature and extent of impacts on participants will depend not only on the nature of the experience, but also on the nature of the participants and their responses to the various aspects of the programmes – the key mechanism (Pawson, 2006). To ignore this contains obvious ideological and pedagogic dangers. It raises important questions about how 'need' and 'development' are conceptualised, and how desired impacts and behavioural outcomes are defined and measured. There is a paradoxical danger of well-meaning projects being based on negative stereotypes of all young people from particular areas, with the attendant danger of misconceived provision, inappropriate performance indicators and subtle forms of racism.

Does participation positively affect the combination of values, attitudes, knowledge and aptitudes contained in a notion of 'development', for all or some?

In both the neo-liberal functionalist and liberationist neo-functionalist perspectives the positive impacts of sports participation are taken for granted. However, our data (Coalter, 2013; Coalter and Taylor, 2010) indicate a wide variety of impacts. Reflecting previous research (Fox, 2000), the data indicate a *general tendency* for those with the weakest or lower-than-average scores for perceived self-efficacy and self-esteem to increase their evaluations. In two East African samples the increases in average perceived self-efficacy scores were statistically significant but with no change in the Indian sample. In only one case was the increase in self-esteem statistically significant – although there were significant cultural variations (Coalter, 2013). However, in all programmes many participants also experienced *decreases* in self-evaluations and some recorded no change. Further, with regard to the traditional sport's hypothesis that strengthened perceived self-efficacy will lead to increased self-esteem, the data indicate that the relationship is contingent and unpredictable (see also, Bowker et al., 2003; Zaharopoulos and Hodge, 1991).

However, the most important finding relates to the view that participation in sport-for-development programmes inevitably leads to 'personal development'. This over-simplifies the varying nature of participants, the differential impact of programmes and the varying strength and direction of their impacts. It seems somewhat obvious to state that, despite certain tendencies in the data, there was no clear and systematic 'sport-for-development effect'. When we move beyond the universalising rhetoric of the conceptual entrepreneurs this is hardly a surprise – the presumption of such a general effect could only exist in the rhetoric of evangelists. As in all forms of social intervention, the nature and extent of impacts were contingent and varied between programmes, participants and cultural contexts.

The mixture of increases, decreases and no change in self-evaluations calls into question the meaning and diagnostic value of the selective individual testimonies and 'heartfelt narratives' (Hartmann and Kwauk, 2011) so often presented as evidence. As it is likely that *any* social interventions will produce individual successes, such testimonies tell us little about *how* various programmes operate and why they have differential and contingent impacts for the wider sample of participants.

How do programmes achieve such impacts and for whom?

Much of the rhetoric of sport-for-development, with its essentialist images of 'sport', ignores the vital distinction between necessary conditions (participation in sport) and *sufficient conditions* – the processes and experiences under which the theoretically potential impacts might be achieved. It cannot be assumed that any, or all, participants will automatically obtain the presumed benefits in all circumstances. Therefore, we need to understand which sports, processes and contexts produce what impacts for which participants. In addition, few sport-for-development organisations seek to achieve their desired impacts and outcomes solely through 'sport', and most can be characterised as 'sport-plus' organisations (Coalter, 2007) – indicating their acknowledgement of the developmental limitations of 'sport'? Consequently, the nature and experience of such programmes will vary widely.

In this regard, Coakley (1998) has distinguished between sport as a *site* for, but not necessarily a *cause* of, socialisation outcomes. Likewise, Hartmann (2003: 134) has asserted that 'the success of any sports-based social intervention programme is largely determined by the strength of its non-sport components'. It is worth noting that the literature reviews by the International Working Group on Sport for Development and Peace – not the likeliest of critics – concluded that 'the evident benefits appear to be an indirect outcome of the context and social interaction that is possible in sport, rather than a direct outcome of participating in sport' (SDPIWG, 2008: 4). More generically, Pawson et al. (2004: 7) have suggested that:

> It is through the workings of entire systems of social relationships that any changes in behaviours, events and social conditions are effected. ... Rarely if ever is the 'same' programme equally effective in all circumstances because of the influence of contextual factors.

Such perspectives emphasise the importance of the need to de-reify 'sport' and to understand middle-range mechanisms (Pawson, 2006; Weiss, 1997). This leads to a shift of focus from *families of programmes* (sport and crime; sport-for-development) to *families of mechanisms*, with apparently diverse interventions possibly sharing common components. This requires the development of a programme theory approach to programme design and evaluation – both via an articulation of providers' theory of change underpinning their programme, and by drawing on a wide variety of sports and non-sports research relating to the components of attitude and behaviour change. The existence of such material and the long history of the use of sport to seek to achieve personal and social change raise questions about assertions that sport-for-development is somehow a new area of study (Kay, 2009; Woodcock et al., 2012) (see Coalter [2013] for a fuller elaboration of this argument).

Do any of the programme impacts result in an intention to change specific behaviours, for all or some, and does this lead to an actual change in behaviour, for all or some?

This relates to the relationship between the impacts of programme participation on *individuals* and the resultant outcomes. One presumes that 'development' is not simply about possible individual changes in perceived self-efficacy, self-esteem and social skills, but that such changes are intended to lead to changed behaviour, opportunities and 'development'. The key question is that, irrespective of the differential impacts of participation in sport-for-development programmes, does any of this 'go beyond the touch line'? Even if sports participation does assist in the development of certain types of values, attitudes and *individual* competence, or even expressed intention to change behaviour, this cannot be taken to imply that these will be transferred to behavioural change, or wider social or community benefits. For example, the transtheoretical theory of behaviour change (Prochaska and Velicer, 1997) illustrates that the relationship between changed attitudes, intentions and subsequent behaviour is not unilinear, and initial behaviour changes are often reversed. Consequently, even if we can illustrate changes in values, attitudes and self-perceptions – more robustly that via the 'heartfelt narratives' – we are still left with the generic methodological problem of relating this to subsequent behaviour change, which surely must be part of any definition of development?

These issues can briefly be illustrated by research on HIV and AIDS – an area where sport-for-development has made substantial legitimating claims about its ability to promote positive change. Some have offered positive evaluations based on sport-for-development programmes' supposed ability to improve knowledge and change intentions about safe sex (Maro and Roberts, 2012; Maro et al., 2009). However, more robust research indicates that the relationship between expressed intention and actual sexual behaviour is relatively weak, with minimal differences between participants and non-participants (Delva et al., 2010). More fundamentally, Jeanes (2011: 13) argues that 'HIV and AIDS education programmes delivered through sport or other mechanisms are unlikely to be effective if targeting young people as if their health behaviour is played out within a social vacuum'. Similarly, Mwaanga (2010: 66) comments that 'to claim that sport can combat HIV and AIDS is not only to overstate the limited capacity of sport but also to dangerously ignore the complexity of HIV and AIDS'.

This leads us to a more fundamental issue that again illustrates the pitfalls of displacement of scope and the extent to which any measured individual impact can be regarded as 'development'.

Does the participants' environment enable desired changes in behaviour?

This issue can be illustrated by considering a factor seen as fundamental to personal development, and one which many associate with sport – resilience. Ungar (2006) has questioned the extent to which resilience can simply be regarded as an individual characteristic. Rather, he suggests that the concern should be the resilient and enabling nature of *environments*. Rather pithily he suggests that it might be better to 'change the odds' rather than try to resource individuals to 'beat the odds' in environments that do not support behaviour change, or fail to offer broader opportunities for 'development' – can encouraging young people to attend poor schools be viewed as development? While some sport-for-development programmes may strengthen the perceived self-efficacy and ambitions of some participants, Ungar's (2006) concerns with the resilience of environments – or Jeanes' (2011) comments about programmes delivered in a social vacuum – raise significant questions for the individualist perspective that underpins much sports evangelism. Again we are reminded of Weiss's (1993) concern with a 'blame the victim' approach that ignores structures and seeks to deal with long-standing, broad-gauge problems via limited-focus programmes of attitude and behaviour change. Further, it echoes Pawson's (2006: 35) generic comment that 'social interventions are always complex systems thrust amidst complex systems' – a complexity not admitted by conceptual entrepreneurs, yet an essential requirement for academics, researchers and practitioners.

Social capital and the economy of affection

Because of space limitations we can only note briefly the more fundamental questions about the relationship between individuals and community and the issues of meso and macro levels of development. The notion of social capital is frequently viewed as a means to somehow address many of these issues, and the displacement of scope connecting such programmes to the wider social structure (Burnett, 2001; Driscoll and Wood, 1999). Ideologies of sport as a neutral, non-political space characterised by communality, mutuality and teamwork combine with decontextualised, romanticised, communitarian generalisations about the supposed 'power of sport' to generate 'social capital' – usually based loosely on Putnam's (2000) concept of bonding social capital. However, as with the individual deficit model, one must beware of the dangers of 'retroactive reasoning' (Portes, 2000: 5) which concludes that the poor are poor simply because they lack collective spirit and solidarity. Secondly, we need to question the extent to which they can be regarded as 'social capital' in an analytical or developmental sense (Spaaij, 2012). Both Putnam (2000) and Coleman (1988–1989) view social capital as a *facilitating* resource – not just a public good, but *for* the public good. In such circumstances, cohesion and mutuality are not viewed as developmental ends in themselves, but as possible means to ends. Consequently, the nature of the *resources* contained in social networks is a major, but frequently ignored, issue (see Burnett [2001] for an analysis of resource-poor networks in sport-for-development). Further, forms of bonding capital in developing societies can obstruct organisational efficiency and economic development – what Calderisi (2007) has referred to as the 'economy of affection' in which consumption is more important than production. Finally, raising issues of displacement of scope and the often ignored distinctions between bonding, bridging and linking social capital, Portes and Landholt (2000) stress the limitations of enforceable trust and bounded solidarity. As with issues of individual behaviour change, collective action is usually only successful in receptive, supportive and non-corrupt environments.

Conclusions

Wagner (1964) has argued that the issue of displacement of scope is inherent in the wide range of sociological subject matters, and this clearly applies to sport-for-development. Perhaps, following Levermore (2008), it might be better to talk of a number of sports-for-developments. For example: sport-for-individual-development in which participation is presumed to change some participants' *specified* values, attitudes, knowledge and aptitudes; sport-for-development-for-behaviour-change in which the focus on the individual is complemented by a concern with the context of behaviour and the extent to which structures are enabling and resilient (the desired behaviour change will need to be specified precisely); sport-for-community-development which deals with issues at a meso level of collective organisation and forms of social capital *relevant to development* rather than simple communality (Burnett, 2001). I am sure that readers can propose other levels of analysis.

Each of these levels raise different methodological issues, serve to acknowledge issues of displacement of scope, and require greater conceptual precision about what is meant by 'development'. The approach would also encourage the use of a range of other academic disciplines and related, but often ignored, sports research that has dealt much more rigorously with such issues, and related programme theories and theories of change (Coakley, 2011; Coalter, 2007; Hartmann and Kwauk, 2011). From this perspective sport-for-development can only be considered 'new' in the narrowest of self-interested senses.

While it is not possible wholly to escape the affective and normative aspects of social theory, there is a clear need to strengthen the cognitive components of sport-for-development. Such an approach would not only better illustrate sport's potential to contribute to more precisely defined 'development', but also theorise its limitations. It would also contribute to the essential work of de-mystifying the mythopoeic approaches of the conceptual entrepreneurs and sports evangelists. However, I remain pessimistic, not just for material reasons and the clear limitations of sport-for-development (Coalter, 2007; Mwaanga, 2010), but also because the opportunistic coalition of interests around sport-of-development brings to mind Pisani's (2008: 300) comment that, in the area of HIV and AIDS, 'doing honest analysis that would lead to programme improvement is a glorious way to be hated by just about everyone' – this was never truer than in sport-for-development.

References

Bandura, A. (1962). *Social Learning through Imitation*. Lincoln, NE: University of Nebraska Press.

Berger, P. (1971). *Invitation to Sociology*. London: Pelican.

Black, D. (2010). The Ambiguities of Development: Implications for 'Development through Sport'. *Sport in Society*, 13(1), 121–129.

Bowker, A., Gadbois, S. and Cornock, B. (2003). Sport Participation and Self-Esteem: Variations as a Function of Gender and Role Orientation. *Sex Roles*, 49(1/2), 47–58.

Burnett, C. (2001). Social Impact Assessment and Sport Development: Social Spin-Offs of the Australia–South Africa Junior Sport Programme. *International Review for the Sociology of Sport*, 36(1), 41–57.

Calderisi, R. (2007). *The Trouble with Africa: Why Foreign aid isn't Working*. New Haven: Yale University Press.

Coakley, J. (1998). *Sport in Society: Issues and Controversies* (6th edn). Boston, MA: McGraw Hill.

Coakley, J. (2011). Youth Sports: What Counts as 'Positive Development?' *Journal of Sport and Social Issues*, 35(3), 306–324.

Coalter, F. (2006). *Sport-in-Development: A Monitoring and Evaluation Manual*. London: UK Sport.

Coalter, F. (2007). *Sport a Wider Social Role: Who's Keeping the Score?* London: Routledge.

Coalter, F. (2013). *Sport for Development: What Game are We Playing?* London: Routledge.

Coalter, F. and Taylor, J. (2010). *Sport-for-Development Impact Study*. London, Comic Relief: UK Sport and International Development through Sport. www.uksport.gov.uk/docLib/MISC/FullReport.pdf

Coleman J. (1988–1989). Social Capital in the Creation of Human Capital. *American Journal of Sociology*, 94, 95–120.

Craib, I. (1984). *Modern Social Theory: From Parsons to Habermas*. Brighton: Wheatsheaf Books.

Darnell, S. and Hayhurst, L. (2012). Hegemony, Postcolonialism and Sport for-Development: A Response to Lindsey and Grattan. *International Journal of Sport Policy and Politics*, 4(1), 111–124.

Delva, W., Michielsen, K., Meulders, B., Groeninck, S., Wasonga, E., Ajwang, P., Temmerman, M. and Vanreusel, B. (2010). HIV Prevention through Sport: The Case of the Mathare Youth Sport Association in Kenya. *AIDS Care*, 22(8), 1012–1020.

Driscoll, K. and Wood, L. (1999). *Sporting Capital: Changes and Challenges for Rural Committees in Victoria*. Melbourne: Victoria Centre for Applied Social Research, RMIT University.

Fox, K.R. (2000). The Effects of Exercise on Self-Perceptions and Self-Esteem. In S.J.H. Biddle, K.K. Fox and S.H. Boutcher (eds), *Physical Activity and Psychological Well-Being*. London: Routledge, 88–117.

Glasner, P.E. (1977). *The Sociology of Secularisation.* London: Routledge and Kegan Paul.

Hartmann, D. (2003). Theorising Sport as Social Intervention: A View from the Grassroots. *Quest,* 55, 118–140.

Hartmann, D. and Kwauk, C (2011). Sport and Development: An Overview, Critique and Reconstruction. *Journal of Sport and Social Issues,* 35(3), 284–305.

Hewitt, J. (1998). *The Myth of Self-Esteem: Finding Happiness and Solving Problems in America.* New York: St Martin's Press.

Jeanes, R. (2011). Educating through Sport? Examining HIV/AIDS Education and Sport-for-Development through the Perspectives of Zambian Young People. *Sport, Education and Society,* First online June 2013, 1–19.

Kay, T. (2009). Developing through Sport: Evidencing Sport Impacts on Young People. *Sport in Society,* 12(9), 1177–1191.

Kay, T. (2011). *Sport in the Service of International Development: Contributing to the Millennium Development Goals.* Paper presented to 2nd International Forum on Sport for Peace and Development. Geneva 10–11 May 2011.

Kidd, B. (2008). A New Social Movement: Sport for Development and Peace. *Sport in Society,* 11(4), 370–380.

Kruse, S.E. (2006). *Review of Kicking AIDS Out: Is Sport an Effective Tool in the Fight Against HIV/AIDS?,* draft report to NORAD, unpublished.

Levermore, R. (2008). Sport: A New Engine of Development. *Progress in Development Studies,* 8(2), 183–190.

Lindsey, I. and Grattan, A. (2012). An 'International Movement'? Decentering Sport for Development within Zambian Communities. *International Journal of Sport Policy and Politics,* 4(1), 91–110.

Maro, C. and Roberts, G. (2012). Combating HIV/AIDS in Sub-Saharan Africa: Effect of Introducing a Mastery Motivational Climate in a Community-Based Programme. *Applied Psychology: An International Review,* 699–722.

Maro, C., Roberts, G. and Sorensen, M. (2009). Using Sport to Promote HIV/AIDS Education for at-Risk Youths: An Intervention Using Peer Coaches in Football. *Scandinavian Journal of Medical Science Sports,* 19, 129–141.

Mwaanga, O. (2010). Sport for Addressing HIV/AIDS: Explaining Our Convictions. *Leisure Studies Association Newsletter,* 85, 61–67.

Nicholls, S. (2008). On the Backs of Peer Educators: Using Theory to Interrogate the Role of Young People in the Field of Sport-in-Development. In R. Levermore and A. Beacom (eds), *Sport and International Development.* London: Palgrave, 156–175.

Nicholls, S., Giles, A.R. and Sethna, C. (2011). Perpetuating the 'Lack of Evidence' Discourse in Sport for Development: Privileged Voices, Unheard Stories and Subjugated Knowledge. *International Review for the Sociology of Sport,* 46(3), 249–264.

Pawson, R., Greenhalgh, T., Harvey, G. and Walshe, K. (2004). *Realist Synthesis: An Introduction.* ESRC Research Methods Programme, University of Manchester. RMP Methods Paper 2/2004.

Pawson, R. (2006). *Evidence-Based Policy: A Realist Perspective.* London: Sage.

Pisani, E (2008). *The Wisdom of Whores: Bureaucrats, Brothels and the Business of AIDS.* London: Granta Books.

Portes, A. (2000). The Hidden Abode: Sociology as Analysis of the Unexpected. 1999 Presidential Address. *American Sociological Review,* 65, 1–18.

Portes, A. and Landholt, P. (2000). Social Capital: Promise and Pitfalls of Its Role in Development. *Journal of Latin American Studies*, 32, 529–547.

Prochaska, J. and Velicer, W. (1997). The Transtheoretical Model of Health Behaviour Change. *American Journal of Health Promotion*, 12, 38–48.

Putnam, R. (2000). *Bowling Alone: The Collapse and Revival of the American Community*. New York: Simon and Schuster.

Spaaij, R. (2012). Beyond the Playing Field: Experiences of Sport, Social Capital and Integration Among Somalis in Australia. *Ethnic and Racial Studies*, 35(6), 1519–1538.

Sport for Development International Working Group (2008). *Harnessing the Power of Sport for Development and Peace*. Right to Play, Toronto.

Ungar, M. (2006). Resilience across cultures. *British Journal of Social Work*, 38(2), 218–235.

Wagner, H.L. (1964). Displacement of Scope: A Problem of the Relationship between Small-Scale and Large-Scale Sociological Theories. *The American Journal of Sociology*, 69(6), 571–584.

Weiss, C.H. (1993). Where Politics and Evaluation Research Meet. *Evaluation Practice*, 14(1), 93–106.

Weiss, C.H. (1997). How Can Theory-Based Evaluation Make Greater Headway? *Evaluation Review*, 21(4), 501–524.

Woodcock, A., Cronin, O. and Forde, S. (2012). Quantitative Evidence for the Benefits of Moving the Goalposts, a Sport for Development Project in Rural Kenya. *Evaluation and Program Planning*, 35, 370–381.

Zaharopoulos, E. and Hodge, K.P. (1991). Self-Concept and Sport Participation. *New Zealand Journal of Psychology*, 20, 12–16.

5
The Ripple Effect: Critical Pragmatism, Conflict Resolution and Peace Building through Sport in Deeply Divided Societies

John Sugden

Introduction: the question

The idea for this chapter comes from a simple question that was asked to me by Dominic Malcolm, fellow Sport Sociologist, during a staff and graduate seminar that I gave at the University of Loughborough in 2006. I had given a presentation about Football for Peace, a cross-community, co-existence programme involving Jewish and Arab towns and villages in Israel that I was directing. When I had finished speaking I was asked a familiar array of questions, mainly concerned with logistical and methodological issues. Then Dominic raised his hand and asked, 'What difference does the fact that you are a sociologist make to your leadership and development of a project like this?'

What a great question! I stumbled through what, on reflection was a pretty vague and incomplete answer saying something like, 'of course it makes a difference, inasmuch as being a sociologist isn't just a job, it's more a vocation, a way of life, and everything you do is filtered through your own sociological gaze. So, inevitably Football for Peace is heavily influenced by that gaze'. While this answer seemed to satisfy the audience, on reflection it did not satisfy me. It is the simple questions that demand the most complex answers. In the intervening years I have been pondering and researching the fuller answer. In this chapter I outline the main features of that answer.

Elsewhere I have had some harsh things to say about what I referred to as the 'fossilisation' of the sociology of sport within the crushing institutionalising embrace of the parent discipline.[1] One of the key elements of this critique focused on the prioritisation of theoretical refinement over the observation and interpretation of people and events in everyday life. This does not mean that I am championing a theoretical and empiricist sociology. On the contrary for me sociological theory – that is evidence-based abstractions that not only help us to understand the what and why of what is and what has been in social relations, but also help us to formulate and give direction to future policy and interventions that change the nature of those relations – is an essential hemisphere of the rounded sociological whole. However, it is important to make it clear from the outset that what follows is both *less* and *more* than the product of a library-based desk top study. It is *less* in as much as it is not built on an exhaustive review of all theories that could 'in theory' be articulated to embrace sport and conflict studies – something that can be found in Simon Gardner's (2012) thought provoking consideration of alternative theoretical approaches in this area which can be found in monograph, *Sport for Development and Peace. A Critical Sociology*. It is *more* because the theoretical direction and selection that informs the following framework has been driven by my seeking to make sense of the lived reality of actually doing sport-based peace work in societies experiencing serious division and conflict.

Thus, in this chapter I outline the key epistemological and theoretical ingredients of this hemisphere as it has emerged through my personal journeys in sport and peace work in Northern Ireland and Israel, supported through extensive conversations with a wide range of practitioners involved in similar interventions in South Africa. This is done in six sections. In the first section I outline the deep ontological and epistemological foundations, or 'deep structure' upon which my own approach is based; the second section is devoted to illustrating the importance of the dynamic relationship between political and civil society in peacebuilding; in the third section I introduce the most influential and relevant theoretical and methodological models that have already been developed in the conflict resolution/peace studies research literature that have informed my thinking; in the fourth section I consider an orientating framework or 'moral compass' for peace work through sport-based on notions of human rights and social justice; in the fifth section I summarise my understanding of research, evaluation and dissemination strategies; and finally, in the sixth section, I present the 'ripple effect' model that depicts how these threads are woven together in articulation with the empirical evidence, to provide a template for planning and executing progressive, sport-based civil society projects in deeply divided societies.

The Sociological imagination and thinking about sport and peace processes

I had already come a long way in my quest to come up with a fully informed answer to Dominic Malcolm's question (subsequently referred to as The Question) when I discovered John Brewer's (2003) monograph entitled, *C. Wright Mills and the End of Violence*. I was drawn to it not only because it focused on two of the regions that feature in this chapter, namely Northern Ireland and South Africa, but also equally importantly because in my formative years as a sociologist I had been heavily influenced by the sociological thinking of Wright Mills. As an Essex undergraduate I had been introduced to his brand of critical interpretation through his classic text, *The Sociological Imagination* (1959). Later, as a postgraduate in the USA at the University of Connecticut, I had taken a whole course dedicated to the sociology of Wright Mills. Hitherto the diet of sociology that I had been fed was increasingly dominated by an intellectual arms race, the weapons of which were hyper-theoretical debate and refinement within various branches of Marxism and neo-Marxism. To me, Wright Mills' more empirically grounded critical sociological accounts of social structure and power in post-war America were refreshingly accessible and plausible. Thus, while I was not fully conscious of it, even before opening the pages of Brewer's book, in my search for answers to The Question I was already drawing heavily on Wright Mill's legacy in my own thinking.

In his book, Brewer uses the framework underpinning Wright Mills' concept of the sociological imagination as a means through which to make sense of the extremely complex web of circumstances that have led two very different societies in serious conflict, namely South Africa and Northern Ireland, down corresponding roads towards peace and reconciliation. Brewer begins by observing that peace processes are exceedingly complex and unpredictable entities, making sense of which involves high levels of informed retrospection. 'Between God and chance you find sociology says Brewer (2003: 152), arguing that Wright Mills' work shows us that sociologists are among the best qualified to engage with and make sense of a world in flux and turmoil. The task for the sociology of conflict resolution and peace building is not to 'discover' or construct a universal theory that explains all peace processes in all theatres of conflict, but is restricted in the (in)applicability of generalised concepts to understand specific intersections of events that exist in real time and space. In this regard, context is everything and history is a critical feature of this context. In different ways, the three empirical case studies that provide the context for this chapter clearly exemplify this. Woe betide any peace activists who attempt to meddle in community affairs in South Africa, Northern Ireland or Israel/ Palestine without having a deep understanding of the confluence of local, regional and national historical currents flowing into the conflicts that they are attempting to help resolve and reconcile.

Furthermore, argues Brewer, making sense of peace processes necessitates focusing on the intersection between biography, social structure and the political process. How in a given moment the actions and interventions of great, good, bad, ordinary and extraordinary individuals articulate within the swirl of transcending institutional forces and movements to contribute to progressive social and political change? In this regard, it is important to show the interaction between the local and the societal by exploring how people experience conflict in their communities, and consequently how this influences an agenda of social activism – what Wright Mills refers to as the dialectic between 'personal troubles' and 'public issues'.

Based on my own reading of Wright Mills, I see it as the task of socially engaged researcher to develop appropriate theoretical explanations and models for action by conducting a dialogue between empirical observations, lived-experiences, and relevant pre-existing bodies of knowledge. In this regard, Wright Mills himself was no slave to theoretical dogma. Rather, guided by his mentor, Hans Girth, he favoured a well-informed critical eclecticism (though he would likely turn in his premature grave should we refer to him as the first postmodernist sociologist!). He had a deep understanding of the classic tradition in sociology, dominated by the three heavyweights, Marx, Weber and Durkheim, with a support cast including Veblen, Spencer, Mosca, Schumpter, Mead, Simmel and Mannheim (Wright Mills, 1960). In terms of his own ontological/epistemological positioning, Wright Mills was highly influenced by the subject of his doctoral studies, pragmatism. Prominent in the works of the American philosophers and educationalists, William James and John Dewy, pragmatism advocates the science of the possible whereby action and intervention are linked to outcomes that are themselves based on a critical assessment of what can be achieved within a given set of situational circumstances (Thayer, 1970). Critical pragmatism places emphasis on theoretical development and refinement through critical, practical, empirical engagement, rather than fixating upon abstract debate and unmoveable theoretical principles. This view recognises that the construction of society is not passively structural, but is an embodied process of individual and collective actions. As Alison Kadlec

(2007: 31) has put it, 'much is missed when we impose artificial arrests on a world in flux, as not only does this impede our ability to perceive deeper and more nuanced relations of power that constrain and repress, this also stunts our ability to perceive and cultivate new possibilities for change'.

The emergence of left realism within critical criminology can in some ways be viewed as a version of critical pragmatism. Disillusioned with conventional theories of crime and deviance emanating from the political right, empiricist and measurement orientated models in mainstream sociology, and the failure of class struggle/revolution-fixated Marxist sociologists to provide the foundation for the development of an agenda for investigation and intervention, scholars developed an innovative, praxis orientated approach. The left-realist paradigm allowed for the mobilisation of a radical and critical sociological imagination in determining strategies for progressive and pragmatic engagement with social problems, with a view to influencing local policies and interventions that could improve the conditions of society's most vulnerable groups. Space does not permit a full discussion on the merits or otherwise of left realism, but that can be found elsewhere (Young, 1991). Suffice it to say that for some radical thinkers and doers, left realism can offer a way out of the inertia so often brought on by an obsession with internecine paradigmatic rivalries. While left realism developed with particular foci on deviance and crime, a similar form of 'praxis' has been advocated in the context of sports activism by the Marxist scholar Ian McDonald, who has argued that rather than being satisfied with armchair critique, 'a radical sociology of sport should be seeking to assist the reconfiguration of the culture of sport by intervening against dominant relations of power'(McDonald, 2002: 105).

This kind of radical thinking and intervention has also been advocated by scholars of international development, including those who focus on fractured community relations and social conflict in divided societies. Gathered loosely under the banner of Critical Development Theory (CDT), academics and practitioners from a variety of disciplines and platforms have expressed concern about the way development studies in recent decades has moved away from its radical, anti-capitalistic roots to adopt more mainstream position within a neo-liberal globalisation agenda. In this regard, the proponents of CDT argue that under cover of the rhetoric of development, best exemplified by the United Nation's MDGs (Millennium Development Goals), international development organisations and related NGOs are peddling new forms of imperialism. CDT involves breaking from this neo-liberal agenda and restoring critical theory as the central component of development studies, which in turn can inform a 'strategic praxeology' or 'pragmatic toolkit' enabling practitioners to ask pertinent, challenging questions and grow strategies for intervention that are appropriate for the local contexts within which they find themselves working.

Sport and peace building as a dialogue between political and civil society

Understanding the role that sport can play in the relationship between political and civil society is a key in understanding any role it can have in promoting progressive social change. Antonio Gramsci's work has been hugely influential in helping us to understand the articulation of power between the institutions of state and civil society actors and organisations, and within and between those cultural formations themselves. An Italian communist and political activist in the 1920s and 1930s, Gramsci's ideas, with their focus on the significance of culture in power relations, represented a break away from more orthodox, econometric Marxist approaches to political struggle and revolution. In this regard a generation of critical sport sociologists have argued that sport is a fiercely *contested* element of 'civil society' – an area of civic culture and popular participation that stands outside the formal institutions of state but is nonetheless vital in securing consensus and control for those occupying the commanding heights of 'political society' (Boham, 2002; Schuurman, 2009).

While Gramsci's analysis was concerned with understanding the dynamics of revolutionary social and political change in the context of capitalism in general, it is nonetheless also useful in helping us to understand the underlying dynamics of peace processes which, in their own way, require a revolution in established social and political relations. While there can be little doubt that the final deals and treaties that are characteristic of the formal phase of a peace process are crafted and agreed in political society, this level of political concord cannot be achieved and successfully implemented without significant support in civil society. Cultural movements are not passive partners in this relationship. As evidenced in the turmoil and revolution that spread across the Near East and North Africa in the early part of the 21st century, at times it is possible that events and movements shaped in civil society outpace and lead to radical change in the circumstances of political society.

Peace processes are messy affairs: hugely complex enterprises that move forwards or backwards according to conditions prevalent in the transcending social and political order. Usually they are driven by activities and actors in political society. However, if there are major social and cultural impediments, 'road maps to peace' that take account of the political sphere alone are doomed to failure. Changes of heart and mind do not ordinarily take place because of political initiatives. Peace is only possible when significant proportions of ordinary people are ready for and open to conflict resolution. By way of illustration, politicians may be in the driving seat but for the 'peace bus' to get anywhere meaningful along its road map there must be passengers willing to climb on board. This comes gradually through social and cultural engagement in everyday life. The challenge for peace activists is to discover ways to join up specific grass-roots, civil society, interventions with more broadly influential policy communities and those elements of political society that hold the keys to peace.

A contribution from peace and conflict studies

If what has been said so far constitutes the deep structure of the theory and method outlined herein, it is now time to turn to the 'surface structure', that is, the most relevant theories and models of practice that have already been developed by other researchers and scholars working in the field of conflict resolution and peace studies. It is not my intention to provide a comprehensive review of all such interpretations and typologies, rather to consider those that are most relevant in informing and strengthening my own critical positioning in relation to my own field experience.

Many of these are based on the pioneering work in Brazil and Chile of Paulo Freire, who in his classic statement on the subject, *The Pedagogy of the Oppressed*, was one of the first to point out that development programmes that are from outside to in and top down in nature, tend to augment rather than ameliorate the circumstances of exploitation and oppression felt by impoverished communities (Freire, 1970) Similarly, Adam Curle drew on fieldwork experiences in the war-torn Balkans in the 1980s and 1990s to advocate the notion of 'peace building from below' – a strategy whereby external forms of intervention and mediation concentrate on facilitating the organic empowerment and active participation of local actors and agencies in conflict resolution and reconciliation (Curle, 1971).

Galtung identifies the interrelationship between visible and less visible violence. He argues that in order to begin conflict transformation and achieve sustainable peace it is necessary to address less visible violence. Building upon this, Marie Dugan developed a 'nested paradigm' model which is a 'sub-system' approach linking the challenges of conflict resolution to the broader necessity of peace-building. At a sub-system level, a peace building strategy could be designed to address both the systemic concerns and problematic issues and relationships existing at a local level. The sub-system approach allows one to shape both grass-root relationships, as well as contribute to wider systematic change.

In concert with the thinking of Dugan, John Paul Lederach (1996) has also theorised a 'web approach' to peace-building. He encourages interventions that explicitly focus on strategic networking or 'web-making', a term used to describe the building of a network of relationships and partnerships with significant local entities and actors, what he refers to as the 'cultural modalities and resources' within the setting of conflict. The model he uses to help us envisage holistic and sustainable peace building is a triangle or pyramid – the apex, or Level One of which, represents international and national political actors. The middle-level features regional political leaders and constituency representatives, including religious, business and trades union leaders and so forth who have connections with and access to Level One actors. Finally, at Level Three, the grass-roots level, there are the vast majority who are most affected by the conflict on a day-to-day basis. Lederach argues that for a peace process to be successful and sustainable it must operate across and include all levels of the pyramid, especially Level Three where conflicts are played out on a day-to-day basis.

Critical for the success of model's like that of Lederach is the facilitation and management of the flow of communication between the three levels. Gavriael Salomon refers to this as 'the ripple effect' through which the impact of peace education programmes spreads to wider social circles of society and eventually permeates overarching institutional and political frameworks. The key values in this process are represented by those middle-level actors who have one foot in community cultures and other in higher level policy-making circles. It is through their input and output that lessons taken from work at the grass-roots can be translated and transferred into constituencies that make use of it in the framing of broader public polices and political agendas (Salomon and Nevo, 2002).

The ripple effect is most effectively created by identifying and building active partnerships with individuals representing organisations that have the proven capacities to operate between levels one, two and three. As middle-level actors, they are ideally located to bring people together and weave dialogue, ideas and programmes across boundaries. By capitalising on key social spaces, they are able to spin a web of sustainable relationships. Critical to all of these approaches is the praxis element and through it the empowerment of subordinate actors and groups through their active participation in peace building programmes and processes. In other words, creating structures through which those experiencing the 'personal troubles' that attend those living in conflict zones can turn these into 'public issues' and be part of creative programmes that allow them to contribute to progressive activities that can make a difference to their everyday lives.

A note of caution is needed here. We would be poor critical scholars indeed if we failed to acknowledge the 'soft power' role played by sport in the spread and maintenance of Western empires in the 19th and 20th century. Indeed, one of the biggest criticisms levelled at Sport for Development and Peace (SDP) work in general is that it not much more than a thinly disguised attempt to continue the exercise of soft power through sport in the post-colonial epoch. I have been acutely aware of this through my own work in Israel where, working closely with the British Council on the one hand, and the Sport Authority for Israel on the other hand, we have faced the double challenge of avoiding being seen to be used by the former organisation as a vehicle for strengthening the British cultural brand in the region, and by the latter as an instrument that contributes to the Israeli state's mission to 'normalise' existing social and political relations there. There is an important lesson here: while the establishment of a network of partnerships through 'middle-level' actors who might favourably influence broader political agendas is an important strategic objective, one has to be acutely aware that this dynamic can also work in the opposite direction inasmuch as pressure exerted by partisan external political influences through network partnerships can undermine the integrity of a given development programme and distort both its operational agenda and external perceptions of its work.

Sport for peace's moral compass

When embarking on civil society interventions in divided societies, to quote the title of Howard Becker's influential 1967 article, there remains the question of 'Whose side are we on?' That is to say, what are and who sets the coordinates of the moral compass that guides our approach to

critical intervention? Becker was one of the first sociologists to articulate what has since become a universally accepted tenet of sociological inquiry, that value-neutrality was neither achievable nor desirable
Becker favoured championing the underdog and the down-trodden, but
as McDonald points out, such an approach is in danger of sacrificing
sociological integrity 'on the altar of partisanship' (McDonald, 2002:
106). What, then, are the ethical principles that guide our 'strategic
praxeology'?

Of course, even with strategies based on critical left realism and CDT,
engagement in social activism of any kind requires those involved to
have an agreed starting position and defined goals to work towards. This
can be a planning minefield, particularly when working in contexts of
deep division and conflict where the antagonistic groups and social
fractions that are brought together espouse antithetical ideologies and
mutually exclusive goals. When this is the case it is vitally important
for practitioners to maintain a neutral stance with regard to those
conflicting goals, while at the same time articulating a rationale for
social and political intervention that does not expose those engaged in
this work to charges of cultural imperialism.

To avoid such eventualities we need unambiguous ethical reference
points, but such reference points are very hard to divine. In this regard,
Peter Donnelly and Bruce Kidd (2000: 135) have argued that 'those of
us committed to opportunities for humane sport and physical activity
ought to resort more systematically to the strategy of establishing,
publicising and drawing upon the charters, declarations and covenants
that enshrine codes of entitlement and conduct' This begs the question
which 'codes of entitlement' and who gives them authority. Article 26
of the UN 1948 Universal Declaration of Human Rights states: 'education shall be directed to the full development of the human personality
and to the strengthening of respect for human rights and fundamental
freedoms. It shall promote understanding, tolerance and friendship
among all nations, racial or religious groups, and shall further the
activities of the United Nations for the maintenance of peace'. As
Donnelly and Kidd went on to argue, the United Nations Charter for
Human Rights is one of the few touchstones for governing activism
that has near universal approval – although account should be taken
of arguments claiming that 'human rights' is a conceptual construction rooted in Western liberal thought and appeals to such 'higher
order' charters and moral principles can be criticised for being at best
idealistic and at worst a form of neo-liberal Kant (Tomuschat, 2008).
However, I am hard pressed to find anything wrong or abhorrent in

the sentiments expressed in the UN's declarations on human rights; neither do they strike me as particularly pro-Western. On the contrary, it seems to be precisely these kinds of sentiments that have fuelled pro-democracy movements across the globe in the late modern era, including and especially in the wider Middle and Near East. Without such principles, when it comes to social and political activism one's hands are tied by the bonds of standpoint epistemology and cultural relativism, which usually means there is limited scope for progressive social and political change and the status quo prevails. For a fuller discussion of this topic see the collection of essays edited by McArdle and Giulionotti (2003).

Yet the question remains: how and where to intervene? To begin with, the notion of 'peace' is itself an elusive and problematic concept embracing a variety of meanings from 'the absence of war' to 'a state of equilibrium and tranquillity', and many things in between. As Coalter and others have argued, paper declarations and accompanying rhetoric are well meaning but useless without intervention (Coalter, 2010). Despite the abundance of rhetoric eulogising sport's innate capacity to do good throughout the world, in and of itself sport has no magical intrinsic qualities, but is a very flexible crucible into which we can pour ideas and ideals based on notions of human rights and social justice. With resounding echoes of Huizinga's (1949) *Homo Ludens*, John Alt's (1983: 95) articulation of how this can be realised through mobilising the emancipating capacities of play, suggests that it can become a central strategy for sports-based, peace building activities:

> Fair play in sport is related to social justice: individuals are free to consciously pursue the potential and limits of their interests, talents, and character while at the same time respecting the rights of others to do likewise. Justice in this sense implies reciprocal fairness in group life and relates to goodness or civility – being loyal, courteous, tolerant and beneficent as ends in themselves and as a means for furthering rightness.

There is a strand within neo-Marxist thought, best represented by the Frankfurt School, that acknowledges the dialectical potential of sport and related play forms within culture. Traces of this can be found in the works of Lukacs, Marcuse and Adorno, but the pre-eminent voice in this tradition is that of Ernst Bloch. In his magnum opus, *The Principle of Hope*, Bloch revived the utopianism present in many of the writings of the younger Marx and grounds it in a critique of the material conditions of everyday life. For Bloch, if progressive social change is to occur, human actors must be able to construct a vision of a better future: in other words to hope. But that vision or hope exists in a dialectical relationship to what already is, rather than in an imagined utopia that floats entirely free from its material reality (Bloch, 1995).

Carefully constructed and executed SDP programmes can provide windows of opportunity through which visions of better futures can be imagined and appetites for progressive movement toward such futures cultivated. Using Bloch's framework to analyse one such sport-based intervention, John Doyle argues that 'Utopia's great gift is to allow us the critical toolkit to imagine how the future might evolve'. Sport as utopia therefore also provides us an opportunity to continue the journey, to glimpse into the future. It gives us a critical framework to assess the development and metamorphosis of sport institutions ... It provides a lens that refracts the future possibilities being created in the present (Doyle, 2013).

Even in the most dire of circumstances when, in terms of conflict resolution and peace-building, the political momentum is driving in the opposite direction, it is important to continue to provide structures and opportunities in civil society for those who feel impelled to counter political inertia and alleviate feelings of powerlessness through activism in their own communities, in other words, providing ongoing linkages between personal troubles and public issues. This certainly reflects my experience in July 2006 when, on the eve of launching a sport-based peace building initiative in Israel, war broke out along its border with Lebanon between the Israeli Defence Force (IDF) and Hezbollah militia based in Lebanon. As missiles rained down on towns and villages in Northern Israel, the SDP intervention had to be cancelled. However, two months after a cease fire had been agreed we re-engaged in the region: not because we (the outside body) insisted we do so, but because our local partners asked us to. When explaining why we should re-engage, the consensus that emerged was that without such initiatives the field was left clear for the war mongers, whereas collaborative civil society peace building ventures such as ours gave local activists the opportunity to articulate their sense of hope through deeds resistance to such hawkishness.

Research, evaluation and dissemination

Space does not permit a full discussion of strategies for research, evaluation and dissemination, but I will attempt to summarise my position on these interlinked areas. Research has a complex, two-way dynamic: first to facilitate in-depth learning about the transcending social and political context that is essential for the critically pragmatic design and development of a given programme of intervention; and, secondly, to provide detailed and ongoing evaluation of the impact of the project at each level, up to and including, where possible, tracking its influence on the transcending social and political context. This circular and inclusive approach to research and evaluation has helped the projects that I have been involved in to develop organically, from the bottom up, as the knowledge and viewpoints gleaned from all key actors and stakeholders have been used to refine and reform interventions year on year. It has also helped to facilitate growing local ownership and sustainability of the project as the communities themselves take increasing responsibility for the design and delivery of interventions, as well as using ideas drawn from this experience in the development of other programmes of cross-community cooperation operating in similar settings.

As Coalter (2010) has pointed out, realistic and objective evaluation is a crucial element of successful SDP programmes. In my experience, multi-layered methodologies that are not restricted by adherence to a limited, positivistic research paradigm are the most valuable. Pre and post surveys can be useful, particularly if they have a longitudinal dimension, but they cannot yield the rich depth of meanings that are held by those both experiencing and implementing SDP programmes. For this an array of qualitative research strategies is needed, including participant observation, diaries and more creative and locally centred information channels, such as auto-ethnography and other forms of story-telling. We are often pressured by funding bodies into using independently 'objective', outside evaluation consultants who are not only very costly, but also lack the grounded interpretative skills of those most directly engaged in project delivery. Utilising the eyes and ears of those who are most closely connected to programme delivery is an evaluation resource that should never be under estimated, and in the programmes with which I have been most closely associated the schooling of volunteers – both international and local – in aspects of research and evaluation is a key part of the training curriculum.

While understanding how best to improve project delivery in a given location is one of the main objectives for research and evaluation strategies, another is to disseminate any lessons learned to local, regional, national and international audiences. One reason for doing so is that other like-minded organisations can learn from one another's successes and failures, and in doing so improve their own programme planning and execution. Another important reason is to contribute to wider debates taking place in the 'policy community' for sport more generally. In this way programmes of grass-roots intervention can escape local boundaries and begin to exert influence on politicians and policy makers who can more effectively make decisions that introduce progressive social change.

Critical pragmatism and the ripple effect

It remains for me to show how all of the different elements of thinking outlined so far in this chapter are woven together to provide a theoretical and methodological reference point for practical engagement in SDP work. The 'ripple effect' model draws on critical pragmatism to depict how this form of praxis can be achieved (Figure 5.1).

In Figure 5.1, the lower quadrant of the outer circle represents a contextualised human rights moral framework, the locus of which is informed by the prevailing transcending social and political context,

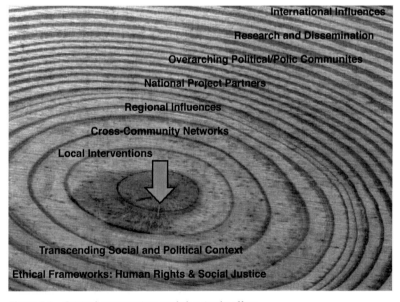

Figure 5.1   Critical pragmatism and the ripple effect

including the status of any overarching peace processes. Taken together they provide a framework upon which to make pragmatic and realistic judgements about the structure and content of any given programme of intervention and its development goals. The inner circle represents the actual grass-roots intervention and values-injection at the local community level. The bull's eye therein represents the target participants: children, youth and adults from different communities; surrounded by trained adult volunteers (international and local) and significant others (relatives, teachers, community leaders, political figures etc.) from the local communities. The nature of the structure, organisation, management and delivery of activities and encounters taking place within this inner circle is crucial in determining the outcomes of any such sport intervention.

In between, working from the middle outwards, the next circle represents the medium of knowledge transfer, comprising active representatives from a network of institutional partners through whom ideas and findings emanating from the project can be articulated within the wider policy community for sport. This in turn may influence processes taking shape in the transcending social and political context and have an impact on the local human rights situation, not only of those directly involved in the project but also further afield. Each level of the process is subject to research and evaluation, and these findings are fed back to inform project modification, growth, and redevelopment, as well as to provide knowledge that can be transferred and disseminated to international audiences. In these ways grass-roots civil society activism can be seen to be influencing the thinking and manoeuvring of powerbrokers operating in political society by creating a ripple effect, the waves from which eventually wash over the shoes of those who walk in the corridors of power. We must bear in mind, however, that just like a stone dropped into a still pool of water, the ripple effect of any community intervention dissipates as it moves further from the centre where the impact is more obviously felt and more easily measured.

Of course, as Michael Mann (1986) reminds us societies 'are much messier than our theories of them' and the lived reality of any peace building intervention is decidedly more fluid, complex and fickle than this rather simplistic, ripple effect model might imply. In many ways the reality is more like Lederach's (1996) 'web approach' to peace building whereby, starting with a small focus, the strategy is to build organic networks of relationships among individuals, communities and institutions around the delivery, development and expansion of that focus.

Like a real spider's web, the more threads there are, the thicker they get and the more anchor points they have will make them more robust, thus enabling them to better withstand potential damage and be more amenable to repair should such damage occur. Finally, the Figure 5.1 is no more than a heuristic representation of what in reality is an embodied process. The success and transferability of any such endeavour will depend on the animation and agency provided by those key actors who operate across and between each level of activity set against the prevailing politics of the times.

Conclusion: the answer

In answer to the question posed at the beginning of this chapter, to operate effectively in the exceedingly complex, multi-layered circumstances that are characteristic of situations of conflict in deeply divided societies, having a highly tuned 'sociological imagination' along the lines summarised herein is a distinct advantage, allowing one to adroitly navigate the challenges presented when working in complex societies in conflict. Thinking of such complexities, I find it useful to envisage peace processes in general as massive, multi-dimensional, jigsaw puzzles that have to be solved without the benefit of having a picture on the box. There are political pieces, economic pieces, military pieces and cultural pieces. Some are violent while others are passive. For the picture to be imagined and completed, all of these pieces will have a part to play and while some, for instance the political corner pieces, may have more significance than others, all the pieces will be necessary for the picture of peace to fully emerge. In the specific contexts of peace processes in deeply divided societies, like South Africa and Northern Ireland, retrospectively we can see that, while not being the most important pieces in each region's complex jigsaw of peace and reconciliation, sport has occupied a significant place in each (partially) completed picture. Currently, in the prevailing circumstances, for Israel and Palestine the picture of the jigsaw of peace may be hard to visualise and nowhere near to being complete. Those of us who choose to try to use sport as a creative forum through which to influence broader agendas do so in the belief that when peace does come to this most troubled of regions, and we look back at the events that contributed to that peace, it is to be hoped that we will be able to identify the positive role played by inter-community sport there.

Note

1. For a fuller rendition of these arguments see *Sport and Peace Building in Divided Societies: Playing with Enemies*. London: Routledge (forthcoming).

References

Alt, J. (1983). Sport and cultural reification: from ritual to mass consumption. *Theory Culture and Society, 1*, 90–107.
Becker, H. (1967). Whose side are we on. *Social Problems, 14*, 239–247.
Bloch, E. (1995). *The Principle of Hope*. Boston, MA: MIT Press.
Boham, J. (2002). How to make a social science practical; pragmatism, critical social science and multiperspectival theory. *Millennium Journal of International Studies, 31*, 449–524.
Brewer, J.D. (2003). *C. Wright Mills and the Ending of Violence*. London: Palgrave.
Coalter, F. (2010). The politics of sport-for-development. Limited focus programmes and broad gauge problems. *International Review for the Sociology of Sport, 45*(3), 295–314.
Curle, A. (1971). *Making Peace*. London: Tavistock.
Donnelly, P. and Kidd, B. (2000). Human rights in sports. *International Review for the Sociology of Sport, 35*(2), 131–148.
Doyle, J. (2013). *Sport as a Mediated Utopia in Peace Building in Israel*, unpublished PhD thesis, University of Brighton.
Freire, P. (1970). *The Pedagogy of the Oppressed*. New York: Continuum.
Galtung, J. (1996). *Peace by Peaceful Means. Peace and Conflict, Development and Civilization*. London: Sage.
Gardner, S. (2012). *Sport for Development and Peace. A Critical Sociology*. London: Bloomsbury.
Huizinga, J. (1949). *Homo Ludens. A Study of the Play Element in Culture*. London: Routledge and Keegan Paul.
Kadlec, A. (2007). *Dewey's Critical Pragmatism*. New York: Lexington.
Lederach, J. (1996). *Preparing for Peace. Conflict Transformation Across Cultures*. Syracuse: Syracuse University Press.
Mann, M. (1986). *The Sources of Social Power*, Volume 1. Cambridge: Cambridge University Press.
McArdle, D. and Giulionotti, R. (eds) (2003). *Sport, Civil Liberties an Human Rights*. London: Routledge.
McDonald, I. (2002). Critical social research and political intervention: moralistic versus radical approaches. In J. Sugden and A. Tomlinson (eds), *Power Games. A Critical Sociology of Sport* (pp. 100–116). London: Routledge.
Mills, C.W. (1959). *The Sociological Imagination*. New York: Oxford University Press.
Salomon, G. and Nevo, B. (2002). *Peace Education. The Concept, Principles and Practices around the World*. New York: Lawrence Earlbaum.
Schuurman, F. (2009). Critical development theory: out of the twilight zone. *Third World Quarterly, 30*(5), 831–848.

Thayer, S. (1970). *Pragmatism, the Classic Writings*. New York: Hackett Publishing.

Tomuschat, C. (2008). *Human Rights: Between Idealism and Realism*. Oxford: Oxford University Press.

Wright Mills, C. (1960). *Images of Man. The Classical Tradition in Sociological Thinking*. New York: G. Braziller.

Young, J. (1991). Left realism and the priorities of crime control. In K. Stenson and M. Cowell (eds), *The Politics of Crime Control* (pp. 147–159), London: Sage.

Part III
From the Field

6
Reflections from the Field: Challenges in Managing Agendas and Expectations around *Football for Peace* in Israel

James Wallis and John Lambert

Introduction

Football 4 Peace (F4P) is a Sport for Development and Peace (SDP) project in Israel that has stood the test of time and found ways of evolving, adapting and reinventing itself in one of the most culturally diverse[1] and politically divided contexts in the world. Since 2001, when it was established, F4P has lived through the Second Intifada, Israel's war with Lebanon, the election of Hamas in Palestine, the 2006 Israel-Gaza conflict, changes in Government spanning the political spectrum, and the Arab Spring. By signposting these events we offer a perspective on the transcending political backdrop to the F4P intervention and give an insight into the scale of the challenges being undertaken and the uncertainty that surrounded every dimension of the project. Knowledge of that context is critical to understanding the nature of a SDP intervention (Sugden, 2006; Coalter, 2007); we provide that in the next section. The chapter then offers some experiential insights into the organisation, application and development of the project. These observations are divided into sections that relate to performance indicators for such interventions; do the actors have shared values and goals? Is there discernible impact at the grassroots level? Are local people empowered and is the programme sustainable? Are the practices ethical? Is the programme evaluation robust? Finally, we provide some examples of where lessons have been learned, highlighting positive and negative aspects, in order to offer some points that may be taken into account and applied in other SDP contexts, each offering their own complex mix of challenges and opportunities.

This chapter is immersed 'in the field'. It is deliberately focused on pragmatics, an on-the-ground approach. It sets out to deliver a critical account of significant managerial, logistical and personal challenges from the perspectives of two practitioners who have played differing, but inter-dependent roles in the development of F4P. Although we acknowledge that we are insiders and provide a perspective based on that subjectivity, our role has provided us with a deeper level of understanding about the functions of F4P than would be possible for an outside researcher (Mercer, 2007). We nonetheless offer a critical, self-reflexive lens: our mission here is not to be self-congratulatory even though, as we acknowledge, F4P can at times provide some inspirational experiences for participants.

A developmental history of F4P

This section is intended to help familiarise readers with the concept of F4P. By mapping a brief overview of the early days followed by F4P project expansion it is designed to facilitate appreciation of some of the demands involved in attempting to establish and embed F4P in Israel. Readers should nonetheless think beyond the text and look for applicability and similarities to their own areas of work; all programmes and projects have challenges. What is laid out in this section requires the reader to consider for themselves the multitude of intricate processes that were navigated on all levels, each step of the way. For example, macro-level budgetary decisions, final editing rights of press releases, the necessary placement of female coaches in Muslim communities and micro-management such as basic coaching equipment, accurate and equitable translation, were all constant challenges that this chapter does not include in its remit, but are an implicit part of work in this particular context.

F4P was conceived 12 years ago by The Reverend Geoffrey Whitfield, David Bedford (athlete and ex-World 10k record holder) and Professor John Sugden of the University of Brighton. F4P uses football as a means to draw together children from across the religious divide in Northern Israel to facilitate peaceful co-existence. As a precursory pilot to future expansion, Ibillin and Misgav, respective Arab and Jewish communities, were chosen to pioneer F4P. The project consisted of an initial four days of football-related activity, with each community hosting the other for two days. A fifth day of activity was conceived as a 'festival of football', as the newly constituted teams would be given the chance to compete against other teams from the project. Composition of teams was cross-community, with coaching and translation by a triad of coaches representing the

UK, Arab and Jewish communities. This facilitated co-operation among people from different communities, rather than competition between them. The inaugural project, while by necessity small in scale, supplied an immediate learning opportunity; it initiated an understanding of the challenges inherent in SDP and illustrated the importance of resilience, adaptability and creativity to practitioners on-the-ground. In 2001, the last minute withdrawal of the Jewish community due to concerns over security when a bus bombing happened nearby meant that the project was based around the integration of Muslims and Christians from different Arab communities. The concept of working across cultural divides was still apparent in the project delivered and the relationships forged were of value to F4P's future.

The project grew from two communities in 2001 (before the withdrawal of Misgav) to 16 communities in 2004: this incorporated Jewish, Muslim, Christian and Druze populations from the Northern Galilee region. Growth continued through to its height in 2009 when F4P included 23 communities and had stretched its remit from Nahariya in the north, six miles from the Lebanese border, through established projects in the Galilee, to Tel Aviv and as far as south Jerusalem and Beer Sheva. Additional features of F4P evolved to include two years of engagement with communities in Jerusalem, involvement of Jordanian children in established projects in the Galilee and an adapted sport-for-development model in Palestine.

The British Council (BC) and the University of Brighton were key partners from the outset, and by 2009 F4P had added two more major stakeholders in the Israeli Sports Authority (ISA) and the German Sports University in Cologne (GSU). The ISA proved to be important partners in that they assumed responsibility for the logistics and organisation of the cross-community partnerships across Israel under the leadership of the ISA Sport Manager for Galilee who was a Bedouin Arab. Surprisingly, this was the ISA's first major involvement in sport-for-peace activity. The GSU invested substantial financial and human resources into the project as well as securing commercial sponsors. The GSU later broke away from F4P as they felt that this investment had not been reflected adequately in decision-making power.

By 2004 a coach training programme had been developed, which was guided by both an on pitch and an off-pitch curriculum that transmitted the core values of F4P: *respect, responsibility, trust, equity and inclusion, and neutrality.* What follows is a critical narrative that examines both the behind-the-scenes practices relating to management, funding and research, as well as the field-based challenges inherent when over 1200 children from 32 communities are being taught values by 150 coaches in a tri-lingual situation. There will be repeated reference to the five core F4P values in terms of how they were modelled on and off the field.

Shared agendas and goals

The aims of F4P are clearly articulated on the official website (www. f4pinternational.eu), in the coaching manual, and in every presentation relating to our enterprise. They provide opportunities for social contact across community boundaries, promote mutual understanding, engender in participants a desire for and commitment to peaceful co-existence, and enhance soccer skills and technical knowledge. The project requires the participants, leaders, managers, coaches and players to place the five core values high in their value system, as these are the values that transcend the whole programme. A relevant question to ask is; to what extent do those involved in F4P at a management level share these aims and model these values? There have been instances when personal agendas have been pursued that conflict with both the stated goals of F4P and its values. As F4P grew it was clear that a significant minority of associates from the EU and Israel were using their involvement as a way of advancing either their career or research profile or both and were showing decreasing interest in matters on the field. These hidden personal agendas led to a lack of *trust* and a resultant fragmentation of F4P.

Sources of funding have always been a crucial consideration within F4P. We can now reflect upon the period of shaky existence as each year's funds were generated from private sponsorship through completing imaginative fund-raising challenges, such as running marathons, and by an increasing demand upon volunteer coaches to contribute financially towards their own passage to Israel. It was a welcome relief when a European Union grant of 400,000 Euros was applied for and gratefully received in 2009. However, this funding came with significant conditions attached which would eventually stretch the relationships of the project partners. The British Council (BC) had headed up the bid and, therefore, had significant influence on how the money was spent. The irony of this was that by then the BC's role in F4P was diminishing while that of the German Sports University, along with their sponsors, was increasing. This caused a tension that ultimately led to an Anglo-German rift in 2010 when the GSU perceived that a body who were contributing little to the logistics of the project was holding most of the purse strings.

Part of the EU money was spent on appointing a salaried adminis-trator based at the BC in Tel Aviv. The person appointed was new to the project which led to tension over whether we should have appointed from within and a perceived lack of *neutrality*. The post holder tried valiantly to co-ordinate the activities of the disparate F4P communi-ties but had no background in SDP work, encountered some resistance from the Arab partners, and never built strong working relationships based on shared interests in the field. This was a person from outside of the project representing an organisation that was becoming increasingly detached from it.

F4P provided a rich source of research data, but this aspect of the project had always been the domain of a small group of academics. Indeed, the lack of a coherent, transparent research strategy led to problems over access to data, intellectual property and academic opportunism. By inviting an academic from one of the sports departments at a prestigious Israeli University, such as the Wingate Institute, to join the F4P research team could have demonstrated a genuine commitment to partnership and *inclusion* in that sphere, as well as embedding the project into the academic culture of its host country. Moreover, while the University of Brighton led the research wing of F4P, neither of us had any access to information on the nature of methods or findings.

Impact

When evaluating the local impact of SDP interventions it is imperative to look for the scale of the project, its longevity, and the detail of activi-ties that directly affect those targeted by the work at grassroots level (Kidd, 2008). The F4P coaching methodology, as laid out in the coaching manual, is based on teaching the five core values through sport (foot-ball) and off-pitch teambuilding activities. It has evolved through action research cycles of action-evaluation-reflection-adaptation (Coghlan and Brannick, 2005; McNiff and Whitehead, 2006), and is unique in that it asks coaches to facilitate, observe and reflect upon the behaviour of the players, rather than their football skills. The coaches are trained in this distinctive pedagogy before the start of the annual project, so that it can be implemented by them with the 1200 children involved.

There are other large scale, long term projects that use football as a medium through which to improve community relations (see e.g. Lea-Howarth, 2006), but none has a dedicated curriculum that places pro-social behaviour as its explicit focus. The assumption is typically that social integration and cohesion will 'just happen' by virtue of attendance. Content of all teaching or coaching programmes resides on an implicit–explicit continuum. Traditional teaching approaches rely heavily on what is overtly (explicitly) said or shown to learners. Other key information is left for learners to subliminally absorb from the environment. In most cases the social message is left as implicit while the sport skills are explicitly coached. The F4P methodology flips the traditional approach by emphasising the learning of human values as its explicit, taught content with the development of football prowess as a secondary, implicit concern. In this respect the coaching methodology applied during F4P sessions is a distinctive feature of our work, and has the potential to be applied to countless other sport contexts with suitably qualified and experienced coaches.

F4P methods have been devised, piloted and adapted over several years, but they rely on delivery from coaches who are familiar and confident with a style that requires them to facilitate situations that lead to value conflict, to stand back and observe behaviour, and finally to reflect upon and reinforce positive examples. For example, a moral dilemma (Hellison, 1995) may be created where players are asked to run their own substitutions, which leads to a decision about whether everyone gets equal game time or the most talented players have more on-field time. The core values of *equity and inclusion* conflict with values related to winning. The coach recognises and praises the players who willingly swap with those on the bench. Applying these coaching strategies necessitates a significant change in practice for the coaches, which some are not able or willing to engage with. Clearly, the F4P manual is an ever evolving working document that supports the work of coaches. However, it should be noted that the manual alone cannot replace the experience of coaches, who are also self-educated and have their own processes for generating value conflict and facilitating debate about it in their sessions.

Because of disparities in the quality of coaching, the availability of translators and local engagement across each twinned Arab and Jewish community programme, the impact of the values-based coaching was variable. We have both worked on successful local projects that comprised a team of trained EU and Israeli coaches, fully committed local sports leaders, and where participants modelled the five core values both in public and private. Conversely, we have experienced F4P projects where children and local coaches are under-recruited, coaches struggle to work with the manual (preferring to revert to traditional coaching methods), there is a lack of basic equipment, and local organisers are involved for the 'wrong reasons'. Most local projects operate along a continuum between the above extremes as they all have different settings, circumstances and challenges. For us, though, it was particularly satisfying to see the development of projects over successive years under the guidance of a consistent local team who genuinely embraced the F4P values in their work. We have confidence that these communities will become the self-sustaining, autonomous legacy of F4P. It would be unrealistic to have expected such commitment from all communities, as some were clearly only interested in their own agendas and box-ticking exercises. In hindsight, there needed to be a process of de-selection of communities who consumed resources but failed to fulfil the shared goals of the project. This process may have been carried out by a committee drawn together from project partners to ensure equity in decisions made. We were, on occasions, too tolerant of some communities who regularly failed to uphold their responsibilities in the delivery of a F4P programme, but would happily advertise and celebrate their involvement in an internationally esteemed sport-for-peace project.

One criticism levelled at F4P is that its impact lasts for five days in July and the participants go back to their communities where they are subjected to confounding values associated with power conflicts and security politics once again. We usually respond by citing those partnerships, such as Ibillin-Misgav-Kowkab that organise cross-community sport and cultural activities all year round. However, it is evident that, while barriers are removed and genuine friendships are forged in those five days, in most cases this is not sustained throughout the year despite communities being situated so close to each other. There was a proposal for a F4P league where teams from each cross-community cluster would play against each other throughout the year presented two years ago but did not come to fruition.

Deliberations concerning the impacts of interventions in sport-for-development projects are commonplace. The need to evidence the integrity, efficacy and value of projects is often necessitated by the demands of sponsors, publicly funded bodies or academia. In many respects such measurements can be perceived as box-ticking exercises to satisfy grant applications or to show outcomes worthy of continued fieldwork (Kay, 2009). Impacts are rarely measured by third parties so objectivity is sacrificed. In addition to this there are questions concerning the fundamental existence of sport-for-development projects. The objectives they set are often immeasurable over the short-term and generally involve interventions that target philosophical, emotional and attitudinal changes that take far longer to embed and catalyse impacts at an individual level.

It is our contention that the effect of F4P resides within each individual and is relative to that individual. F4P has targeted behavioural, attitudinal and emotional change. It can be argued that F4P can, at least in part, be measured by numbers of children or coaches educated or its longevity, but this would be missing a much larger point. The learning process is so implicit that participants themselves are unaware of effects until there is opportunity for personal reflection on attitudes and values, along with introspection on the moral impact on behaviour. A leap of faith is required in order to accept that our efforts may not necessarily be overtly apparent at the time of project delivery, and to trust the transformative potential of our work in years to come. Through our personal involvement with the project we believe that F4P has the potential to be transformative. We are drawn to the theory of transformative learning popularised by Jack Mezirow (1990, 2000, 2009), which recognises that negative or contradictory experiences can become positive learning experiences over unspecified amounts of time. This process may take many years depending upon the person's readiness and willingness to reflect and learn. In this respect, F4P acts as the lived experience which can be reflected upon over time as attitudes and behaviours mould and shift. In time, F4P may lead to attitudinal shifts as generations of participants reflect upon relationships initiated on the football pitch. In essence, F4P may have sown a seed that could make a significant contribution to individual attitudes, emotions and behaviours. At the very least, F4P has been a medium for inter-community contact that is often otherwise denied. Contact has, at times, been in conflict with preconceived value judgements, but according to Mezirow the process of subjecting somebody to this contradiction initiates learning, with time and reflection on experience doing the rest. Measuring impact is a challenging exercise for any SDP initiative due to the choice of suitable outcome criteria, the appropriateness of methodology, and other logistical considerations. Add to these dilemmas the argument that value change in individuals may not manifest itself until years later and evaluation becomes highly problematic.

Empowerment and sustainability

It is commonplace for SDP projects to have objectives concerning future sustainability and local ownership at their heart. A sense of handing over, a gradual shift of control, governance and decision-making to indigenous personnel are necessary hallmarks of an exit strategy (Lederach, 1997; Schulenkorf 2010). To reject this notion raises questions of who stands to benefit from continued occupation, and undermines the whole definition of development (Black, 2010). Under these circumstances a project's aims are diluted, it becomes self-proliferating, and can conflict with the fundamental principle of its existence; to provide support as a basis for self-development. The 'Donor-Client' model has been widely dismissed by researchers (Hognestad, 2006) as disempowering and Neo-Colonialist.

A critique of the aid programme to the 'global south' by NGOs has been presented by Dambisa Moyo (2009) who uses the example of aid to Africa in the form of millions of mosquito nets to areas of high prevalence of malaria – which subsequently undermines the local production of nets and causing the closure of family businesses. It is her contention that Western aid in Africa since the 1980s has undermined local production, generated economic apathy and destabilised governments. The tenets of Moyo's arguments can be used as an analogy for ill-conceived SDP initiatives that fail to develop genuine partnerships with local actors and allow them a voice.

After 12 years we are just reaching the stage where the local Arab and Jewish communities, under the leadership of the Israeli Sport Authority, feel that they are ready to assume autonomy and break loose from their EU partners. While we are critical of NGOs who 'parachute' in, set up SDP programmes (usually with the funding and the research access they require), then leave after a couple of years, we admire those that are in it for 'the long haul' (Martinek, 2006) and believe that autonomy-supportive actions should have been implemented with F4P much earlier. In this respect the 12-year lifetime of F4P in Israel could be interpreted in one of two ways; either a runaway success or failure to achieve a more comprehensive handover during this time. How long is too long? How do you gauge the speed of handover? Who does jurisdiction transfer to? The answers to these questions, and others, are all contextually bound, and, in the case of F4P, contributed to the challenges of making ourselves dispensable.

It is accepted that offering greater autonomy to less experienced coaches runs the risk of diminishing immediate outcomes. Highly trained EU coaches were in a better position to deliver the F4P methodology than Israeli coaches by virtue of their experiences of value-based work and opportunity to practice. It was tempting to adopt this modus operandi as projects could then be centrally managed and present a facade of excellence, features that may well have been appealing to some with other vested interests in the project. From a practitioner's perspective there are constant deliberations concerning the practical implications of a sustainable model and the continued reliance upon an external, finite resource. Up to this point the key personnel in both coach education and the delivery of F4P projects were senior university lecturers and their student volunteers. A visual representation of this model would locate senior staff at the centre, EU volunteers in close association with Israeli coaches radiating from the centre, with proximity to the centre representing their level of involvement. Concerns over the paradigm that places EU staff at the centre and locals on the margins began to develop. As projects grow they attract profile, external interest and become worthy of territorial battles over ownership and personal positioning. The fundamental principle of the project can become marginalised, indeed almost forgotten as creative minds and expert practitioners lose their focus on the task on hand. These can be inevitable conclusions where rivalling agendas exist and centre stage becomes worth contesting.

As questions of autonomy surfaced, the emphasis needed to shift to a more sustainable use of resources that could deliver the F4P methodology to children while providing the F4P coaching methodology to community coaches. The 'Cascade' principle rejected nationality as a way of separating coaches and instead divided them by their level of experience and training in the F4P methodology. Coaches were tiered and given responsibilities for project planning and delivery that were in keeping with their level of training. This change of emphasis in coach education from training that was dominated by a narrow group of experienced EU coaches towards a three tier coach mentoring system that fully involved the locals was a turning point. From 2010 onwards the training week, which traditionally had taken place in the UK or Germany in April ten weeks prior to the project in July, was based on autonomy-supportive lines in accordance with self-determination principles (Deci and Ryan, 1985). It was attended by mainly young Tier 1 coaches, new to F4P methods, from sports courses at the University of Brighton and the GSU alongside similarly novice coaches from Arab and Jewish locations in Israel. The Tier 2 and 3 came from the rest of the coaches present; which category they were in depended on their level of F4P experience. The Tier 3 mentored the Tier 2 who, in turn, trained and mentored the new Tier 1 coaches. This cascade programme, which was used by the locals in Israel to train the 50 coaches who did not travel to Europe, allowed for devolved *responsibility* and led to an increase in perceived competence, relatedness and autonomy (Patrick et al., 1993). In other words, by progressively handing over *responsibility* to the locals, we had moved from a team of passive, dependent Israeli coaches to a cohort of independent, trained practitioners confident in delivering the values-based curriculum on and off the football field.

An obvious question needs to be asked. Why did we allow the local coaches and leaders to become so disengaged from the project that they took on the mere secondary roles of translating and organising equipment? In reality the EU leaders and coaches adopted practices that maintained control over every aspect of the project, including the on and off-pitch activities, due to a lack of *trust* in some local coaches and, in some cases, to maintain a power differential in order to more easily pursue personal agendas. The F4P Coaching Manual sets out the project aims which inform the learning activities and pedagogy; research conducted in 2005 showed, however, that very few local coaches had seen or read the manual, which exemplifies the lack of ownership felt by the Israelis. The manual had been translated to Hebrew but was not available in Arabic until 2008, which raises issues of *equity and inclusion*.

Ethical practices

There are examples of partner communities in F4P that both facilitate high quality values-based on and off-pitch activities and have developed enduring friendships across the religious and political divide. The Ibillin-Misgav-Kowkab partnership has been a shining example since 2001. In contrast, a small number of local communities have been found to work in unethical ways that are counter to F4P aims and values. One local organiser collected money from the families who sent children, despite a declared F4P open access policy in line with our *equity and inclusion* values. Few Arabs attended that particular project, which was populated by middle class Jews. More generally, all communities receive funding to cover facilities and equipment costs on the understanding that all leaders and coaches are volunteers. We have worked at local venues that did pay certain coaches and leaders and, not surprisingly, there was a lack of balls, cones and bibs. These unethical practices betray a lack of engagement with and *respect* for conflict prevention goals, and usually result in either the local personnel changing or the community ceasing to be part of F4P.

   While the vast majority of students and academics who worked on F4P were involved for ethically sound reasons, and thus to fulfil the aims of the intervention, there has been a minority whose actions were motivated by self-interest. One academic, for example, was admitted on to the management team in order to write grant applications and join the research team. In reality that person and their Masters students attended only one single project in Israel in 2008, gathered the data they required and then travelled to conferences around the World presenting about F4P, using it as a vehicle to raise their international SDP profile.

On a positive note, it is reasonable to assert that the opportunities and status of female coaches and players was advanced by F4P in a country where women are particularly under-represented in sport. The numbers involved in the girls' project grew each year and we assigned a female coach to every local project. The emergence of the female dimension of F4P was not without cultural problems in some localities with Muslim councils but we managed to develop opportunities for the girls to take part while paying due regard to religious sensitivities. The performance of both female players and coaches enhanced their reputation both within and outside F4P, and provided impetus for future growth.

Robust evaluation

Those bodies investing in SDP projects usually require some evidence, often in the form of impact reports, to demonstrate that their time and money has been invested wisely. Commonly, this evaluation is justifiably written as a condition into the funding agreement. If not carefully managed, impact reports can be a problem to both those providing the money and the recipient organisation. Invariably, the NGO delivering the SDP intervention is reliant on the grant to maintain levels of local investment in terms of the scale of the project and quality of the work that places pressure on those conducting the evaluation.

Those of us who have been F4P insiders for several years have experienced the problems of local disengagement, uneven rigour in recruitment of EU coaches, off-pitch activities that have been so disorganised that they have created conflict, and an end-of-project tournament that has been hijacked by outsiders seeking PR opportunities. However, these have been either overlooked in the annual evaluations or no action was taken to remedy them. While there has been some qualitative research on the impact of F4P on coaches and children, this is small-scale, short-term and selective. The aim behind this research has often been to provide data for research degrees and journal articles rather than to rigorously investigate the project's impact and feed back into project design.

Finally, we admit that changes in an individual's value system and consequent attitudes are difficult to measure. However, there are instruments (Schwartz and Bardi, 2001) that can provide empirical data before and after an intervention that can detect initial changes in value systems, even if the full effect of F4P on a participant may not manifest itself until many years down the line. It is, therefore, surprising that until today, no attempt has been made to measure value change considering that this is a key aim of F4P.

Lessons learned

As previously stated, this critique of F4P is intended to highlight the aspects of success and areas to improve upon, as well as offer recommendations to likeminded people who are attempting to use sport as a tool make a modest but important contribution to community relations in their chosen setting. Some lessons learned from F4P are:

- Build genuine relationships with all partners based on shared aims and an underpinning set of values, thus creating a social web (Lederach, 2005) at all levels. Model the values on and off the field.
- Focus on the interface between practitioners and participants throughout. Develop a curriculum that, if delivered in an appropriate way by trained coaches, will alter the value systems and attitudes of your target group in a desired way (Lambert, 2006). It is not only what you do that matters but also how you do it. Teaching and coaching methods are as important as content.
- From day one there should be planned strategies that empower the host country's coaches, organisers and significant others within the intervention, this leading to local self-sustaining infrastructure and eventual project withdrawal of external change agents (Coalter, 2010; Lederach, 1997, Schulenkorf, 2010). Self-determination theory (Deci and Ryan, 1985) contends that motivation derives from three sources: (1) autonomy or control over proceedings, (2) perceived competence and (3) a sense of relatedness or belonging to the environment. Without interventions that could facilitate the growth of these three constructs, the likelihood of local engagement or a phased hand over is limited.
- Women can be the biggest victims of conflict and are often marginalised in sport. Involve women in roles that are culturally relevant and that will empower them (Mazurana and McKay, 1999).
- Every community wishing to be involved in the project should sign a binding agreement to abide by a set of mutually agreed overarching

principles that includes rules on expenditure, a commitment to activities that span the whole year, and a minimum level of player recruitment and coach training. Adopt a de-selection policy for non-fulfilment of key principles.

- The research programme that supports the project should have clear direction that includes a comprehensive evaluation of impacts that relate to its aims, a code of ethics and a transparent structure. SDP organisations must guard against 'research parasites' who gain short-term access to projects for personal academic prestige and a 'regime of truth' (Darnell, 2010), and where a narrow self-interest group is privileged.

At best F4P has been a life-enhancing experience for all of us, especially the sports coaches and teachers who have applied the skills, knowledge and, most importantly, values to their future work in the United Kingdom, Germany, Israel and beyond. The lasting partnerships and friendships have transcended social and cultural barriers due to involvement in F4P. That is a legacy to celebrate.

Note

1. At the time of writing the population of Israel is just under 8 million people. The biggest proportion is Jewish with 70 per cent being Israeli born and 5 per cent Jewish migrants, themselves from diverse ethnic backgrounds. Around 20 per cent of the population are often clumsily labelled 'Arab Israeli' but this does little to capture the distinctive identities of a range of ethnic and religious differences such as; Muslim, Christian, Druze, Bedouin. It is estimated that the remaining 5 per cent are comprised of Armenians, non-Jewish migrants and foreign workers.

References

Black, D.R. (2010). The Ambiguities Of Development: Implications For Development through Sport. *Sport in Society*, 13(1), 103–117.

Coghlan, D. and Brannick, T. (2005). *Doing Action Research in Your Own Organization.* London: Sage publications.

Coalter, F. (2007). *A Wider Social Role for Sport: Who's Keeping the Score.* Oxon: Routledge.

Coalter, F. (2010). The Politics of Sport for Development: Limited Focus Programmes and Broad Gauge Problems. *International Review of the Sociology of Sport*, 31, 295–314.

Deci, E. and Ryan, R. (1985). *Intrinsic Motivation and Self-Determination in Human Behaviour.* New York: Plenum Press.

Darnell, S. (2010). Sport, Race and Bio-Politics: Encounters with Difference in 'Sport for Development and Peace' Internships. *Journal of Sport and Social Issues,* 34, 396–417.

Hellison, D (1995). *Teaching Responsibility through Physical Activity.* Champaign, IL: Human Kinetics.

Hognestad, H. (2006). *Whose interests? Some dilemmas of understanding and using sport as a tool for development,* paper presented at Discussion Forum on Sport for Development and Peace, 19th September 2006, Norwegian School of Sport Sciences.

Kay, T. (2009). Developing through Sport: Evidencing Sport Impacts on Young People. *Sport in Society,* 12(9), 156–171.

Kidd, B. (2008). A New Social Movement: Sport for Development and Peace. *Sport in Society,* 1(4), 123–138.

Lambert, J. (2006). The Football for Peace Coaching Manual: A Values-Based Approach to Coaching Sport in A Divided Society. In J. Sugden and J. Wallis (eds), *Football for Peace? Teaching and Playing Sport for Conflict Resolution in the Middle East.* London: Meyer and Meyer, 13–33.

Lea-Howarth, J. (2006). *Sport and Conflict: Is football an appropriate tool to utilise in conflict resolution, reconciliation or reconstruction?* Unpublished MA dissertation, University of Sussex.

Lederach, J.P. (1997). *Building Peace: Sustainable Reconciliation in Divided Societies.* Washington: US Institute of Peace.

Lederach, J.P. (2005). *The Moral Imagination: The Art and Soul of Building Peace.* New York: Oxford.

Martinek, T. (2006). The Development of Compassionate and Caring Leadership among Adolescents. *PE and Sport Pedagogy,* 11(2), 141–157.

Mazurana D. and McKay S. (1999). *Women and Peacebuilding. Montreal: Rights and Democracy.* International Centre for Human Rights and Democratic Development.

McNiff, J. and Whitehead, J. (2006). *Action Research.* London: Sage.

Mercer, J. (2007). The Challenges of Insider Research in Educational Institutions: Wielding A Double⬛Edged Sword and Resolving Delicate Dilemmas. *Oxford Review of Education,* 33(1), 1–12.

Mezirow, J. and Associates (1990). *Fostering Critical Reflection in Adulthood: A Guide to Transformative and Emancipatory Learning.* San Francisco, CA: Jossey-Bass.

Mezirow, J. (2000). Learning to Think Like An Adult. Core Concepts Of Transformation Theory. In J. Mezirow and Associates (eds), *Learning as Transformation. Critical Perspectives on a Theory in Progress.* San Francisco, CA: Jossey-Bass, 3–33.

Mezirow, J. (2009). An Overview of Transformative Learning. In K. Illeris (ed.), *Contemporary Theories in Learning, Learning Theories in their Own Words.* Abingdon, England: Routledge.

Moyo, D. (2009). *Dead Aid; Why Aid is not Working and Why there is Another Way for Africa.* London: Penguin.

Patrick, B.C., Skinner, E.A. and Connell, J.P. (1993) What Motivates Behaviour and Emotion? Joint Effects of Perceived Control and Autonomy in the Academic Domain. *Journal of Personality and Social Psychology,* 65(4), 781–791.

Schwartz, S. H. and Bardi, A. (2001). Value Hierarchies Across Cultures: Taking A Similarities Perspective. *Journal of Cross-Cultural Psychology*, 32, 268–290.

Schulenkorf, N. (2010) The Roles and Responsibilities of A Change Agent in Sport Event Development. *Sport Management Review*, 13(2), 118–128.

Sugden, J. (2006). The Challenge of Using A Values-Based Approach to Coaching Sport and Community Relations in Multi-Cultural Settings. The Case of Football for Peace (F4P) in Israel. *European Journal for Sport and Society*, 3(1), 7–24.

www.football4peace.eu (retrieved 20 September 2012).

7
Indigenous Discourses in Sport for Development and Peace: A Case Study of the Ubuntu Cultural Philosophy in EduSport Foundation, Zambia

Oscar Mwaanga and Kabanda Mwansa

Introduction

In recent times, the international community has begun to gain 'consciousness of the full magnitude of sport's potential as a tool in achieving development goals' (Beutler, 2008: 359). Consequently, the global expansion of Sport for Development and Peace (SDP) interventions with the backing of international organisations has occurred. The sub-Sahara Africa (SSA) has been a key site for SDP activities (Beacom and Levermore, 2008). By the beginning of 2013, the International Platform on Sport for Development and Peace had officially registered about 182 projects and 448 organisations that are involved in one way or another in the SDP movement. Of all these initiatives, 71 projects and 161 organisations were in Africa (www.sportanddev.org, 2013). It is claimed that within this innovative model of development, sport provides a legitimate contribution in the quest to improve global health, education, development and peace (UN, 2006).

Currently, international development predominantly involves the supposedly apolitical but 'developmental' transposition of resources from donor (Global North) to implementer (Global South)[1] (Briggs, 2008). These include the less tangible resources such as Global Northern knowledge, world views, philosophies, practices, values and ideals, which are typically transposed in a unidirectional pattern from the North to the South. Undoubtedly, the distribution of the less tangible resources as listed above consequently standardises and shapes the legitimate ways of perceiving and making development (Sidaway, 2008). Indeed, while SDP policy rhetorically endorses the inclusion of other development perspectives, the reality is that perspectives from the Global South are highly generally marginalised or excluded (Hayhurst, 2009). This disparity could be seen as re-establishing or reimposition of colonial ideologies in a post-colonial setting, thus extending a notion of colonial discourse: that the power to define truth and knowledge lies naturally with the North. This asserts a view that the South lacks knowledge, skills or ideals of its own and thereby forecloses local decision-making channels (Hayhurst, 2009). This tendency within SDP, argues Darnell, is 'based on racialised and spatialised notions of superiority' and outsider expertise, whereby Northern characteristics are taken to signify the *raison d'être* of development in Southern contexts (2007: 562).

However, this assumed superiority of Northern knowledge is never totalised, in that Southerners will inevitably adopt and/or re-interpret such notions by modifying or even countering them with indigenous worldviews and values of their own, leading to social betterment on the basis of local knowledge (Black, 2010). Thus, one may inquire: what cultural discourses do Southerners identify with and how do they interact with, for instance, the predominance of neo-liberal objectives threaded through Northern SDP interventions (Darnell, 2010: 66)? It is irrepressible to deduce that Southerners are still located in a Northern influenced space where their own cultures and worldviews are seldom, if ever, taken into account beyond their folkloristic aspects (Breidlid, 2013: 3). Besides the work of a small number of Northern academics, notably Nicholls et al. (2010) and Lindsey and Grattan (2012), interactions between Northern and Southern worldviews are rarely considered within SDP. This means that localised discourses within Southern contexts tend to be subjugated and find little voice. However, one aspect of Southern indigenous knowledge that is gaining ground in the Northern discourse is collective accomplishment as opposed to 'individualised notions of success and achievement' (Darnell, 2010).

In order to understand how alternative development perspectives could influence SDP research and practice, this chapter introduces and examines the indigenous SSA cultural philosophy of Ubuntu as it is applied within the EduSport Foundation[2] context (Broodryk, 1997; Louw, 1995; Shutte, 1993).The Foucauldian discourse and the post-colonial perspectives are the key notional tools with which the theoretical analysis is engaged. This chapter's critique is essentially located within three primary sources. First, it is grounded in the recent body of work in critical sociology of sport and development (see Darnell, 2010; Hayhurst,

2009; Nicholls et al., 2010; Lindsey and Grattan, 2012). Second, the chapter draws on the PhD research of the first author (Mwaanga, 2012). Third, this critique is underpinned by both authors' prolonged involvement in the SDP movement in an SSA context as activists and practitioners working with the EduSport Foundation in Zambia.

The EduSport Foundation in context

EduSport Foundation is a Christian non-governmental organisation (NGO) based in Zambia. Having operated in the targeted Zambian communities already by 1996, it was formally registered as an NGO in 1999. EduSport Foundation is the first SDP NGO in Zambia and among the first in SSA (EduSport, 2006). It aims at empowering under-served and other vulnerable communities. The Foundation strives to archive this through the use of sport and other physical activities that may work towards the empowerment of underprivileged youth groups (EduSport, 2001). Through its' work, EduSport aims at equipping local communities with skills, resources and knowledge that may be needed to develop local initiatives that increase control in the individual lives of the participants. EduSport also aims at developing indigenous leadership and knowledge in the various communities it works with as one document report that:

> Solutions to the problems in the broken down communities are with local people ... and sport is one of the most effective ways to not only reach the under-served. ... but also a way to genuinely involve them in the reconstruction of their communities. EduSport (2006: 2)

Simultaneously, one of the objectives of the EduSport Foundation is to use sport as a means to foster programmes that build bridges across people of different socio-economic backgrounds and to break down prejudices against race, tribe and gender, thus bringing about transformation at individual and societal level (EduSport, 2001). The main delivery strategy EduSport uses is peer influence especially at youth level. Therefore, EduSport identifies and trains young people to become peer educators or peer coaches as they are called in the EduSport context. The peer coaches are then assigned to lead groups of younger peers towards developing vital life and leadership skills through EduSport programmes. The principles and values of Christianity and Ubuntu form the ideological bed rock of the work and responsibilities that the peer coaches do (EduSport, 2013).

Given the overwhelming presence of HIV/AIDS in the communities EduSport is engaged with, the Foundation has come up with a deliberate programme of mitigating the scourge. Kicking Aids Out (KAO)[3] is the official name for all HIV/AIDS programmes in EduSport. In Zambia, the KAO programme is found in communities that have close ties with the EduSport Foundation (EduSport, 2013). However, KAO has since been adopted by other local and international organisations that are also implementing it. On the other hand, KAO has become a network of international organisations that use sport as a medium through which HIV/AIDS education and awareness is circulated (EduSport, 2013; Mwansa, 2011). Other key programmes for EduSport include the girl's empowerment programme called Go-Sisters[4] and the GreenSport programme that utilise sport as a tool to educate people about diverse environmental concerns.

Theoretical frameworks

In order to disinter the extent to which the Ubuntu cultural discourse presents an alternative SDP discourse, this section examines its tenets. Furthermore, the section applies Foucauldian discourse analysis and post-colonial theoretical perspectives to support the exploration. These bring to the fore, important historical, social, power and political issues that must be examined to achieve the kind of critical understanding we have advocated for.

The tenets of Ubuntu

What is Ubuntu? Bhengu (1996: 10) defines Ubuntu as the art of being a human being. This common African aphorism is often translated as 'a person is a person through other persons' (Ramose, 1999: 49). This proverb identifies its central concept, Ubuntu, which variously means humanity or humanness (Shutte, 1993). At the core of the Ubuntu worldview is the ideal of being with others; that human beings should relate to one another with respect and compassion (Broodryk, 2002). Ubuntu is believed by many authors to be the general philosophical worldview underpinning the way of life for many SSAs (Broodryk, 2002; Ramose, 1999). However, Ubuntu is a highly contested term because diverse views have been applied to its praxis with little compromise (Bhengu, 1996; Broodryk, 2002; Ramose, 1999; Shutte, 1998; Van der Merwe, 1996). Nonetheless, there is much consensus on the roots of Ubuntu: that it is an ancient African worldview with roots deeply anchored in traditional African ways of life (Broodryk, 2002: 56). Equally important to stress here is that Ubuntu is a worldview of hybridity because it has been negotiated with other worldviews; this is because SSAs have historically interacted with other worldly peoples. For example, the Christian worldview has influenced Ubuntu in its contemporary existence. Indeed, many SSAs also follow the Christian religion with varying blend of traditional African concepts such as Ubuntu. In Zambia, the hybridity of Christianity and traditional African ethos is highly significant during burials and marriage ceremonies.

Ubuntu relates 'to the concepts of ontological being and identity' that come to signify the centrality of relationships for the African worldview (Forster, 2010: 244). According to Ubuntu, it is through the relationships found within community life that development for both the individual and the community depend upon each other (Zondi, 1996). This seems to corroborate with the notion that the sub-Saharan culture radically differs from Northern individualism (Kay and Spaaij, 2011). Indeed, compared with Northern individualism, stemming from thinkers such as Kant who deemed the achievement of enlightenment to be through the freedom from guidance of others, to understand through one's own individual rationality; Ubuntu and its 'radical statements of ontological interdependence' serves almost as individualism's antithesis (Praeg, 2008: 372). Therefore, Ubuntu is the capacity in African culture to express compassion, reciprocity, dignity, harmony and humanity in the interests of building and maintaining community tranquillity (Nussbaum, 2003). Ubuntu speaks of our interconnectedness, our collective humanity and the obligation to each other that goes with our connection (Mwaanga, 2012). However, on the contrary, other scholars such as Van Binsbergen (2001) argue that Ubuntu runs the danger of denying other possibilities of identification among some Africans, hence, causing tension that is a recipe for conflict. Van Binsbergen's (2001) stance could be viewed within the xenophobic attacks that rocked South Africa in May 2008. These attacks on innocent immigrants from other African countries could have been ignited to a larger extent by serious identification issues (Mwakikagile, 2008).

Foucauldian discourse theory and SDP

Foucauldian discourse theory is conducive for providing an understanding into how certain ideals within SDP become marginalised. In doing so, it gives precedence to subjugated views, with the potential for such perspectives to inform SDP policy (Danaher et al., 2000). Foucault's theory holds that the generation of truth/knowledge is informed and constrained by the processes of power (Foucault, 1980). Truths are socially constructed and produced through struggles over meaning; a truth's validity is never totalised, but rather occupies a space in hierarchy wherein multiple discourses exist, all being 'highly articulated around a cluster of power relations' (Foucault, 2004: 520). The Foucauldian theory posits development as a discursive formation. According to Rossi (2004), a discursive formation is a historically rooted system in which particular statements and acts make more sense and seem more natural than others. Thus, this development is seen as a historically and culturally specific form of rationality, which is inseparable from related regimes of practice and configurations of power (Rossi, 2004). However, to fully appreciate the notion of discursive formations, it is imperative to familiarise oneself with the fundamental Foucauldian concept of discourse itself. Foucault defines a discourse as a group of statements that are made possible and indeed explicable by featuring in the same discursive space, meaning that they are texts not bound by physical/ geographical arenas. Discourse possesses material formed by virtue of being recognizably different from other texts and narratives (Scott and Marshall, 2005).

Discourse and discursive formations are productive in supporting the understanding of the ways in which discourse transmits power (Rail, 2002). However, even if power is multi-directional according to the Foucauldian theory, it is seductive and coercive, establishing some sort of dependence among those that are coerced by it (Breidlid, 2013: 96). Part of the reason is that mostly development practices do not exist without a certain regime of rationality (Foucault, 1991). This is in fact historically rooted and working as a structure of knowledge. It allows, at any particular time, certain events and patterns of agency (for example, sending sport volunteers from the Global North to the Global South to work in refugee camps), and rendering [others] unthinkable, unsayable and undoable (e.g. zero acceptance of innovative approaches in SDP stemming from the Global South). It is undoubtedly within discourse that the relationship of meaning and power may be reinforced or challenged. Discourses concerning sport and SDP practices privilege a particular form of rationality that reflect and legitimatise relations of power, whereby the Northern development paradigms dominate SDP policy and practice. For example, although the KAO approach was a holistic (applying wide ranging discourses) approach when it was initi-ated at the EduSport Foundation as HIV/AIDS education through sport, once it became internationalised (Northernised), it focused more on the behavioural change discourse framed within neo-liberal development frameworks. The discourse approach to the analysis of power relations within SDP also urges us to think in terms of a plurality of discourses. In his analysis, Foucault raises questions pertinent to situations common in SDP:

> Which individuals, which groups or classes have access to a particular kind of discourse? How is the relationship institutionalized between the discourses, speakers and the destined audience? How is the relationship of the discourse to this author between classes, actions, linguistic cultural or ethnic collectivities? (1975: 15)

In the preceding quote, Foucault acknowledges the hierarchically stratified subjectivities reacting to and manipulating discourses; however, he does not reconcile these views. Nevertheless, it should be noted that resistance is a form of power and that marginalised discourses have the opportunity to resist dominant discourses and subsequently force change (Pringle, 2005). Resistance here is said to be the mechanism, whereby those who experience oppression on the basis of race, gender, age and sexual preference challenge the multiple axes of power. This is well captured in Rossi's articulation:

> This is particularly evident in the field of development, where actors (especially the recipients 'of polices and interventions') are faced with discourses to some degree external to their language, culture, and society. Relative distance' from the sources of development rationality increases the room for maneuver available to the actors involved … But negotiations do not take place between equals. While it is important not to characterize less powerful actors as passive, there is a difference between framing the terms of reference for discursive struggles and being at best able to manipulate dominant orders of discourse subversively. (2004: 26)

Consequently, the hegemony of Global Northern development discourses framing SDP, leave few examples for illuminating alternative development perspectives within SDP (Levermore and Beacom, 2009). However, the SSA cultural philosophy of Ubuntu has been brought to light through this chapter, as a rare attempt to address this concern. Accordingly, we shall highlight how the Ubuntu perspective compliments and/or clashes with dominant development perspectives imposed on EduSport, particularly through conditions attached to financial donations made by

Northern donors such UK Sport, Commonwealth games (Canada) and the Norwegian Confederation of Sport and Olympic committee (NIF).

Nonetheless, criticisms of this post-modernism argues Foucault's approach to power renders resistance problematic since truth claims of the subjugated can not be more legitimate as the truth to which they resist (Parfitt, 2002). However, this viewpoint somewhat avoids the notion of self-determination: that Southern practitioners and SDP policy recipients seemingly do not hold the right to mediate their truth(s) despite SDP having 'profound material effects' upon the dynamics of their lives and those connected with their interventions (Levermore and Beacom, 2009; Siddiqi, 2005: 66). Therefore, while Foucault's theoretic may be characterised as being *deconstructive* in nature, it also possesses the capability to inform new processes of *constructing* knowledge democratically through the participation of alternative discourses (Blaikie, 2000). Hayhurst et al. (2010: 12) acknowledge as much, suggesting that while prima facie SDP represents a univocal agenda through, for instance, the movement's alignment with mainstream development goals, SDP scholars must 'consider whether a cohesive movement might neglect issues of [...] domination [and] marginalisation'.

Post-colonial theory and SDP

Many commentators agree that post-colonial theory is a specific intellectual discourse that consists of reactions to and analyses of the cultural legacy of colonialism (Hall, 2007; Sharp, 2008). This conceptualisation of post-colonialism is useful through locating post-colonialism as a continuation of colonialism, albeit through the different or new relationships concerning power and the control/production of knowledge (Sharp, 2008). Conceptualising post-colonialism as a temporal concept, meaning the time after colonialism has ceased, or the time following the politically determined independence on which a country breaks away from its governance by another state, can be problematic because the 'once-colonised world' is full of 'contradictions, of half-finished processes, of confusions ... and liminalities' (Dictionary of Human Geography, 2007: 561). For example, colonialism involves interruption and destruction of native culture by European imperialism (Smith, 1999). Gilbert and Tompkins (1996) urge that the debate and understanding of post-colonialism must be less a chronological construction of post-independence and more a discursive experience, wherein we engage and contest the colonial discourses, power structures and social hierarchies that remain somewhat a congealed second nature. The earlier conceptualisation of post-colonialism implies structural domination: a system of discursive control and oppression whereby the dominant discourse privileges white, patriarchal knowledge, deeming inferior the knowledge stemming from non-whites (Darnell, 2007). Post-colonialism touches on one of the central issues within development – the concept of power, and how power shapes developmental thinking and policy (McKay, 2004).

How then can we make sense of post colonialism within the SDP context? We would suggest that post-colonialism allows cognisance of a veil propagating, through institutions and policies, an overwhelmingly simplistic and Eurocentric view of development. McKay (2004: 64–65) argues that 'the West with its blind faith in technology and the effectiveness of planning has treated the Third World as a child in great need of guidance.' Of particular concern to post-colonialism, then, is the way that the Global South, within SDP literature and the media, is portrayed in a negative, derogatory and stereotypical manner (McEwan, 2002; Mwaanga, 2012; Mwansa, 2011; Said, 1978). To redress these concerns, development thinking in the Global South requires the inclusion of more local, indigenous understandings/inputs. Such interventions will radically or moderately disrupt entrenched systems of (Northern) knowledge, which creates an air of immutability over development practices (and their representation). The critical essence of post-colonial theory (within the SDP project) entails, then, a destabilising of Global Northern ways of thinking; a creation of space for marginalised groups to speak and produce alternatives to the dominant discourse. The first and leading Zambian indigenous NGOs EduSport Foundation applies the SSA cultural philosophy of Ubuntu to guide their programming, consequently somewhat countering Westernisation in their work.

In failing to acknowledge alternative ideals, the SDP movement effectively replaces 'one reality with another' (Wai, 2007: 73). Indeed, the Northern denial of African philosophy has only served to reinforce this ambivalence (Omobowale, 2007). However, African philosophy irrevocably exists and may be fundamental in shaping the praxis of SDP (Kaphagawani and Malherbe, 2003). Within the EduSport Foundation context, the cultural philosophy of Ubuntu may be regarded as discursively significant in this regard.

Ubuntu and the EduSport Foundation

The EduSport Foundations' Roadmap 2005–2010 document clearly highlights a number of unique organisational tenets. Two aspects relevant to this chapter stand out, that is, empowerment and Ubuntu. In terms of empowerment, EduSport's organisational mission statement is framed within the empowerment framework: 'To empower communities through sport' (EduSport Road Map 2005–2010, 2004: 1). It is important to note that the paradigm focus is towards how sport can help increase access to important resources and how sport can help to influence the wider society, the wider goal being for the socio-economically disadvantaged youth to have greater control and a sense of self-esteem in their lives. This is part of the aims of the organisation as earlier alluded to and sets forth a holistic approach that does not solely focus on behavioural change interventions. This is the opposite of some of the Northern SDP organisations and funding partners that come to implement single-goal initiatives in Africa. For example, Grass Root Soccer (grassrootsoccer, 2012) has a deliberate programme with a sole focus on behavioural change for the youth, completely overlooking other contextual factors that may add value to their goal. The belief in EduSport is that of maintaining a holistic approach in all of its programmes. For example, EduSport cannot embark on a behavioural change programme before a thorough consideration of social structures that make a long-term contribution to young people's lives such schools and churches. Thus, EduSport supports the creation of community schools by directly working with the target communities. The other platform EduSport has created in order to positively contribute to behavioural change for the youth is that of economic empowerment. Through the distribution of loans to help youths start small-scale businesses, EduSport believes that economic empowerment is a crucial factor for behavioural change. Research has shown that lack of economic resources can force youths to engage in risky behaviours in order to survive (Mwansa, 2011; Kalipeni et al., 2006).

Furthermore, it is apparent that EduSport has adopted and continue promoting values of the SSA cultural philosophy of Ubuntu, with a primary focus on the needs of the people as a community. Unlike international NGOs, 'EduSport programs are centered on the interests and needs of the people the organization serves' (EduSport, 2013). The understanding of the need is achieved over time through dialogue with the affected target populations and communities. The approach translates and explains why many EduSport programmes (e.g. Go-Sisters; school sponsorships; etc.) are prioritised to consolidate work with families and build strong social bonds among the youth. EduSport sees family involvement as an extension of its work into smaller and manageable clusters that could help drive a point home by captivating this from a holistic point of view. With this perception, Kay and Spaaij

(2011) have been rare exceptions in moving beyond individualised research foci by acknowledging African ontological interdependency by investigating effects of the family in SDP interventions. Therefore, in light of Ubuntu, considerations into how community discursivities impact upon SDP interventions is a good example of how an indigenous discourse may provide an alternative trajectory on SDP research and practice. However, one must be careful not to bring 'unanimism' to the African context that there exists a single unproblematic and uncontested indigenous African attitude, as explained previously, Ubuntu is a contested term and there is a multiplicity of cultures and discourses within indigenous communities that is partly influenced by Northern discourses (Wai, 2007: 91).

Clearly, this central resolve of EduSport to adopt Ubuntu as a discourse in its own right is a fundamental part of the organisation; hence, its relevance to SDP ought to be captured in any research on the organisation. In this regard, Levermore and Beacom (2009) identified EduSport Foundation as one of the few indigenous NGOs that show some evidence of adopting alternative SDP practices as they were echoing on the paucity of indigenous SDP organisations. However, there are still uncovered issues as to why the Ubuntu ontological position of EduSport has eluded countless Global Northern academic reports. As argued earlier, the privileging of Global Northern forms of knowledge leads to the systematic marginalising of others within SDP. In support of this, Sharp (2008) posits that other forms of knowing are marginalised by Global Northern thinkers, who usually refer to these alternative options of knowing as myth or folklore. Ironically, the academic front wants to know more about the marginalised people's experiences, but within SDP, the academic powerhouse is not interested in the latter's own explanations of those experiences. Hooks (1990) and McKay (2004) question the Northern academics engagement with the other. To truly engage with the marginalised or colonised other, they argue, an academic would need to decentre him/herself as the expert (Hooks, 1990; Joanne, 2008; McKay, 2004). Breidlid (2013) writes that the common culture in the Global North favours scholars as guardians of the truth. For example, the on-going SDP knowledge development is dominated by Global Northern academics who spend limited time with the researched people in SSA, relying heavily on the academic competencies and approval of their peers to establish themselves and their knowledge. As expected, the SSA sport for development subject becomes subordinated and known through the representations of Global Northern academics.

Hooks concludes that the relationship between the academic and the marginalised subject is as follows:

No need to hear your voice when I can talk about you better than you can speak about yourself. No need to hear your voice. Only tell me about your pain. I want to know your story. And then I will tell it back to you in a new way. Tell it back to you in such a way that it has become mine, my own. Re-writing you I write myself anew. I am still author, authority. I am still colonizer the speaking subject and you are now at the center of my talk. (1990: 241)

Against this background, it is argued that those Global Northern academics that are willing to position themselves as co-learners and co-inquirers with the research subjects are better positioned to appreciate and capture non-Global Northern discourses (Mwansa, 2011) such as the SSA philosophical worldview of Ubuntu. Equal research collaboration between the Global North and the Global South should be appreciated within SDP in order to stimulate alternative discourses. Far too few Northern academics are willing and courageous to fully adopt a decentred approach in the research. One good example in SDP that stands out in this regard is the work by Lindsey and Gratten where SDP practitioners in Zambia were involved at key stages of the research. This included dissemination of findings with the publication of article in the Leisure Studies Association Journal recognising the SDP practitioners as co-authors (Lindsey et al., 2010).

Having this said, Ubuntu and its application within EduSport programmes is not flawless. Some have challenged Ubuntu on the grounds that its emphasis on collectivism can easily tip into oppressive communalism (Teffo, 1994). Louw (1995) concurs, but simultaneously maintains that 'true' Ubuntu incorporates dialogue: It therefore incorporates both relation and distance. It preserves the other in his/her otherness, in his/her uniqueness, without letting him/her slip into the distance (Shutte, 1993). If the ideals of Ubuntu are the destination, then dialogue is the transport to that end. In EduSport, Ubuntu is perceived as a work in progress so that in situations when its principles are compromised, social meetings (called Indaba/Insaka) are convened in order for the community members to discuss how to refocus on Ubuntu ways in their SDP programmes. In KAO movement games, a red card in a game is not taken as punishment as such, but an avenue through which the affected player will leave the playing area to meet a peer counsellor on the sidelines for a serious dialogue about the best ways of playing and interacting.

Because of limited examples and studies that openly advocate the inclusion of non-Northern discourses in SDP work particularly in SSA, the current analysis is rather descriptive than expansive. The arguments put forth thus far will only hold if what has been described is consistent with EduSport practice. However, do EduSport participants adhere to the Ubuntu's ideals or, at least, aspire to do so? And if so, to what extent is this apparent? These are controversial issues. For example, when an individual in EduSport fosters personal ambitions at the expense of the interest of the collective, then how can we reconcile Ubuntu in this context? In fact, one may wonder whether Ubuntu can survive (*or has survived*) within the poverty-stricken SSA environment, where living by individualist approaches is perhaps more plausible because of the probability of success it offers to people. Much more can and needs to be said in response to these questions. Louw (1995: 8) makes a thoughtful point by stating that, like other philosophies, Ubuntu is just not a given way of thinking, it is also clearly a task. Ubuntu is primarily an ethical ideal, that is, something that continuously needs to be realised, although encouraging examples already exist (Shutte, 1998: 20).

Through our work with EduSport thus far, we can attest to that there are many examples of youth leaders exercising and building their Ubuntu muscles on a daily basis. Unlike the neo-liberal worldview wherein the individual's development interests rule supreme, wherein others within a society are regarded as a means to an end (Khoza, 1994), the Ubuntu worldview maintains that an individual's existence is only possible through relationships with others. This is why within the EduSport context, it is not strange to hear how a community football team contributed money to buy food for needy team members or to pray and support a funeral of EduSport member's friends or families in ways that only churches and extended families have historically done in the Zambian setting. Prayer is something EduSport teams use as a harnessing tool to consolidate team spirit. Essentially, Christianity and Ubuntu principles in EduSport reciprocate and determine each other, rendering a very symbiotic margin at the point of interaction. For example, as mentioned earlier, EduSport teams come together in the name of Ubuntu when there is a funeral in the community, but while there, teams will engage in Christian prayers and songs to console the bereaved and fellow community members at the funeral.

Teams intentionally and/or unintentionally utilised their Ubuntu cultural knowledge to give physical, social and spiritual support at a funeral, replicating formal structures. Not only does Ubuntu provide the knowledge around which to frame how to react to other people's needs in the community such as a funeral, Ubuntu's cultural orientation predisposes EduSport teams to engage in ways that emphasise love, peace and unity. The preceding principles are correspondingly emphasised in the Bible that has equally reshaped the ways of Ubuntu in EduSport and generally in Zambia. Furthermore, EduSport teams take time off sport to clean and tide up the physical surroundings of local clinics and other public utility spaces. Teams have cared for the needy children in orphanages and have fetched water for old people for domestic use. Helping the vulnerable such as the old and the orphaned is not just an Ubuntu principle, but something that the Bible emphasises on. While it can be claimed from a post-colonial theoretical perspective (Young, 2003) that Christianity was an enforced religion and therefore not fitting for native Zambians, for the EduSport peer coaches, their belief in the Christian faith is crucial in dealing with community challenges. In rural settings, EduSport teams have contributed towards the sinking of community bore holes (water articulation points) and building of local community schools. Teams in consultation with the local authorities have planted trees in an effort to contribute positively to their environment through the GreenSport program.

Conclusion

The theoretical analysis and the authors' views as Global Southern SDP activists and practitioners applied in this chapter brought to the fore a number of key issues for SDP praxis. First, it places the SDP agenda to unfortunately show a biasness that is deeply rooted in the hegemonic colonising practices just like a lot other international development programs. This has necessitated an interrogation of power according to Foucauldian discourse theory, emphasising that in order for people to interpret their life situation, they need a frame of reference, which is contextual to their situation (Rail, 2002), shaping the ways of thinking and the meaning of their world. Ubuntu stresses this school of thought as demonstrated by EduSport. Thus, the chapter advocates that SDP should deliberately eliminate rather than promote the impediments to alternative discourse shaping the ways of thinking and meaning in the Global South context such as Ubuntu. In practice, the authors have shown how the EduSport Foundation has negotiated a hybrid discourse that has somewhat acknowledged concepts from both the Global North and Global South. Furthermore, the chapter has pinpointed that it is correct to perceive that alternative perspectives like Ubuntu underpin particular or contextual aspects of SDP practice. Regrettably though, knowledge of 'indigenous' or alternative perspectives on the development agenda remain inadequately appreciated and refined to suit the demands of the prevailing global trends in SDP.

In the final analysis, the chapter warns SDP not to completely fall into the trap of behaving as a medium to silence the non-economically sound institutions in the Global South. To redress this and other concerns, the chapter presents some development thinking about what the Global South requires, that is, the support of more local, indigenous understandings/inputs in order to drastically or reasonably unsettle deep-rooted structures of (Northern) understanding, which generate an air of immutability over development practices (and their representation). Thus, local research by indigenous scholars and practitioners should be promoted as opposed to the influx of Northern researchers that come with a Western frame of reference and, as a result, see local participants as mere subjects. This chapter highlighted the potential that indigenous development discourses may have in helping us to envisage new development trajectories within the wider SDP movement, without which SDP will only continue to reproduce international development approaches that have failed to deliver tangible outcomes to many local communities in Africa and other parts of the Global South.

Notes

1. The binary of Global North and Global South is 'of course, geographically inaccurate and too generalised to encompass the complexities within and between nations, but it is perhaps the least problematic means of distinguishing between relatively wealthy countries and continents [Europe] and relatively poorer ones [Africa]' (McEwan, 2009: 13–14).
2. EduSport (Education through Sport) Foundation is the first ever indigenous SDP NGO utilising education through sport interventions in socio-economically under-served communities in Zambia.
3. Kicking AIDS out is an international network of sport for development NGOs, organisations and national sport structures working as a collective to raise awareness about how sport and physical activity programs can be adapted to promote dialogue and education about HIV and AIDS and to facilitate life-skills training. A major focus of the network is to support locally run initiatives in building up capacity of youth leaders as (http://www.kickingaidsout.net).
4. The Go-Sisters program aims at contributing to the achievement of the MDG3 in Zambia – promoting gender equity and empowerment – by increasing the number of girls in the target communities adopting leadership roles at the community and district levels (http://www.uksport.gov.uk/pages/edusport-case-study).

References

Beacom, A. and Levermore, R. (2008). International Policy and Sport-in-Development. In V. Girginov (ed.), *Management of Sport Development*. Oxford, UK: Butterworth-Hienemann, 225–242.

Beutler, I. (2008). Sport Serving Development and Peace: Achieving the Goals of the United Nations through Sport. *Sport in Society*, 11(4), 359–369.

Bhengu, M.J. (1996). *Ubuntu: The Essential of Democracy*. Cape Town, South Africa: Novalis Press.

Binsbergen, V. (2002) Ubuntu and the Globalization of Southern African Thought and Society. In P. Boele Van Hensbroek (ed.), *African Renaissance and Ubuntu Philosophy, special issue of Quest: An African Journal of Philosophy*.

Black, D.R. (2010). The Ambiguities of Development: Implications for 'Development through Sport'. *Sport in Society* [online], 13(1), 121–129. Available: Ebscohost (accessed 10 March 2011).

Blaikie, P. (2000). Development, Post-, Anti-, and Populist: A Critical Review. *Environment and Planning A* [online], 32, 1033–1050. Available: Ebscohost (accessed 7 March 2011).

Breidlid, A. (2013). *Education, Indigenous Knowledges, and Development in the Global South*. New York: Routledge.

Briggs, J. (2008). Indigenous Knowledge and Development. In V. Desai and R.B. Potter, eds. *The companion to Development Studies* (2nd edn). Hodder Education, London: UK, 107–111.

Broodryk, J. (2002). *Ubuntu: Life Lessons from Africa*. Tshwane, South Africa: Ubuntu School of Philosophy.

Broodryk, J. (1997). *Ubuntuism as a Worldview to Order Society*. Unpublished doctoral dissertation. Pretoria, South Africa: UNISA.

Danaher, G., Schirato, T. and Webb, J. (2000). *Understanding Foucault*. SAGE, ST Leonards: Australia

Darnell, S.C. (2010). Power, Politics and 'Sport for Development and Peace' Investigating the Utility of Sport for International Development. *Sociology of Sport Journal*, 27(1), 54–75.

Darnell, S.C. (2007). Playing with Race: Right to Play and the Production of Whiteness in Development through Sport. *Sport in Society*, 10(4), 560–579.

Dictionary of Human Geography (2007). *Dictionary of Human Geography*. London, UK: Blackwell Publishing.

EduSport Foundation (2013). www.edusport.org.zm (accessed 19 January 2013).

EduSport Foundation (2001). *Strategies and Frameworks*. Lusaka: EduSport.

EduSport Foundation (2004). *EduSport Road Map 2005–2010*. Lusaka: EduSport.

EduSport Foundation (2006). *About EduSport: Framework Paper*. Lusaka: EduSport.

Forster, D.A. (2010). African Relational Ontology, Individual Identity, and Christian Theology: An African Theological Contribution towards an Integrated Relational Ontological Identity. *Theology* [online], CxIII(874), 243–253. Available: Sage Journals [accessed 1 February 2011].

Foucault, M. (2004). The Incitement to Discourse. In A. Jaworski and N. Coupland (eds), *The Discourse Reader*. Routledge London: UK, 514–522.

Foucault, M. (1980). *Power/Knowledge: Selected Interviews and Other Writings*. New York, US: Pantheon.

Foucault, M. (1975). *Discipline and Punish – The Birth of the Prison*. London: Penguin Books.

Foucault, M. (1991). Governmentality. In G. Burchell, C. Gordon, P. Miller (eds), *The Foucault Effect: Studies in Governmentality*. Hemel Hempstead, UK: Harvester Wheatsheaf, 87–104.

Gilbert, H. and Tompkins, J. (1996). *Post-Colonial Drama: Theory, Practice, and Politics*. New York, US: Routledge.

Grassrootsoccer http://www.grassrootsoccer.org/ (accessed 07 September 2012).

Hall, S. (2007). The West and the Rest: Discourse and Power. In T.D. Gupta, C.E. James, R.C.A. Maaka, G.E. Galabuzi and C. Andersen (eds), *Race and Racialization: Essential Readings*. Toronto, Canada: Canadian Scholars Press, 56–60.

Hayhurst, L.M.C. (2009). The Power to Shape Policy: Charting Sport for Development and Peace Policy Discourses. *International Journal of Sport Policy*. [online], 1(2), 203–227. Available: Ebscohost (accessed 27 February 2010).

Hayhurst, L.M.C., Wilson, B. and Frisby, W. (2010). Navigating Neoliberal Networks: Transnational Internet Platforms in Sport for Development and Peace. *International Review for the Sociology of Sport*. [published online], 1–15. Available: Sage Online Journals (accessed 23 February 2011).

Hooks, B. (1990). Marginality as a Site of Resistance. In R. Ferguson, M. Gever, M. Trinh and C. West (eds), *Out There: Marginalization and Contemporary Cultures*. Cambridge, UK: MIT, 241–243.

Joanne, S. (2008). *Geographies of Post Colonialism: Can the Subaltern Speak?* Glasgow, UK: Sage Publications.

International Platform for Sport and Development, www.sportanddev.org (accessed 11 September 2012).

Kalipeni, E., Craddock, S., Oppong, J. and Gosh, J. (2006) *HIV/AIDS in Africa: Beyond Epidemiology*. Victoria: Blackwell publishing.

Khoza, R. (1994) The Need for an Afrocentric Approach to Management. In P. Christie, R. Lessem and L. Mbigi (eds), *African Management Philosophies, Concepts and Applications*, Randburg: Knowledge Resources.

Kay, T. and Spaaij, R. (2011) The Mediating Effects of Family on Sport in International Development Context. *International Review for the Sociology of Sport*, 47(1): 77–94.

Kaphagawani, D.N. and Malherbe, J.G. (2003). African Epistemology. In P.H. Coetzee and A.P.J. Roux (eds), *The African Philosophy Reader* (2nd edn). Routledge, London: UK, 219–229.

Levermore, R. and Beacom A. (2009). *Sport and International Development*. Basingstoke, UK: Palgrave.

Lindsey, I. and Grattan, A. (2012). An 'International Movement'? Decentering Sport-for-Development within Zambian Communities. *International Journal of Sport Policy and Politics*, 4(1), 111–124.

Lindsey, I., Namukanga, A., Kakome, G. and Grattan, A. (2010). 'Adventures in Research': Community Impact through Sport for Development Research. *LSA*, 85, 56–61.

Louw, D.J. (1995). Decolonization as Post Modernization. In J.G. Malherbe (ed.), *Decolonizing the Mind*. Pretoria, South Africa: Research Unit for African Philosophy, UNISA.

McEwan, C. (2002). Post Colonialism. In V. Desai and R.B. Potter (eds), *The Companion to Development Studies*. London, UK: Hodder Education, 127–131.

McEwan, C. (2009). *Postcolonialism and Development*. Oxon, UK: Routledge.

McKay, J. (2004). Reassessing Development Theory: Modernisation and beyond. In D. Kingsbury, J. Remenyi, J. Mckay and J. Hunt (eds), *Key Issues in Development*. Basingstoke, UK: Palgrave Macmillan, 53–58.

Mwaanga, O. (2012). Understanding and Improving Sport Empowerment for People Living with HIV/AIDS in Zambia. Unpublished PhD Dissertation. Leeds Metropolitan University, Leeds.

Mwakikagile, G. (2008). *African Immigrants in South Africa.* UK: New Africa Press.

Mwansa, K. (2011). *Contextual Realities of Sport for Development: An Analysis of HIV/AIDS Education Conducted through Sport and PE in Zambia.* Beau Bassin, VDM Publishing House Ltd.

Nicholls, S., Giles, A.R. and Sethna, C. (2010). Perpetuating the 'Lack of Evidence' Discourse in Sport for Development: Privileged Voices, Unheard Stories and Subjugated Knowledge. *International Review for the Sociology of Sport.* [first published online], 1–16. Available: Sage Online Journals (accessed 23 February 2011).

Nussbaum, B. (2003). Ubuntu: Reflections of a South African on Our common humanity. *Reflections.* Massachusetts Institute of Technology, 4(4).

Omobowale, A.O. (2007). Capitalism, Globalisation and the Underdevelopment Process in Africa: History in Perpetuity. *African Development.* [online], 32(2), 97–112. Available: CODESRIA (accessed 8 February 2012).

Parfitt, T. (2002). *The End of Development: Modernity, Post-Modernity and Development.* Pluto Press, London: UK.

Praeg, L. (2008). The Aporia of Collective Violence. *Law and Critique,* 19(2), 193–223.

Pringle, R. (2005). Masculinities, Sport and Power: A Critical Comparison of Gramscian and Foucauldian Inspired the Oretical Tools. *Journal of Sport and Social Issues,* 29(3), 256–278.

Rail, G. (2002). Postmodernism and Sports Studies. In J. Maguire and K. Young (eds), *Theory, Sport and Society.* Oxford, UK: JAI, 179–207.

Ramose, M.B. (1999). *African Philosophy through Ubuntu.* Harare, Kenya: Mondi Books.

Rossi, B. (2004). Revisiting Foucauldian Approaches: Power Dynamic in Development Projects. *Journal of Development Studies,* 40(6), 1–29.

Said, E. (1978). *Orientalism.* London, UK: Routledge.

Scott, J. and Marshall, G. (2005). *Oxford Dictionary of Sociology.* New York: Oxford University Press.

Sharp, J. (2008). *Geographies of Post Colonialism.* London, UK: Sage Publications.

Shutte, A. (1998). African and European Philosophising: Senghor's Civilization of the Universal. In P.H. Coetzee and A.P.J. Roux (eds), *Philosophy from Africa: A Text With Readings.* Johannesburg, South Africa: International Thomson Publishing, 428–437.

Shutte, A. (1993). *Philosophy for Africa.* Rondebosch, South Africa: UCT Press.

Sidaway, J. (2008). Post-Development. In V. Desai and R. B. Potter (eds), *The Companion to Development Studies,* 2nd edn. London, UK: Hodder Education, 16–19.

Siddiqi, Y. (2005). Edward Said, Humanism, and Secular Criticism. *Alif: Journal of Comparative Poetics.* [online], 25, 65–88. Available: JSTOR (accessed 15 April 2011).

Smith, L.T. (1999). *Decolonizing Methodologies: Research and Indigenous Peoples.* London, UK: Zed Books.

Teffo, J. (1994). *The Concept of Ubuntu as a Cohesive Moral Value.* Pretoria, South Africa: Ubuntu School of Philosophy.

United Nations (UN) (2006). *Sport and Peace: Report on the International Year of Sport and Physical Education.* Geneva: UN.

Van Binsbergen, W. (2001). Ubuntu and the Globalization of Southern African Thought and Society. *Quest*, XV(1–2), 53–91.

Van Der Merwe, W.L. (1996). Philosophy and the Multi-Cultural Context of (Post) Apartheid South Africa. *Ethical Perspectives*, 3(2), 1–15.

Wai, Z. (2007). Whither African Development? A Preparatory for an African Alternative Reformulation of the Concept of Development. *African Development.* [online], 32(4), 71–98. Available: CODESRIA (accessed 6 February 2011).

Young, R.J.C. (2003). *Post Colonialism: A Very Short Introduction.* New York, US: Oxford University Press.

Zondi, K.M. (1996). Peace and Development: Challenges and Role of Youth. *Cradles of Peace and Development: Ubuntu Conference.* Pretoria: Kagiso Publishers, 61–64.

8
Promoting Gender Empowerment through Sport? Exploring the Experiences of Zambian Female Footballers

Ruth Jeanes and Jonathan Magee

Introduction

Sport-for-development initiatives have expanded in the last decade at a phenomenal rate. As researchers working in Africa over the last six years, it has not only been challenging for us to keep up with changes to work on the ground, but also the ever expanding and increasingly sophisticated debates that now occur regarding this somewhat contentious development area. As Levermore and Beacom (2009) suggest, this body of work has extended from a fairly descriptive outline of the potential of sport to achieve development goals and the possible ways it may do this, to a more critical examination of the capacity of sport to achieve the ambitious goals attributed to it (Coalter, 2007, 2010). Subsequent analyses have also reviewed the position of sport within broader development politics, particularly the role of sport in maintaining or increasing hegemonic global power relations (Darnell, 2007; Darnell and Hayhurst, 2011; Hayhurst, 2009). This body of literature has provided an excellent basis for repositioning and critiquing the sport-for-development movement. However, we argue that there continues to be a gap in knowledge that articulates and examines the experiences of those at the receiving end of sport-for-development initiatives (Hayhurst, 2009). Only a limited number of studies (e.g. Fokwang, 2009; Guest, 2009; Kay, 2009; Lindsey and Gratton, 2012; Okada and Young, 2011; Schulenkorf, 2010; Spaaij, 2011) have directly sought the views of participants and local communities to examine how policy plays out in practice, that is, in the lives of those where sport initiatives are intended to benefit. As Guest (2009: 1348) suggests, to complement existing research,

> It would be useful to know more about the diversity of actual experiences of individuals and communities as related to development through sport programmes. What aspects of global rhetoric are internalised, resisted and negotiated at local level? What local forces and meanings reshape the development through sport endeavour? The current proliferation of development through sport programmes should provide a rich and critical opportunity for scholars to address diverse experiences with sport at both individual and community levels.

Our chapter is placed within this knowledge gap, and seeks to provide a critical exploration of the experiences of young Zambian women who played football (soccer) within the context of a broader NGO-led gender empowerment/HIV/AIDS education initiative. Undertaking research directly with participants is essential for raising the prominence of local understanding; indeed, it is only by doing this that researchers can begin to contribute effectively to the decolonising of sport-for-development research and practice (Darnell and Hayhurst, 2011; Hayhurst, 2009; Kay, 2009). The chapter explores whether sport – and in this case football – provides a useful vehicle for promoting broader development goals of gender equity and female empowerment; it does so by examining the experiences of Zambian women.

The research context

The women who took part in our research ($n = 14$) were aged between 14 and 27 and had been playing football for at least two years – some for up to a decade. Several of the women had played at junior and senior international levels, as well as for their NGO team. All of the women had grown up in various compound communities within Lusaka, Zambia's capital city. The women played for a team supported by an NGO that was a part of a wider NGO initiative to use football to promote and encourage gender equity and female empowerment, and to provide a setting for delivering HIV/AIDS education. The NGO, unlike many operating in Zambia, was initiated and developed by Zambians, and was first registered as an NGO in the late 1990s. The organisation's staff has been extremely successful in attracting continued funding from a variety of external agencies, including Norwegian and UK government sporting agencies, as well as from global corporations such as Nike (Banda, 2011).

The overall aim of the NGO is to use sport to enhance the lives of young people living in impoverished communities across Zambia, although the majority of its work is focused in urban areas and particularly the capital Lusaka. Because of the ferocious impact of the HIV/AIDS pandemic within Zambia, a great deal of their activities has focused on providing education and encouraging preventative health behaviours among young people. More broadly, however, the NGO uses sport as a means to help young people develop 'life skills', including team work, cooperation and negotiation, and to consider ways to collectively improve both their communities and their own lives.

The NGO also provides scholarships for some young people to be able to access ongoing education. All of its work is based around a peer education model, whereby NGO staff train young people from communities to become peer leaders. These young people then have responsibility to develop sport and educational activities within their local areas. The activities are usually based around four sports (football, basketball, netball and volleyball), although indigenous games are incorporated into HIV/AIDS education. The sport-for-development programme has led to the development of youth sports teams within many communities who play competitive matches against teams from other communities. From these, the NGO has also established central teams that recruit talented players from various communities and enter into established sports leagues operating in Lusaka. The young women we spoke to played for the central NGO team, as well as within their local communities, and participated in a women's football league coordinated by the Football Association of Zambia.

The gender empowerment initiative the young women in our research were taking part in utilised a similar peer leader model. The aims of the project were to raise the profile of women within local communities; encourage intolerance for gender-based violence; empower young women to be able to assume greater control of their own lives and equip young women with skills that help them minimise damaging health behaviours. The young women not only generally came together to play football, but would also take part in peer-led education activities including discussions and debates, and through this process received information from 'guest speakers' on particular topics. Some of the girls were also able to access NGO-funded school scholarships that allowed them to attend local schools. The peer leaders were encouraged to involve young males from their local communities in educational activities; this was a strategic attempt to engage them in a process of challenging gender stereotypes about young women. NGO staff also held parents forums that were similarly aimed at changing parental views towards the position of female daughters within both the household and community more broadly.

Football was introduced to Zambia during British colonisation. Initially only played within formal club structures by white males of European background, its popularity spread within the indigenous population – particularly the townships (Liwena, 2006). Historically, football within Zambia has been constructed, both in perception and practice, as an almost exclusively masculine domain. Notwithstanding that patriarchal dominance, it is now widely considered to be the country's national sport. Meier and Saavedra (2009: 1159) describe the 'contemporary Zambian "sportscape" as being dominated by men's football, with perennial hopes for World Cup advancement despite significant deficits in infrastructure and programme resources at all levels.' The status of men's football recently reached unprecedented status within Zambian society after the national team's triumph over Ghana in the final of the 2012 African Cup of Nations.

Organised female football began in Zambia in the 1970s, with a national team established in 1976 (Liwena, 2006; Meier and Saavedra, 2009). Saavedra (2009: 225) illustrates the difficulties of establishing female football within African countries more broadly, indicating that

> the immense popularity and weighty social meaning of the men's game in Africa, has made it that much harder for a women's game to develop. Even where other sports for women, such as netball, handball, athletics and basketball, have flourished, women's football has been met with scepticism, neglect and sometimes, outright hostility. Yet, women's football has nonetheless emerged.

Within Zambia, the development of women's football has been fragmented, with various teams established during the early 1980s that fell away towards the end of the decade (Liwena, 2006). The emergence of the sport-for-development movement in the 1990s provided significant financial resources to establish gender empowerment initiatives that indirectly supported the expansion of female football in Lusaka (Meier and Saavedra, 2009). Teams began to emerge within compound communities (these are high-density housing areas on the edge of Lusaka, whose inhabitants experience extreme levels of poverty), with a women's league consisting of NGO and business-sponsored teams. Many of them continue to run today: indeed, the women in this research have been playing in this league. The female game is therefore growing within

Zambia, and is heavily intertwined with the sport-for-development movement and the associated social aims and objectives linked to these. Community teams for women do exist in Zambia, such as those attached to local businesses, but the majority of participation occurs via sport-for-development programmes. The following section discusses gender equity and empowerment within sport-for-development to provide further context for our own research.

Gender and sport-for-development

Zambia was a patriarchal society well before the arrival of European invaders. However, colonisation is largely responsible for the nature of contemporary gender relations. Current gender norms are, in that respect, a legacy of male/female expectations established during the colonial era (Hansen, 1990; Parpart, 1994). Within Zambia, British colonial officers established gender norms mirroring traditional Victorian values that positioned women as having limited power or voice within public life; this has been maintained in the independent era. Within contemporary Zambia, males dominate public and private spaces, with women expected to be subservient and dutiful to males within their families and communities (Schlyter, 1999). As with all gender relations, however, men and women are continually renegotiating gender discourses and behaviours. Middle-class, educated urban women in particular are gaining greater status within Zambian society, and do have some access to well-paid employment and opportunities to contribute to decision making (Gough, 2008). Women's gender status within compound communities has, however, remained more static, with an adult female's primary role centred on the home. Families there place limited priority on educating young women; what little financial resources they have are usually invested in educating male children. Meanwhile, marriage at a young age remains a relatively common practice for girls and women. Communities tolerate, and to an extent normalise, violence against females by males within the compounds (Hansen, 2005). Gender inequity has created considerable social challenges within Zambia, particularly in relation to HIV/AIDS, and infection rates among young women continue to be higher than that among young men (9% compared to 5%, UNICEF 2010). Price and Hawkins (2002) have explained this variation by highlighting the difficulties young women face in negotiating safe sexual behaviour with men, and within some impoverished families elder members force young women into prostitution to provide the family with a source of income.

However, even without this pressure, prostitution may be the only way that young women in the compounds can secure a living (Magnani et al., 2002). More broadly, because of discourses and cultural norms that position women as subordinate to men, women may experience difficulties exerting choice within their relationships. A 2002 survey of eight African countries that included Zambia suggested that 18 per cent of women had experienced 'intimate partner violence' (Andersson et al., 2007). These gender dynamics, therefore, make it difficult for women to say no to sex or demand safe sex practices, such as using a condom (Nshindano and Maharaj, 2008).

Gender empowerment initiatives within Zambia have emerged within this context, but there have been limited studies examining the role of sport in challenging unequal gender relations in the Global South. Saavedra (2009: 124) has critically appraised the role of sport within development programmes, suggesting that 'seeking to empower females through sport is somewhat paradoxical given that the world of sport can be a bastion for male privilege and power.' However, others have suggested that the potential of sport to disrupt established hegemonic gender relations emerges from its very position as a masculine domain (Mean, 2001). If women can display sporting competence that challenges perceptions of their capability in this arena, there may be potential for this to spill over into other social settings (Beutler, 2008). Kay (2009) has conducted one of the few studies examining the experiences of young women in sport-for-development initiatives. Her research indicates the positive benefits that young Indian women gained from participation in the programme, including improved physical and mental health, increased education and increased status and respect within their families and communities.

Meier and Saavedra (2009), however, highlight a more complex picture, suggesting that those who are set to lose power often strongly resist female empowerment through sport-for-development initiatives, which can lead to women becoming further marginalised and disempowered within their community. The authors provide an extreme example of how those in power continue to resist female equity in the case of Eudy Simelane, a South African female footballer, who was gang raped and stabbed to death. Meier and Saavedra (2009) outline how her attackers described the crime as a 'corrective rape' for her disregard of appropriate gender and sex relations; she had openly identified her sexual orientation as lesbian. Donnelly et al. (2011: 598) suggest that gender-based sports interventions can indeed have unintended negative consequences,

Such assumptions [regarding the benefits of gender equity as under-stood in Global North terms] may be interpreted as neo-colonialist if projects have been initiated without adequate consultation or regard for local culture and the current status of gender relations. As a consequence, young women may be punished for behaving in [what is considered to be] inappropriate ways by participating in sport.

Existing research, therefore, presents a mixed picture of the relationship between gender development goals and sports initiatives. Sport does seemingly have the potential to contribute towards raising the profile of women in communities and foster some feelings of empowerment, as evidenced by Kay's research (2009). However, sport interventions may not easily disrupt the deeply entrenched nature of hegemonic gender relations within Global South countries, and so the positive impacts observed by Kay ought to be understood in context, not as evidence of a general phenomenon (Saavedra, 2009).

More broadly, we can construct the fostering of gender equity through sport-for-development as a further example of neo-colonial ideology, a point that has been discussed extensively in the critical work of Darnell and Hayhurst (Darnell, 2007; Darnell and Hayhurst, 2011). Gender empowerment initiatives can be organised unquestion-ingly within local communities by well meaning, but nonetheless patronising Global North funding agencies who have limited under-standing of the complexities of social structures and the nuances of existing relations. Black (2010: 123) argues that this can severely disrupt communities, de-stabilising 'social relations and ways of life'. Indeed, Donnelly et al. (2011) indicate that such initiatives can lead to women experiencing more extreme forms of repression rather than liberation. The relationship between sport and gender development goals is therefore complex and fraught with tensions. Work in this area is essentially seeking to challenge deep-rooted social relations and therefore requires transference of power. Those set to lose authority are always highly resistant to such changes (Foucault, 1975), presenting a considerable challenge for sport-for-development policy makers and practitioners. The experiences we discuss in this chapter are within this broader context, and contribute to Hayhurst's (2009: 223) call for a greater illustration of 'how those on the "receiving end" of SDP poli-cies are affected and challenged by taking up the solutions and tech-niques prescribed to them.'

Methodology

The study drew on a feminist post-colonial lens to assist with interpreting the experiences of the young women. The feminist lens prioritises the voices of young women while also acknowledging that, as a source of knowledge, they are marginalised within the research process (Mills, 2003). This approach, combined with a post-colonial social perspective, assisted us to recognise the nature and extent of disempowerment that young women in Zambia experience (Trinh, 1997). Research utilising a feminist post-colonial perspective helped to ensure that we were sensitive to notions of power and inequity in our particular study. In addition, we made a concerted effort to learn how the women in Zambia constructed their identities (Hayhurst, 2009). A post-colonial perspective acknowledges that while women may be disempowered and repressed by global and local discourses, there is always potential for them to be resisted and re-negotiated (Mills, 2003). Feminist post-colonialism also encourages researchers to commit to fostering change via research. This transformational goal relies upon giving voice to those who have previously been unheard, and therefore enables investigators to construct knowledge through engagement with these research actors. As Darnell and Hayhurst (2011: 192) explain,

> As a method then, postcolonial feminisms attempt to confront institutionalised forms of oppressive power that are immersed within imperial and Eurocentric discourses that foreground intersectional analyses that reconstruct how race, class, sexuality and nationality interact to frame social institutions.

Fourteen young women participated in the study, who were recruited via a snowball sampling approach. Our initial contact was made through a participant who was taking part in the existing research work. One of the co-authors spoke with her about the possibility of doing some in-depth research regarding female experiences of participating in football and sport-for-development programmes. Kate (pseudonym) was very enthusiastic about the possibility of taking part in the research, and in particular the potential opportunity it gave the rest of her team to share their views and experiences. We were very aware of the negative power relationships that can potentially exist within our research as white middle-class individuals from the Global North seeking to work with highly impoverished women in the Global South. In an attempt to minimise coercion or obligation to take part in the research, we asked Kate if she would discuss the research with her team-mates, and, if they were interested in taking part, were welcome to contact us to talk about it further. As the initial approach did not come from us, we were unaware who had been contacted, and as a result we hoped that potential participants would not feel unduly obliged to participate in the research. This was indeed the case, as Kate informed us of subjects who had willingly consented to take part after her discussion with them. Subsequently, interviews were organised at locations convenient to the young women, such as next to football pitches, at their homes and in the middle of market places. The decision to use interviews was made with consideration of several issues. Firstly, for logistical reasons, it was often easier for us to meet with individual participants at locations that best suited them rather than having to travel to a central point for a focus group. Secondly, our previous research in Zambia suggested that young people were often willing to talk extensively about their experiences, and this richness can become diluted in a focus group setting where not all participants have as much chance to talk as in an individual interview context. Finally, while the young women seemed willing to share often sensitive information with us, as outsiders, about their lives, we were advised by Kate that they may not always be so open in front of some team-mates. Individual interviews therefore seemed the most appropriate method to use. We did, however, indicate to all young women that if they would prefer to talk to us with a friend or family member, this would be completely acceptable.

While all of the young women spoke excellent English, we offered them the option of speaking to us in Nyanja, their local language. We had discussed this with Kate, who suggested that if the young women wanted to do this, she would be happy to assist us with translation. In practice, on the women's request, all of the interviews took place in English. The interviews were between 45 and 90 minutes long and were audio recorded with permission from the participants. All interviews were transcribed verbatim. We initially analysed the transcripts individually, using an inductive approach and manual open coding to identify the key themes emerging. We compared these and identified the most prominent themes; subsequently, we reanalysed the data to identify and explore relevant sub-themes (Creswell, 2003). On a subsequent research visit, one of the co-authors had the opportunity to meet with several of the young women, discuss with them our findings and seek clarification of our interpretations. We recognise that it is a limitation of our study that we were unable to gain the views of all participants as to the reliability of our interpretations, but feel those we were able to speak to assisted with establishing some elements of trustworthiness to our data. Our chapter is organised around the key themes emerging from that data, and will first examine how much young women felt their participation contributed to development aims of equity and empowerment, before moving on to discussing the tangible benefits as well as issues and challenges of involvement.

Findings

Gender equity and empowerment through sport: young women's experiences

The initial part of our interviews focused on talking to young women about their experiences of playing football and what they felt it contributed to their lives. The young women repeatedly discussed feeling 'empowered' as a result of their participation. We spent some time during the interviews asking them to discuss this further, and particularly illustrate how such empowerment played out in practice. To interpret their empowerment experiences, we have drawn on Rowlands' (1997) conceptualisation of power, which enables us to understand empowerment as a fluid, incremental process at both an individual and a community level. Rowlands (1997) suggests that there are four dimensions of power: (1) power over (controlling power/domination of marginalised groups); (2) power to (generate new possibilities without domination); (3) power with (collective power, power created by group process) and (4) power from within (spiritual strength to inspire, to be able to think and see alternative ways of existing). She suggests that transformative agency/empowerment will only occur for individuals and groups when they have access to all of the types of power outlined. Our data suggest that young women had mixed experiences of empowerment resulting from their participation. Many young women discussed feeling personally empowered. Several of the young women talked about gaining physical strength, feeling 'fit' and 'strong', which created feelings of well-being, confidence and security. This physical strength contributed to greater feelings of individual well-being and a belief that they could exert greater control over their lives. As Angel articulated,

> I know I am strong and healthy; I have got my strength from playing football. It makes me fit and strong.

Livy explained further,

> Football has made me strong and fast, it makes me feel good. It makes me feel like I can do things, I can say listen to me I am a strong Zambian woman.

They outlined how, traditionally, Zambian women are constructed as vulnerable and fragile. The participants highly valued their new capacity to create a feminine identity for themselves that incorporated, via football, elements of physical strength and fitness. The young women acknowledged that their participation was in opposition to traditional stereotypes of lower-class women as home-makers and inactive beyond that context. As Rowland's (1997) theorised, they were aware that their participation in football provided them with the opportunity to develop alternative representations of female identity that challenged traditional gender discourses. Some felt that they were changing beliefs regarding the capabilities of women in their community, since football, one of the key bastions of masculinity within Zambia, provided a particularly potent arena for altering beliefs about women's position within sport and Zambian society more broadly. Marlaya explained that,

> In [her community] they think football, it is only for the men. But, we have shown them that women can also play and we can do the same things as men. It is making them [community] change how they see women here.

The young women's comments reflected beliefs articulated by practitioners and policy makers of the social value of sport, and there is the suggestion, therefore, that through playing football young women were also developing a 'collective power' to 'generate new possibilities within their local communities, which is consistent with Rowland's (1997) theoretical approach.

However, the young women's discussions also highlighted less positive experiences that arose from their participation, for many of them had to negotiate considerable challenges to be able to play regularly. Although several young women discussed how they felt their participation was changing community attitudes, others were subjected to continuous derogatory comments. They talked about members of the wider community questioning their behaviour, accusing them of being shameful and disrespecting conventional cultural values and norms. Nari explained that

I have had men say to me I should be ashamed, I don't behave like a woman should. They say I am trying to be like a man and it is wrong. ... they say these things as I walk down the street.

A number of young women repeatedly had to endure accusations that they were homosexual and therefore deviant. With homosexuality illegal in Zambia, many felt under pressure to emphasise their femininity to dissuade this belief, and were anxious to dissociate themselves from any allegations. Similar to players in the Global North, young women sought to emphasise traditional forms of femininity away from football (see also Jeanes, 2011). Several players talked about keeping their hair long, and it seemed particularly important not to participate in other perceived 'masculine' behaviour. Kate talked about wanting to dissociate herself from young women who, as she put it:

They just let themselves go, they wear their hair short and they do not care what they look like. They play football and then they want to do other things that men do so they go drinking in bars and they smoke, they are loud. ... this is not good behaviour, this is not how a girl should be behaving. It makes others think that if we play football we will become badly behaved ... it is important for us to show we are not like that. We still know how to behave as a woman.

This quote illustrates the fine balance that many of the young women felt they had to navigate as both Zambian women and footballers. They felt comfortable and able to contest particular stereotypes. However, this was restricted and did not necessarily translate into other areas of their lives, indicating that there was perhaps limited impact beyond the sport setting.

A number of young women had family members who were unsupportive of their participation in football. This ranged from forbidding young women to play, to continually discouraging young women from maintaining participation. While several had family members (usually mothers and grandmothers) who had actively encouraged their involvement, for at least half of the young women participation had met with disapproval. The young women talked about different reasons for their family's resistance, which were usually linked to broader cultural expectations,

My father he says that young women should not play football, it is for boys and that if I play it brings shame on him. People will think he has not raised me well. ... he thinks no one will want to marry me if I play football.

My auntie says that I do not have time to be playing games, I need to be helping her in the house and with my siblings.

Most young women negotiated their participation by offering a range of compromises,

> My father, he did not want me to play, he said I should be at home and helping my mother with my sisters ... I told him that I would do my jobs in the morning before I went to the ground and once we had finished I would come straight home ... in the end he let me play but sometime I can't because my mother needs me to do work for her.

Shani, in the quote above, illustrates that to be 'allowed' to play she had to demonstrate that gender ideologies away from the football pitch remained constant, again reinforcing the limited impact on gender relations beyond the football pitch. The team captain found the difficulties young women had in terms of committing regularly to football understandable but frustrating,

> The only way some can play at all is to show that it will not affect the family home but then some don't come to training or to games when they say they will play because they have to do jobs in the home ... if they say no or say but I have to play they will not be allowed to play at all so we get used to it.

Several of the young women felt that their families were stricter with them and gave them more responsibilities in the home to emphasise that they could not compromise their domestic and family life by football participation. The young women suggested that via football participation and the collective education they had participated in, they were more aware of their current repressed position (as females), and felt they were beginning to make public statements that contradicted dominant notions of how women should behave in Zambia. However, their experiences were, as illustrated, constrained by broader cultural expectations. They were unable to disrupt significantly, what Rowlands' (1997) defines as 'power over'.

Reflecting this, the young women's discussions suggested that they struggled to gain significant agency within their communities, and for at least half of the participants within the home setting. Although they felt they were physically stronger, they still considered themselves relatively powerless to challenge abusive behaviour. Two of the young women talked about encountering violence, one within the family home from an uncle and one from a boyfriend. Despite stating that playing football had made them more confident and the broader educational element of the initiative had taught them about their right to 'stand up for themselves', they indicated that this did not translate into being able to negotiate a way out of these unequal relationships,

> I do feel stronger and I am angry with [Uncle] but if I say no this is not right for you to do this to me I know he will only beat me more. It is easier to say nothing....I have to live in his house.

More generally, although some young women suggested that their participation was changing perceptions of how females were seen within their communities, others were more critical of the possibility for them to change patriarchal power dynamics. They did not necessarily believe their participation could significantly alter their position in society without considerable social upheaval occurring,

> Yes I play football and I feel strong and we are showing those in our community then we can do the things that men do. ... but they [men] do not include us in community matters, we still have no say in what happens. It is changing a little but very slowly.

Again, the young women's discussions on this topic illustrate the complexity of their involvement and how their participation was generally tolerated in ways that seemed to provide a series of small gains, or perhaps no gains beyond the football pitch. They were participating regularly in what had previously been an exclusively masculine setting, and in doing so were able to make some semblance of a statement within their community that countered traditional perceptions of what young women were capable of. However, despite this, many restrictive gender ideologies remained intact while for some, as Donnelly et al. (2011) suggest, dominant ideologies intensified, resulting in some young women having to contribute more to their home lives to be able to play.

Moving beyond equity and empowerment

Both academics and policy makers have increasingly advocated the need for sport-for-development initiatives to 'prove' they work and provide 'hard evidence' of what they achieve. Against this background, it would be easy to suggest that the young women's football participation was failing to meet ambitious development outcomes. However, as Kay (2009) noted elsewhere, detailed interviews allow researchers to understand what young women themselves sought to gain from their participation. Darnell and Hayhurst argue that

> Prioritizing shared 'local' understandings of development issues remains paramount within a decolonizing methodology ... for example if the targets of sports based development programs ... are principally concerned with getting jobs, it may be unreasonable for decolonizing activism 'based on sport' to make the most important contribution (2011: 192).

While challenging gender stereotypes, reducing violence against women and increasing opportunities for themselves outside of the home were all aspirations they felt were worthy, the young women did not necessarily believe that participating in football would lead to such outcomes. They had other expectations from their participation, with ambitions focused around wanting to develop their athletic skills, play well and, for some, to work towards playing at or continuing to play at the elite level, including the international arena. They wanted funding agencies to provide them with ongoing resources to be able to continue their participation, develop their skills and maintain the friendship network they had been able to create through playing. Similar to Guest's (2009) work, there appears to be a mismatch between what the young women desired from the project and what funding agencies wanted to occur. While the young women's ambitions were not necessarily at odds with the broader sport-for-development agenda, they were more modest and reflective of the realities of their lives. Football was an enjoyable activity and they were appreciative of the opportunity to participate, but impact beyond the immediate participation setting was far harder to achieve.

The young women talked most extensively about the strong friendships and connections they had made with each other as being a key outcome of their participation. As Kayla explained, 'my team is like my family, my team-mates are very important to me.' Describing team-mates as family was common and it was clear that they viewed them as an important source of social support,

> Yes, things are difficult sometimes and you have many challenges in your life, it is good to have the ground [football pitch] to go to and

be able to talk to my team-mates. They give me help with problems
I have.

All of the young women interviewed felt that the social networks
they developed through their participation were the most important
outcome from playing. While playing football was seemingly unable to
promote significant changes to repressive gender relations, it provided a
safe space where young women could escape these challenges and gain
some respite for a period of time. As indicated, for some young women
abuse and violence was a regular part of their daily lives, but playing
sport allowed them time away from these realities, even if only for a
short period. Aylina discussed such breaks as critical for managing the
difficulties she faced,

> It is very hard, my life at home is difficult and I can get very upset. …
> it helps to know that I will see my team mates and once I am playing
> I forget everything. All I want to do is make a good pass or score a goal
> … it helps me forget.

Football provided young women with a regular support structure,
something to focus on and look forward to, and in doing so provided
them with a sense of hope in a community where they faced significant
challenges.

Conclusion

The opinions and views that we have outlined in this chapter illustrate
the complexity of lived experiences within sport-for-development initiatives. As Black suggests,

> In ambitious and usually well-intentioned rhetoric extolling a partic-
> ular set of virtues for sport, programmes tend to oversimplify the
> complicated realities of development in diverse settings in Africa.
> (2010: 1339)

Willis (2000: 844) questions whether sport in the Global South 'can
provide a unique opportunity to break down patriarchal structures,
leading towards more equality'. Our study would suggest that the
highly ambitious aims of many gender empowerment programmes are
not readily achieved via participation within sport, even when this is
combined with educative elements; this is due to the strength of existing

patriarchal structures and the extreme disruption of the existing social order that is required for major changes to occur. Extensive research on female participation, disruption and contestation of repressive gender values in the Global North also suggests that women's participation often fails to challenge the status quo (e.g. Dworkin and Messner, 2001; Mennesson, 2000). It therefore seems naive to assume that young women's participation in football in the Global South will be any less complicated or have greater success at challenging deeply entrenched notions of appropriate masculinity and femininity in Zambia.

We must, however, recognise the advances that have been made in altering cultural expectations that have resulted in women being able to play football, and with this more or less being tolerated within their local communities. To an outsider, women are participating and doing so regularly, hence they are questioning patriarchal structures. However, as the young women's accounts have illustrated, this participation is contested and negotiated within the confines of more repressive gender ideals. As Donnelly et al. (2011) and Meier and Saavedra (2009) each discuss, there is potential for gender empowerment programmes to have unintended negative consequences. We have indicated how some girls had to overcompensate within the home environment to be able to participate regularly. Football takes place within current gender relations rather than leading to a reshaping of ideologies. As illustrated, many of the women had to engage in a constant battle to be able to play; this involved compliance with gender expectations in other areas of their lives. The earlier quote from Kate demonstrates that many of the young women were concerned about challenging gender beliefs 'too much', and crossing over into what they perceived to be 'overly' masculine and sexually deviant behaviour. These concerns continually regulated what they did away from the football pitch. Black's (2010) point that instead of 'assuming sport will transmit values,' it may be more realistic to conceptualise sport-for-development as a site where 'meanings are negotiated', and is valuable for interpreting the young women's experiences. Alternative meanings of femininity were navigated via football, but gender equity, authority and power were not 'transmitted' via their participation, or even as a result of the educative elements of the initiative that sought to help the young women achieve this.

As several other studies have illustrated, women's participation provided empowerment at an individual level (Rowlands, 1997); they felt fitter, stronger and better about themselves, but through this were not able to change particular social structures to significantly alter their position within their communities. Initiating broader social and cultural change is a difficult process mediated by numerous forces beyond the sport-for-development agenda. As Akindes and Kirwin (2009: 241) indicate, 'SDP has been hampered by rather than challenging broader, systematic relations of social and economic power.' Darnell and Hayhurst (2011: 189) similarly conclude that 'football in development cannot "solve" the political and social constraints and limitations to which development attends' and will not necessarily 'challenge the socio-political status quo' (190).

As discussed, within sport-for-development, there has been an increasing call to demonstrate the impact of programme initiatives. Various frameworks and models have been advocated to assist with identifying the aims and goals defined by policy makers and funding agencies, and examining if these have been met. Assessing the outcomes that the young women experienced, alongside the development goals intended from their participation, would suggest that football is providing them with limited benefits. However, the value of talking to young women directly and in detail is that we can begin to understand what they want, value and need from their participation. The findings demonstrate that friendship, socialising and a 'safe space' (Brady, 2005: 40) to escape everyday realities were of greater importance to them as opposed to more ambitious programme-driven outcomes. Other studies that have captured the voices of participants indicate similar findings (Burnett, 2001: Okada and Young, 2011).

Measurement is not everything. Willis suggests that for young people in Mathare, their sport-for-development programme became the 'social epicentre of their lives' (Willis, 2000: 844) that provided a sense of hope that was 'impossible to quantify' (Willis, 2000: 848). Similarly, for our young women we cannot underestimate the importance of the networks created through football for helping them manage (although not prevent) challenges in their wider lives. We also argue that while we have high-lighted some of the current limitations of sport-for-development initiatives in catalysing the transformative agency necessary for wider social change, these friendships and networks could potentially provide a platform through which collective empowerment, or Rowlands' (1997) concept of power to develop alternatives, may develop, albeit on a small scale. Coalter (2010: 1383) suggests that such connections can 'play a significant role in local social regeneration – for example, as an essential first step towards building collective confidence, cohesion and coopera-tion'. The educational element of the programme, alongside meeting regularly with other young women via football, had undoubtedly raised the consciousness of the participants. They recognised that they occupied a subordinate position within their communities and wanted to change this. However, they had not as yet been able to turn this heightened critical consciousness into collective action (Freire, 1970). Such a process is likely to be slow and gradual, and may require the use of more transformational pedagogical approaches (Spaaij and Jeanes, 2012) than those currently utilised. The time required to achieve substantial change is also often in opposition to the requirements for 'quick hits' that funding agencies insist from sport-for-development practitioners.

In summary, we argue that only through prioritising the voices of participants within research and policy development can we begin to understand the nuances of experience and understand what sport-for-development actually does (and does not do) within local communities. The women's accounts assist with highlighting the positive aspects of participation, the negatives and the challenges of involvement as well as the quest for support and acceptance by family members and the wider community. They also illustrate how development ambitions do not always align to the expectations from participation, and thus both researchers and practitioners need to consider the latter carefully when attempting to determine 'what is best' for intended recipients.

References

Akindes, G. and Kirwin, M. (2009). Sport as international aid: assisting development or promoting under development in sub-Saharan Africa? In R. Levermore and A. Beacom (eds), *Sport and International Development*. Basingstoke: Palgrave Macmillan, 219–245.

Andersson, N., Ho-Foster, A., Mitchell, S., Scheepers, E. and Goldstein, S. (2007). Risk Factors for Domestic Violence: Eight National Cross-Sectional Household Surveys in Southern Africa. *BMC Women's Health*, 7, 1–13.

Banda, D. (2011). International Development through Sport: Zambia. In B. Houlihan and M. Green (eds), *International Handbook for Sport Development*. Oxon: Routledge, 323–336.

Beutler, I. (2008). Sport Serving Development and Peace: Achieving the Goals of the United Nations through Sport. *Sport in Society*, 11(4), 359–369.

Black, R. (2010). The Ambiguities of Development: Implications for `Development through Sport'. *Sport in Society*, 13(1), 121–129.

Brady, M. (2005). Creating Safe Spaces and Building Social Assets for Young Women in the Developing World: A New Role for Sports. *Third World Quarterly*, 33, 35–49.

Burnett, C. (2001). Social Impact Assessment and Sport Development: Social Spin Offs of the Australia–South Africa Junior Sports Programme. *International Review for the Sociology of Sport*, 36(1), 41–57.

Coalter, F. (2007). *A Wider Role for Sport: Who's Keeping the Score?* London: Routledge.

Coalter, F. (2010). Sport for Development: Going beyond the Boundary? *Sport in Society*, 13(9), 1374–1391.

Creswell, J. (2003). *Research Design: Qualitative, Quantitative, and Mixed Methods Approaches*. Thousand Oaks, CA: Sage.

Darnell, S. (2007). Playing with Race: Right to Play and the Production of Whiteness in 'Development through Sport'. *Sport in Society*, 10(4), 560–579.

Darnell, S. and Hayhurst, L. (2011). Sport for Decolonization: Exploring a New Praxis of Sport for Development. *Progress in Development Studies*, 11(3), 183–196.

Donnelly, P., Atkinson, M., Boyle, S. and Szto, C. (2011). Sport for Development and Peace: A Public Sociology Perspective. *Third World Quarterly*, 32(3), 589–601.

Dworkin, S. and Messner, M. (2001). Just Do What? Sport, Bodies and Gender. In S. Scraton and A. Flintoff (eds), *Gender and Sport: A Reader*. London and New York: Routledge, 17–29.

Fokwang, J. (2009). Southern Perspectives on Sport in Development: A Case Study of Football in Bamenda, Cameroon. In R. Levermore and A. Beacom (eds), *Sport and International Development*. Basingstoke: Palgrave Macmillan, 198–218.

Foucault, M. (1975). *Discipline and Punish: The Birth of the Prison*. New York: Random House.

Freire, P. (1970). *Pedagogy of the Oppressed*. New York: Continuum.

Gough, K. (2008). 'Moving Around': The Social and Spatial Mobility of Youth in Lusaka. *Geografiska: Series B, Human Geography*, 90(3), 243–255.

Guest, A. (2009). The Diffusion of Development through Sport: Analyzing the History and Practice of the Olympic Movement's Grassroots Outreach to Africa. *Sport in Society*, 12(10), 1336–1352.

Hansen, K.T. (1990). Body Politics: Sexuality, Gender and Domestic Service in Zambia. *Journal of Women's History*, 2(1), 120–142.

Hansen, K.T. (2005). Getting Stuck in the Compound: Some Odds against Social Adulthood in Lusaka, Zambia. *Africa Today*, 51(4), 2–16.

Hayhurst, L. (2009). The Power to Shape Policy: Charting Sport for Development and Peace Policy Discourses. *International Journal of Sports Policy and Politics*, 1(2), 203–227.

Jeanes, R. (2011). 'I'm into High Heels and Make up but I Still Love Football': Exploring Gender Identity and Football Participation with Preadolescent Girls. *Soccer and Society*, 12(3), 402–420.

Kay, T. (2009). Developing through Sport: Evidencing Social Impacts on Young People. *Sport in Society*, 12(9), 1177–1191.

Levermore, R. and Beacom, A. (2009). Sport and Development: Mapping the Field. In R. Levermore and A. Beacom (eds), *Sport and International Development*. Basingstoke: Palgrave Macmillan, 1–25.

Lindsey, I. and Gratton, A. (2012). An 'International Movement'? Decentering Sport-for-Development within Zambian Communities. *International Journal of Sport Policy and Politics*, 4(1), 91–110.

Liwena, R. (2006). *The Zambian Soccer Scene*. Lusaka: Liwena Publishing and Printing House.

Magnani, R., Mehryar Karim, A., Weiss, L., Bond, K., Lemba, M. and Morgan, G. (2002) Reproductive Health Risk and Protective Factors Among Youth in Lusaka, Zambia. *Journal of Adolescent Medicine*, 30, 76–86.

Mean, L. (2001). Identity and Discursive Practice: Doing Gender on the Football Pitch. *Discourse & Society*, 12(6), 789–815.

Meier, M. and Saavedra, M. (2009). Esther Phiri and the Moutawakel Effect in Zambia: An Analysis of the Use of Female Role Models in Sport for Development. *Sport in Society*, 12(9), 1158–1176.

Mennesson, C. (2000). 'Hard Women and Soft Women' the Social Construction of Identities Among Female Boxers. *International Review for the Sociology of Sport*, 35(1), 21–33.

Mills, S. (2003). Gender and the Colonial Space. In R. Lewis and S. Mills (eds), *Feminist Postcolonial Theory: A Reader*. New York: Routledge, 692–719.

Nshindano, C. and Maharaj, P. (2008). Reasons for Multiple Sexual Partnerships: Perspectives of Young People in Zambia. *African Journal of AIDS Research*, 7(1), 37–44.

Okada, C. and Young, K. (2011). Sport and Social Development: Promise and Caution from an Incipient Cambodian Football League. *International Review for the Sociology of Sport*, First published online, doi: 10.1177/1012690210395526.

Parpart, J.L. (1994). 'Where Is Your Mother?' : Gender, Urban Marriage and Colonial Discourse on the Zambian Copperbelt, 1924–1945. *The International Journal of African Historical Studies*, 27(2), 241–271.

Price, K. and Hawkins, K. (2002). Researching Sexual and Reproductive Behaviour: A Peer Ethnographic Approach. *Social Science & Medicine*, 55(8), 1327–1338.

Rowlands, J. (1997). *Questioning Empowerment: Working with Women in Honduras*. Oxford: Oxfam.

Saavedra, M. (2009). Dilemmas and Opportunities in Gender and Sport in Development. In R. Levermore and A. Beacom (eds), *Sport and International Development*. Basingstoke: Palgrave Macmillan, 124–155.

Schlyter, A. (1999). *Recycled Inequalities: Youth and Gender in George Compound, Zambia*. Motala: Nordiska Afrikainstitutet.

Schulenkorf, N. (2010). Sport Events and Ethnic Reconciliation: Attempting to Create Social Change between Sinhalese, Tamil and Muslim Sportspeople in War-Torn Sri Lanka. *International Review for the Sociology of Sport*, 45(3), 273–294.

Spaaij, R. (2011). *Sport and Social Mobility: Crossing Boundaries*. London: Routledge.

Spaaij, R. and Jeanes, R. (2012). Education for Social Change? a Freirean Critique of Sport for Development and Peace. *Physical Education and Sport Pedagogy*, First published online, 10 July 2012, doi: 10.1080/17408989.2012.690378.

Trinh, T. Minh-ha (1997). Not You/Like You: Postcolonial Women and the Interlocking Questions of Identity and Difference. In A. McClintock, A. Mufti and E. Shohat (eds), *Dangerous Liaisons: Gender, Nation and Post Colonial Perspectives*. Minneapolis: University of Minnesota Press, 415–419.

UNICEF (2010). UNICEF 2010 Annual Report, http://www.unicef.org.au/downloads/Publications-(1)/Unicef-Anual-Report_2011_FINAL_screen.aspx

Willis, O. (2000). Sport and Development: The Significance of Mathare Youth Sports Association. *Canadian Journal of Development Studies*, 21(3), 825–849.

9
Sport-for-Development Programme Objectives and Delivery: A Mismatch in Gulu, Northern Uganda
Justin Richards and Charlie Foster

Introduction

Stakeholders in the Sport-for-Development (SFD) sector currently implement a broad array of intervention designs and claim various cross-cutting positive results (SDPIWG, 2008). However, there is limited evidence that these programmes are effective, and thus a more focused analysis of any claimed impacts is needed (Cronin, 2011). With these points in mind, this chapter features a case study of the peace building and health-related outcomes of a SFD intervention for adolescents implemented in Gulu, Uganda – a post-conflict context in a low-income African country. The SFD sector claims to achieve social cohesion and peace building outcomes in similar settings (Kidd and MacDonnell, 2007), while SFD stakeholders also claim to positively influence physical and mental health outcomes in post-conflict populations. However, these proponents primarily cite evidence from studies conducted in adult populations living in peaceful and high-income countries (Zakus et al., 2007), so the contexts are very different. This is a crucial point: an understanding of local contexts and needs is an important part of developing and implementing SFD interventions in low-income and post-conflict settings. That same principle applies to the monitoring, evaluation and assessment of SFD programmes.

The gap in the evidence base for SFD interventions is accompanied by a paucity of programme theory (Coalter, 2010). Identifying programme objectives and developing a model for implementation processes that outlines the steps towards achieving these is essential for understanding how an intervention can, in theory, work (Nutbeam and Bauman, 2006). However, there is rarely a concerted focus on specific objectives in the SFD sector, while the interaction between various stakeholders is often poorly understood (Kidd, 2008; Levermore, 2011). Instead, programme implementers typically describe broad aims based on unsubstantiated claims about the positive effect of sport on development outcomes (Coakley, 2011). These are often adapted to the expectations of SFD funders, rather than being informed by a community needs analysis and formative evaluations that identify specific objectives and/ or a target population (Coalter, 2011; Coakley, 2011; Kidd, 2008). The final outcomes are presumed to occur despite a typical lack of conceptual understanding of the processes, mechanisms and causal sequences that provide guidance for SFD programme monitoring and evaluation (Coalter, 2010).

This chapter explores the disconnect between various stakeholders in the 'problem definition' → 'solution generation' → 'innovation testing' stages of programme development to evaluate the delivery of an SFD intervention in Gulu (Nutbeam and Bauman, 2006). A novel model for programme implementation was developed prior to the intervention, and used to guide a mixed-methods evaluation that explores how dysfunction in these processes can lead to a profound mismatch between programme objectives and delivery. This has implications that may explain some of the detrimental final outcomes observed in the case study presented in this chapter.

Problem definition

Local context

Gulu is located in Northern Uganda. It is currently a post-conflict region after more than 20 years of civil war that ended in 2006. The conflict was between an insurgency group known as the Lord's Resistance Army (LRA) and the Ugandan government forces. The LRA initially benefitted from local support for its objective to form a new government based on the Ten Commandments of the Christian Bible, but this waned as the war progressed and high levels of internal displacement and child abduction occurred in Northern Uganda. It has been estimated that one-third of all boys and one-sixth of all girls in Gulu were abducted to serve as equipment carriers, child soldiers or 'wives' for the LRA (Annan et al., 2006, 2008). Government soldiers were also widely accused of severe human rights violations before they successfully expelled the LRA from Uganda (Branch, 2008).

The post-conflict period has brought to Gulu many of the typical challenges associated with building peace after an extended period of war. These include reintegrating people into their communities, recon-structing infrastructure and reviving productive livelihoods (UNDG, 2005; UN, 2006). In the process, Gulu has undergone relatively rapid socio-economic development and urbanisation. This has been supported by international aid agencies and the national government (Branch, 2008). Gulu municipality now has approximately 150,000 inhabitants, which makes it the largest city and the primary commercial hub in Northern Uganda.

Local needs

During the war, many adolescents were abducted by the LRA and forced to commit atrocities against their families and local communities (Annan et al., 2006, 2008). This has contributed to negative stigmatisa-tion of former abductees by the wider community and may account for persistent high levels of mental health disorders and emotional distress in adolescents from Gulu during the post-conflict period (Annan et al., 2006, 2008; Betancourt et al., 2009; McMullen et al., 2011). Consequently, there appears to be an ongoing need for peace building and mental health initiatives targeted at young people in Gulu.

Some observers contend that rapid development in Gulu may catalyse changes in its epidemiological profile (Roberts et al., 2012; Yusuf et al., 2001a, 2001b). This hypothesis is supported by health data collected by the Gulu District Health Office (DHO). Although communicable diseases continue to be the primary cause of deaths in Gulu, cardio-vascular disease and hypertension are emerging health problems in the population (DHO, 2008, 2009). Limited opportunities to be physically active are likely to be a major contributing factor (Lee et al., 2012). Development and urbanisation are associated with changes in trans-port, vocation and recreation that, in combination, often reduce phys-ical activity levels (Yusuf et al., 2001a, 2001b). There is also evidence that physical education is poorly implemented in Ugandan schools (Hardman, 2005). When this is coupled with the infrastructure limita-tions that are evident in Northern Uganda, there are clearly significant barriers to adolescents participating in sufficient amounts of physical activity to promote health (Figure 9.1).

The claimed impacts of the SFD sector position it well to address both the peace building and the emerging physical and mental health needs in Gulu. Enthusiasm for sport and social goals is not new to Gulu, with various organisations having previously harnessed the positive percep-tion of SFD to deliver leagues, camps and one-day festivals. Although

Figure 9.1   Homemade football and sports field in Northern Uganda
Source: Photos taken by Justin Richards – Northern Uganda 2010.

these programmes had broad objectives that included peace building and health-related outcomes, their effectiveness was not rigorously evaluated. Previous interventions tended to be responsive to donor demands and opportunities rather than follow an established model, and they failed to develop sufficient local capacity to maintain a SFD legacy in Gulu. At the time of the current evaluation, several organisations claiming (though yet to demonstrate) a broad range of peace building and health outcomes were planning to re-establish SFD activities for local adolescents.

Solution generation

Sport-for-Development intervention

The SFD intervention evaluated in this case study was the inaugural season of a nine-week community based, competitive football (soccer) league that took place at two central locations in Gulu municipality. The programme plan described by the implementing partners comprised three seasons per year, with each including 160 girls and 240 boys. The authors observed the inaugural season, which comprised two age groups (under 12 and under 14) and a total of 32 teams playing football games (approximately 40–45 minutes) each week. They also performed a peace building activity (approximately 15–20 minutes) before each game that addressed a broad range of topics (e.g. domestic violence, gender equity, conflict resolution) using various methods (e.g. structured debate, theatrical performance, poetic presentation). The participants also participated in at least one training session (1.5 + hours) per week that combined football and peace building activities.

Adolescents living in Gulu aged 11–14 years were eligible to register for the league by voluntarily attending a registration day at the start of the programme. All of the girls who registered were included in the programme. However, there were more boys registered than places available, so some of them were randomly selected to be wait-listed for the next season. The points system for the league was designed to promote peace building activities and encourage participation in football as a form of physical activity that would benefit physical and mental health (Table 9.1).

Table 9.1 The points allocation system for the SFD intervention in Gulu

Activity	Points awarded
Football league and tournament (*Maximum 30 points*)	Teams awarded points according to results: • League (7 weeks): win = 3 points, draw = 1 point, loss = 0 points • Tournament: 1st = 9 points, 2nd = 8 points, 3rd = 7 points, 4th = 6 points, 5th = 5 points, 6th = 4 points, 7th = 3 points, 8th = 2 points
On-field behaviour (*Maximum 25 points*)	Teams commenced the season with maximum points (25) and deductions were made for poor on-field behaviour: • Deduct 3 points for a red card • Deduct 1 point for a yellow card
Peace building activities (*Maximum 25 points*)	Teams awarded points based on attendance and engagement in the peace building activities taking place before each game: • Maximum of 3 points before each league game • Maximum of 4 points for parental participation on the parents' day
Community service (*Maximum 20 points*)	Teams received 4 points for each community service activity (approximately 1 hour) completed as an inclusive group (up to maximum of 20 points). Maintenance and slashing of club training grounds could contribute to community service points

The programme was funded by aid agencies from Canada, Australia and the United Kingdom. It was implemented by two organisations that forged a partnership shortly before the programme commenced. The first of these was a local community based organisation that had previously focussed on broad peace building initiatives. The second partner was a non-governmental organisation that had its headquarters in Kampala, but had previously implemented sport leagues in Gulu. Each of the implementing organisations contributed resources to support the programme that was coordinated by six paid personnel and 32 volunteer coaches. The volunteers received a written manual and one week of training in football coaching and peace building prior to the league commencing. This comprised morning lectures and afternoon practical workshops that trained the volunteers in methods to become coaches of basic football skills. It also provided the volunteers with tuition in the peace building content of the programme, and training on how to facilitate this component of the intervention. Weekly meetings were conducted with the volunteers throughout the programme to reinforce these football coaching and peace building skills.

Evaluation of the peace building outcomes was completed internally. It included anecdotal observations made by programme staff and a rudimentary pre–post participant questionnaire that had not been previously pilot tested to assess metric quality. However, the physical and mental health outcomes were assessed more rigorously as part of an observational study and randomised controlled trial conducted by an independent evaluation team. This comprised a group of five local research assistants who were trained by the authors to apply validated metrics and quantitative evaluation methods. Full details of these study protocols are reported elsewhere (Richards, 2011b).

Prior to commencing the intervention, a series of planning meetings with the delivering partners and evaluation team were conducted to develop a model for programme implementation processes. In the absence of previous rigorous evaluation of local SFD interventions, this model drew heavily on the prior experience of the contributing stakeholders in various contexts (i.e. diverse programme designs delivered in different locations, populations and environments). Therefore, despite the need for local specificity, the consensus reached when developing the model for programme implementation processes was necessarily based on several assumptions about the generalisability of SFD interventions. It was intended that this model would provide a roadmap for the delivery and process evaluation of the current intervention, as well as have a broader utility for the implementation and objectives of other SFD programmes (Figure 9.2).

This model of programme implementation processes is underpinned by stakeholder theory. It focuses on harmonising the interests of all stakeholders in an attempt to optimise the intervention outcomes (Freeman, 1984). The programme aims and objectives are the central starting point and should be developed in consultation with the local community by stakeholders that are typically active in developing SFD interventions:

- Public sector (i.e. local, district and national governments).
- Private sector (i.e. profit- and market-oriented organisations).
- International organisations (i.e. agencies of the UN and regional unions).
- Non-government organisations (i.e. independent non-profit organisations).
- Sport organisations (i.e. organisations that focus on sporting achievement).
- Academic institutions (i.e. education centres and institutes for learning and research).

Although these stakeholders often have interdependent aims and objectives, they each have their own agenda and function (Levermore, 2011; SDPIWG, 2008). The programme aims and objectives are determined by the underlying purpose of each participating organisation (e.g. funder, implementer or evaluator). They are typically also influenced by the expectations of the funding source (Coalter, 2011; Kidd, 2008). According to stakeholder theory, it is important that these aims and objectives are also *formed in response to local needs and the intended reach of the SFD programme* (Figure 9.2).

After establishing objectives, the stakeholders proceed to implementing actions and realising the subsequent intermediary outputs. These stages are generic to all SFD objectives and resemble other SFD logic models previously described in the literature (Coalter, 2006). However, in this model for programme implementation processes, there is interdependence within and between each of the described levels. The chronological relationship between these levels is multi-directional and responsive to downstream feedback (i.e. actions determine outputs and feedback from these outputs influence subsequent actions), as well as the status of concurrent actions and outputs.

According to stakeholder theory, there needs to be concerted support for the actions required to establish a holistic SFD programme (Freeman, 1984). However, certain organisations typically take a lead role depending on the skills and expertise required. The actions can and should be tailored according to the programme objectives and the organisations involved. The intermediary outputs are accomplished as joint ventures led by the stakeholders that pilot the associated actions. They link the actions with the final outcomes of SFD interventions by developing the necessary environment, knowledge and capacity to establish a sustainable programme.

The outcomes in the model refer to the broad array that are claimed by the SFD sector. The application of the model should be a flexible process that becomes less generic; in fact, it varies depending on the underlying intervention objectives and the local context. In the Gulu case study, the programme components were planned prior to completing a comprehensive formative evaluation of the proposed methods and potential intervention mechanisms in the target population. Therefore, this component of the model was not informed by locally relevant data or evidence specific to Gulu. It was assumed that the intervention would have a clinically significant impact on activity levels that would in turn influence physical and mental health directly as well as indirectly through improved fitness (Bouchard, 2001; Zakus et al., 2007). It was also assumed that the design of the intervention would enable effective promotion of the desired peace building objectives (Table 9.1). A subsequent formative evaluation conducted in Gulu prior to implementation provided the first indication that these assumptions may not have been locally relevant for achieving the intended outcomes.

Formative evaluation

The formative evaluation assessed the quality of the case study methods and the viability of delivering the intervention in the local context. It also provided an initial feasibility assessment of the mechanisms described in the model for programme implementation processes. This was completed by an independent evaluation team for the physical and mental health outcomes, and the results are described in more detail elsewhere (Richards, 2011a). No formative evaluation was completed for the peace building objectives.

In summary, the results of the formative evaluation indicated that the metrics for evaluating the health-related outcomes were valid and reliable. This was the first time that the proposed methods had been used in Gulu, and they proved to be robust to the relatively unpredictable local environment. The programme proposal appeared to be well received by the community. Barriers to implementation were primarily confined to negotiations over the reimbursement of expenses for volunteers, and securing appropriate locations for the programme activities. Local businesses were capable of assisting with the procurement of the necessary resources, and in accordance with stakeholder theory there appeared to be widespread support from all of the key partners described in the model for programme implementation processes (Freeman, 1984).

The adolescent population in Gulu demonstrated varied levels of physical health when assessed as part of the formative evaluation. This appeared to be amenable to change depending on barriers and opportunities for participating in physical activity. Therefore, the objective of improving physical health by facilitating participation in football appeared to be feasible and appropriate. However, scatterplots demonstrated no relationship between physical and mental health indicators measured in a cross section of Gulu adolescents prior to the intervention (Richards, 2011a). Contrary to the current evidence, which is primarily based on research from high-income and peaceful communities, this suggested that it was unlikely that mental health would improve in response to simply increasing physical activity in Gulu. Consequently, there was a mismatch between the mental health objectives and the proposed mechanism of how these would be achieved. In other words, in contrast to the claims of the SFD sector cited by the implementing organisations, it appeared that programme impacts on the mental health of Gulu adolescents would require an approach that involved more than just increased participation in physical activity.

It is important to note the implications of the retrospective nature of this formative evaluation. At the time it was completed, the programme objectives and design had already been finalised in order to secure funding for the programme. This highlights an important 'chicken and egg' scenario where programmes are often granted funding based on ambitious objectives that have been developed without appropriately considering their efficacy in a local context (Levermore, 2011). Funders typically require clearly articulated objectives from implementing partners prior to approving their proposals, but insufficient resources often prevent evaluators from contributing to the planning process. Implementers may also perceive evaluators as potential threats who divert resources from interventions, and are only necessary for satisfying the accountability demands of funders (Levermore, 2011). This perspective does not acknowledge the positive contribution that evaluators can make to refining objectives and improving programme delivery (Nutbeam and Bauman, 2006).

Innovation testing

Outcome evaluation

Forensic details about the outcomes of the intervention are not the focus of this chapter, but are reported in detail elsewhere (Richards et al., 2013). That said, some of these results are important contextual elements for understanding the discussion of programme implementation processes. The programme had differential physical and mental health effects on adolescents in Gulu according to gender and level of programme engagement (i.e. intervention versus wait-list control versus non-registered comparison groups). These may be explained by changes in local capacity, perceived opportunity in the community and the nature of personal interactions during the intervention. As previously described, the outcome evaluation used validated metrics and quantitative methods. The results can be summarised as follows:

- The intervention had a *negligible* effect on the physical and mental health of the participating girls when compared to the non-registered comparison group.
- The intervention had a *negligible* effect on the physical health of the participating boys when compared to both the non-registered comparison and wait-listed control groups.
- The intervention had a *negative* effect on the mental health of the participating boys when compared to the *positive* change seen in the wait-listed control group and *negligible* change in the non-registered comparison group.
- Internal logistical challenges prevented the completion of the peace building impact evaluation and there were no results reported.

Process evaluation

The process evaluation drew on ethnographic observations of intervention delivery that were recorded in the field diaries of the evaluation team. The model for programme implementation processes was used as a framework for exploring the relationships between the objectives, actions and intermediary outputs of the relevant stakeholders (Figure 9.2).

Programme objectives

At the centre of the model for programme implementation processes are the *aims and objectives formed in response to local needs and the intended reach of the SFD programme* (Figure 9.2). All stakeholders need

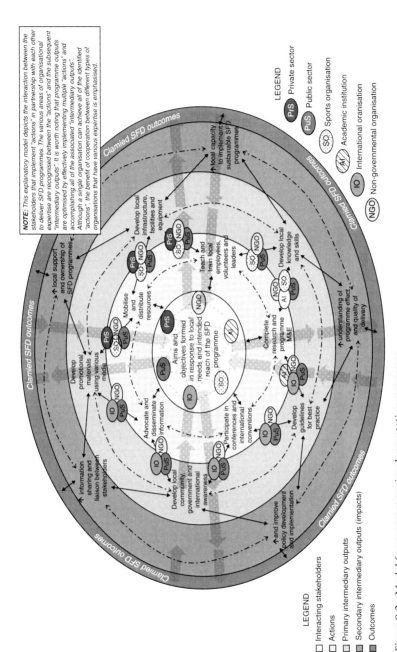

NOTE: This explanatory model depicts the interaction between the stakeholders that implement "actions" in partnership with each other to deliver SFD programmes. The various areas of organisational expertise are recognised between the "actions" and the subsequent "intermediary outputs". It is worth noting that programme outputs are optimised by effectively implementing multiple "actions" and accomplishing all of the associated "intermediary outputs". Although a single organisation can achieve all of the identified "actions", the benefit of cooperation between different types of organisations that have various expertise is emphasised.

Clamied SFD outcomes

Clamied SFD outcomes

Clamied SFD outcomes

Clamied SFD outcomes

Develop local infrastructure, facilities and equipment

local capacity to implement sustainable SFD programmes

local support and ownership of SFD programmes

Mobilise and distribute resources

Teach and train local employees, volunteers and leaders

Develop local knowledge and skills

Develop promotional materials using various media

Aims and objectives formed in response to local needs and intended reach of the SFD programme

Complete research and programme M&E

understanding of programme effect and quality of delivery

information sharing and liaison between stakeholders

Advocate and disseminate information

Participate in conferences and international conventions

Develop guidelines for best practice

Develop local community government and international awareness

and improve policy development and implementation

LEGEND

PrS Private sector
PuS Public sector
SO Sports organisation
AI Academic institution
IO International or;anisation
IO Non-governmental organisation
NGO Non-governmental organisation

LEGEND

☐ Interacting stakeholders
☐ Actions
☐ Primary intermediary outputs
▨ Secondary intermediary outputs (impacts)
▨ Outcomes

Figure 9.2   Model for programme implementation processes

to contribute to this process, and consultation with the community is critical for identifying their priorities and promoting sustainability through local ownership (Akhbari et al., 2010; Coalter, 2011; Nutbeam and Bauman, 2006). Programme objectives are ideally informed by effective problem definition that, according to stakeholder theory, directs all stakeholders towards common objectives (Freeman, 1984; Nutbeam and Bauman, 2006).

In this case study, formulating the programme objectives was complicated by the partnership of two previously independent implementing organisations that were supported by multiple donors. This union avoided intervention replication in Gulu, and was the most economical use of resources to increase the programme size. However, there was some diversity in the objectives of the organisations, and these may have been diluted when the partnership was formed. One organisation was a 'plus sport' organisation that used football as a means to attract participants for peace building initiatives (Coalter, 2007). It lacked previous evaluation and had not established a model for programme implementation processes. In contrast, the other local partner came from the opposite end of the SFD spectrum. It was a 'sport plus' organisation that originally focused on football development for young people, but had diversified its objectives in response to donor demands to include reintegration of previously abducted children and improvement of health-related outcomes (Coalter, 2007).

A compromise was eventually reached between the two implementing organisations that fused the objectives of their previous programmes. The aim was to implement a football intervention that provided a vehicle for delivering peace building initiatives and promoted the broader benefits of physical activity on health. There was a particular focus on mental health because it bridged the peace building and health agendas of all stakeholders and has been associated with physical activity levels in other populations reported in the academic literature (Freeman, 1984; Roberts et al., 2012).

In accordance with stakeholder theory, a series of meetings were conducted in Gulu prior to commencing the intervention activities (Freeman, 1984). Representatives from the local government, schools, sports clubs and NGOs were consulted. However, the primary purpose of these meetings was to gather the support of the community for an intervention that had already been designed and funded. The local stakeholders did confirm the importance of several of the planned programme activities (e.g. the choice of football rather than netball for girls). However, the retrospective nature of these meetings with regard to programme planning compromised local ownership of the intervention and the potential for traction within the community. Perhaps most importantly, failing to appropriately engage the local population during the initial planning phases of the intervention meant that their concerns were displaced by the priorities of the other stakeholders (Kidd, 2008).

Programme delivery

The actions and outputs of the model for programme implementation processes can be tailored to the original intervention objectives and outcomes of interest (Figure 9.2). Ideally, programme delivery can be tracked using process indicators that are developed during the formative evaluation of an intervention (Nutbeam and Bauman, 2006). When the programme processes are well established, these are the stepping stones that describe how a SFD intervention is intended to work (Coalter, 2006). Although failure to establish an appropriate model for programme implementation does not inherently preclude the success of an intervention, it does hinder targeted delivery and process evaluation, as well as the full engagement of local stakeholders (Nutbeam and Bauman, 2006).

In this case study, the intervention personnel and volunteers appeared to implement all of the actions described in the model for programme implementation processes. However, the delivery of each of these varied in quality when comparing the health and peace building objectives.

The intervention did effectively *mobilise and distribute resources*, as well as *advocate and disseminate information* for football participation in Gulu (Figure 9.2). The provision of resources and capacity appeared to catalyse a broader engagement in football in schools throughout the community. The same was not observed for the peace building agenda. This may reflect the universal appeal of sport that features in the SFD rhetoric (SDPIWG, 2008). However, it is also likely that this difference was influenced by the efforts of the football logistics coordinators to *teach and train local employees, volunteers and leaders* throughout the programme (Figure 9.2). In contrast, the peace building personnel made a more dubious contribution to training the volunteer coaches. They also failed to rigorously *complete research and programme M&E* for the peace building objectives and only the football coordinators *participated in conferences and international conventions* in the form of coaching workshops (Figure 9.2).

As indicated in the model for programme implementation processes, achieving the primary intermediary outputs is related to the delivery of the associated actions. Therefore, it follows that the intervention effectively developed *local infrastructure, facilities and equipment* for football participation (Figure 9.2). It also contributed to *local knowledge and skills* that were specific to coaching sport and developing local football (Figure 9.2). However, the peace building objectives were notably neglected for all of the primary intermediary outputs because the associated actions were poorly implemented. Consequently, a 'sport plus' intervention was not successfully delivered because although the football components of the programme were well developed, the peace building facets remained elementary (Coalter, 2007). This was particularly evident in the effective development of *promotional materials using various media, guidelines for best practice* and *local community, government and international awareness* (Figure 9.2).

The initial stages of programme implementation had subsequent downstream repercussions for the secondary intermediary outputs. It follows that *local capacity to implement sustainable SFD programmes* was well established for the 'sport' components, but not for the 'plus' facets of the proposed intervention in Gulu (Figure 9.2). Similarly, *understanding the programme effect* on participation in physical activity improved and the *local support and ownership* for the football component of the intervention also developed (Figure 9.2). The subsequent *policy development* and *information sharing between stakeholders* also focussed on the football component and, unfortunately, continued to neglect the peace building agenda (Figure 9.2).

In summary, all of the actions and intermediary outputs described in the model for programme implementation processes were accomplished for promoting the football components of the intervention. The programme that was finally delivered was essentially a competitive league that focussed on winning games rather than the peace building or physical and mental health objectives. This was particularly evident in the attitudes and behaviours of the participants and coaches from the boys' leagues. Although the focus on winning football games did not appear to hinder player participation in physical activity, it signified a clear departure from the original objectives of the programme. This shift may explain some of the detrimental programme impacts identified in the outcome evaluation that were summarised previously (Richards et al., 2013).

Conclusions and recommendations

It was intended that the intervention in this case study would address both the physical and mental health objectives of the implementing partners (Bouchard, 2001; Zakus et al., 2007). However, the formative evaluation exposed the limitations of the programme model when applied to mental health objectives in Gulu. Since the formative evaluation was completed retrospectively by an independent team, it did not inform the design and implementation of the intervention. Consequently, there was a mismatch between the mental health objectives and the proposed mechanism by which these would be achieved. Although this explains a lack of positive effect on mental health outcomes, it does not account for the relative deterioration of the boys participating in the programme (Richards et al., 2013). This surprising outcome warrants further evaluation in future research. One possible explanation could be that the highly competitive nature of the boys' leagues contributed to the negative mental health outcomes observed in the intervention group (Burnett, 2001; Siegenthaler and Gonzalez, 1997). Therefore, if mental health objectives remain a priority in Gulu, the merit of league-based SFD programmes that have the propensity to become highly competitive and compromise the nature of personal interactions is questionable.

There is clearly a need to increase resources for prospective formative evaluation as part of SFD intervention planning (Hartman and Kwauk, 2011; Levermore, 2011). This should focus on establishing locally relevant models for programme implementation processes that harmonise all stakeholder objectives as part of intervention development (Coalter, 2011; Freeman, 1984; Nutbeam and Bauman, 2006). The model presented in this chapter can be used and adapted to fit different contexts (Figure 9.2).

Upon reflection, an effective and prospective formative evaluation in Gulu would have identified the need to more thoroughly address the peace building objectives prior to commencing the programme. It may have also mitigated the negative impact that the intervention had on mental health by identifying the need to develop alternative mechanisms for achieving this objective. This could have included a shift towards delivering a 'plus sport' intervention by training local psychosocial 'peer leaders' and adapting the volunteer coach tuition to increase the focus on the mental health objectives (Coalter, 2010; Schulenkorf and Sugden, 2011). The implemented actions could have been subsequently adjusted to follow a programme model that had been specifically developed for the desired mental health and peace building outcomes. Although this may have diluted the actions of programme delivery and weakened the physical health impact, it would have addressed the multiple objectives of the implementing partners more effectively.

References

Akhbari, M., Kunz, V., Selvaraju, U. and Wijesekera, R. (2010). *Sport and Development: A Summary of SAD's Experiences and Good Practices.* Bienne: Swiss Academy for Development (SAD).

Annan, J., Blattman, C., Carlson, K. and Mazurana, D. (2008). *The State of Female Youth in Northern Uganda: Findings from the Survey of War-Affected Youth (SWAY).* Kampala: UNICEF.

Annan, J., Blattman, C. and Horton, R. (2006). *The State of Youth and Youth Protection in Northern Uganda: Findings from the Survey for War Affected Youth.* Kampala: UNICEF.

Betancourt, T. S., Bass, J., Borisova, I., Neugebauer, R., Speelman, L., Onyango, G. and Bolton, P. (2009). Assessing Local Instrument Reliability and Validity: A Field-Based Example from Northern Uganda. *Social Psychiatry and Psychiatric Epidemiology*, 44, 685–692.

Bouchard, C. (2001). Physical Activity and Health: Introduction to the Dose-Response Symposium. *Medicine and Science in Sports and Exercise*, 33, S347–S350.

Branch, A. (2008). Gulu Town in War ... and Peace? Displacement, Humanitarianism and Postwar Crisis. *Crisis States Research Centre Working Papers.* London School of Economics: Destin Development Studies Initiative.

Burnett, C. (2001). Social Impact Assessment and Sport Development: Social Spin-Offs of the Australia–South Africa Junior Sport Programme. *International Review for the Sociology of Sport*, 36, 41–57.

Coakley, J. (2011). Youth Sports: What Counts as 'Positive Development?' *Journal of Sport and Social Issues*, 35, 306–324.

Coalter, F. (2006). *Sport-in-Development: A Monitoring and Evaluation Manual.* London: UK Sport.

Coalter, F. (2007). *A Wider Social Role for Sport: Who's Keeping the Score?* London: Routledge.

Coalter, F. (2010). *Sport-for-Development Impact Study – A Research Initiative Funded by Comic Relief and UK Sport and Managed by International Development through Sport.* In D.O.S. Studies (ed.), Stirling: University of Stirling.

Coalter, F. (2011). Sports Development's Contribution to Social Policy Objectives. In B. Houlihan and M. Green (eds), *Routledge Handbook of Sports Development.* New York: Routledge.

Cronin, O. (2011). *Comic Relief Review: Mapping the Research on the Impact of Sport and Development Interventions.* Manchester: Orla Cronin Research.

Gulu District Health Office (DHO) (2008). *Gulu DHO Annual Workplan 2008–2009.* Gulu: Gulu DHO.

Gulu District Health Office (DHO) (2009). *Gulu DHO Annual Workplan 2009–2010.* Gulu: Gulu DHO.

Freeman, R.E. (1984). *Strategic Management: A Stakeholder Approach.* Boston: Pitman.

Hardman, K. (2005). *An Update on the Status of Physical Education in Schools Worldwide: Technical Report for the World Health Organisation (WHO).* Geneva: WHO.

Hartman, D. and Kwauk, C. (2011). Sport And Development: An Overview, Critique, and Reconstruction. *Journal of Sport and Social Issues*, 35, 284–305.

Kidd, B. (2008). A New Social Movement: Sport for Development and Peace. *Sport in Society*, 11, 370–380.

Kidd, B. and Macdonnell, M. (2007). Peace, Sport and Development. *Literature Reviews on Sport for Development and Peace*. Toronto: Sport for Development and Peace International Working Group (SDPIWG).

Lee, I.M., Shiroma, E.J., Lobelo, F., Puska, P., Blair, S.N. and Katzmarzyk, P.T. (2012). Effect of Physical Inactivity on Major Non-Communicable Diseases Worldwide: An Analysis of Burden of Disease and Life Expectancy. *Lancet*, 380, 219–229.

Levermore, R. (2011). Sport in International Development. In B. Houlihan and M. Green (eds), *Routledge Handbook of Sports Development*. New York: Routledge.

Mcmullen, J.D., O'Callaghan, P.S., Richards, J.A., Eakin, J.G. and Rafferty, H. (2011). Screening for Traumatic Exposure and Psychological Distress Among War-Affected Adolescents in Post-Conflict Northern Uganda. *Social Psychiatry and Psychiatric Epidemiology*, 47(9), 1489–1498.

Nutbeam, D. and Bauman, A. (2006). *Evaluation in a Nutshell*. Sydney: McGraw-Hill.

Richards, J. (2011a). *Evaluating the Impact of a Sport-for-Development Intervention on the Physical and Mental Health of Young Adolescents in Gulu, Uganda – a Post-Conflict Setting within a Low-Income Country*. DPhil, University of Oxford.

Richards, J. (2011b). *Study Protocol (Methods): Evaluating the Impact of a Sport-for-Development Intervention on the Physical and Mental Health of Young Adolescents in Gulu, Uganda – A Post-Conflict Setting within a Low-Income Country*. University of Oxford.

Richards, J., Foster, C., Townsed, N. and Bauman, A. (2013). Physical and Mental Health Impact of a Sport-for-Development Intervention in a Post-Conflict Setting: Randomised Controlled Trial Nested within an Observational Study of Adolescents in Gulu, Uganda. *Unpublished paper*.

Roberts, B., Patel, P. and Mckee, M. (2012). Noncommunicable Diseases and Post-Conflict Countries. *Bull World Health Organ*, 90, 2–2A.

Schulenkorf, N. and Sugden, J. (2011). Sport for Development and Peace in Divided Societies: Cooperating for Inter-Community Empowerment in Israel. *European Journal for Sport and Society*, 8, 235–256.

Sport for Development and Peace International Working Group (SDPIWG) (2008). *Harnessing the Power of Sport for Development and Peace: Recommendations to Governments*. Toronto: SDPIWG.

Siegenthaler, K.L. and Gonzalez, G.L. (1997). Youth Sports as Serious Leisure: A Critique. *Journal of Sport and Social Issues*, 21, 298–314.

United Nations (UN) (2006). *Post-Conflict Stabilization, Peacebuilding and Recovery Frameworks*. Geneva: UN Disarmament, Demobilization and Reintegration Resource Centre.

United Nations Development Group (UNDG) (2005). *United Nations Development Assistance Framework (UNDAF) – Post-Conflict Transition*. New York: UNDG.

Yusuf, S., Reddy, S., Ounpuu, S. and Anand, S. (2001a). Global Burden of Cardiovascular Diseases: Part I: General Considerations, the Epidemiologic Transition, Risk Factors, and Impact of Urbanization. *Circulation*, 104, 2746–2753.

Yusuf, S., Reddy, S., Ounpuu, S. and Anand, S. (2001b). Global Burden of Cardiovascular Diseases: Part II: Variations in Cardiovascular Disease by Specific

Ethnic Groups and Geographic Regions and Prevention Strategies. *Circulation*, 104, 2855–2864.

Zakus, D., Njelesani, D. and Darnell, S. (2007). The Use of Sport and Physical Activity to Achieve Health Objectives. *Literature Reviews on Sport for Development and Peace*. Toronto: Sport for Development and Peace International Working Group (SDPIWG).

10

Lessons Learned from Monitoring and Evaluating Sport-for-Development Programmes in the Caribbean

Zachary Kaufman, Brooke Page Rosenbauer and Gabriela Moore

Synopsis of chapter

Sport-for-development (SFD) programmes have proliferated in the Caribbean over the last decade because of increased funding and growing interest in the field. With few donors directly financing programmes or expecting formal, independent evaluation, many organisations rely on data collected through internal monitoring and evaluation (M&E) to document their effectiveness. In-depth interviews with coordinators of two SFD programmes – *A Ganar* and *Deportes para la Vida* – in six Caribbean countries were carried out to understand organisational practices, successes and challenges pertaining to M&E. Interviews revealed the importance of feedback loops, the inspirational role that M&E data can play for staff and volunteers and various M&E challenges related to time, staff capacity and geography. Recommendations are provided for improving M&E systems and practices in the two highlighted programmes, with implications for other SFD programmes in the Caribbean and beyond.

Introduction

This chapter features voices from the field that articulate the experience of monitoring and evaluating SFD programmes in the Caribbean, specifically Dominica, Haiti, Jamaica, St. Kitts and Nevis, St. Vincent and the Grenadines, as well as the Dominican Republic (DR). The chapter focuses on two programmes – *A Ganar* and *Deportes para la Vida* (DPV) – both of which fall within the 'plus-sport' model articulated by Coalter (2008) and Levermore (2008), in which development programmes focusing on health, education, employment or other themes add a sports component to better engage their target audience and mobilise communities. We draw from in-depth interviews with six local practitioners and a Caribbean-based SFD coordination/advocacy organisation, as well as from our own experiences of monitoring, managing and evaluating SFD programmes in Africa, Latin America, Central America and the Caribbean, to document M&E-related challenges and successes. We then make recommendations for improving systems and processes.

SFD in the Caribbean

Sport has deep cultural roots in the Caribbean, dating back to its colonial origins and the inclusion of sport and physical education in the formal school system. Historically, sport has played a culturally and politically important symbolic role. It has also played significant role in the identity formation of young people, with both amateur and professional athletes representing cultural 'heroes' (McCree, 2005). Today, international superstars such as Usain Bolt, Pedro Martinez and Adonal Foyle captivate the islands' hearts through a diverse array of sporting activities including football, cricket, baseball, netball, volleyball, basketball and athletics. The recent 2012 London Summer Olympics highlighted the region's vigorous spirit for its track and field athletes; the successes of Usain Bolt and Yohan Blake brought pride not only to Jamaica but also to the entire region. Although many differences exist among the Caribbean countries, their shared enthusiasm for sport is pervasive.

In the Caribbean, SFD precedes the United Nations' 2001 appointment of a Special Advisor on Sport for Development and Peace. The Commonwealth Heads of Government recognised the potential for sport to combat poverty and promote development. These aspirations were discussed at regional meetings of The Council for Human and Social Development on Sport in the late 1990s and early 2000s. As a result of these meetings, numerous youth and health policy frameworks in the region started to include sport-based initiatives (CARICOM, 2003). With the help of international programmes such as the Commonwealth Sport Development Programmes and international donors such as AUSAID, which includes the Caribbean in their Australian Sports Outreach Programme (ASOP), SFD programmes have proliferated throughout the Caribbean. AUSAID has been supporting SFD programmes in the Caribbean since 1998 (AUSAID, 2012). Currently, the Government of Australia spends AUD$8 million per year on SFD in the Pacific and Caribbean and is seen as an international leader in the arena. Furthermore, the Commonwealth Games of Canada (CGC) organisation is focused on 'International Development through Sport'.

Programmes of CGC in the Caribbean include *Trinidad & Tobago Able and Ready*, which is focused on youth with disabilities, *Bowling out aids!* and *Kicking AIDS Out* (Commonwealth Games, 2012). These latter initiatives exemplify the widespread support for SFD in the region.

Although many SFD programmes have been implemented in the Caribbean in the past decade, historically, formal evaluations have been sparse. One exception is an evaluation conducted by CARICOM in 2003, which highlighted a number of prominent SFD programmes in the region. The evaluation revealed that the programmes were generally 'disparate and uncoordinated' and needed to 'build capacity to continuously evaluate programme delivery and impact'. As a consequence of limited resources, an 'absence of evaluation and impact assessment components' existed because staff took 'shortcuts to get to the program delivery stage' (CARICOM, 2003).

M&E in the field of SFD

While numerous M&E toolkits have been developed for SFD organisations (Cronin, 2011; Coalter, 2008), little research on SFD organisations perceptions and experiences of M&E has been carried out worldwide. As an exception, the Denmark-based Network for Sport and Development (NSD) documented the M&E experiences of 12 SFD organisations', citing constraints on time and resources, as well as lack of adequately trained staff, as key M&E challenges (NSD, 2009). A comic-relief-supported mapping of SFD research – in which 12 SFD practitioners at eight organisations were interviewed – revealed similar challenges with limited capacity, time and funds (Cronin, 2011). At the time of writing, no official research is available that investigates the M&E experiences in a Caribbean context.

During our practical experience of monitoring, evaluating and managing SFD programmes in Africa, Central and Latin America as well as the Caribbean over the last five years, we have become aware of and concerned about two dangerous tendencies that threaten the long-term success of the field. The first is a tendency to not hold SFD interventions to the same evidence standards as other health, education and youth development interventions. This is partly caused by a perception that SFD is 'an emerging field' in its nascent stages (IWG SDP, 2008). The perception is false. Organisations have been using sport as a strategic development tool since the 1970s. *Partners of the Americas*, for example, has done so through exchange programmes. More generally, there have long been supportive policies around the use of sport-in-development interventions, while sport-based HIV prevention programmes have been delivered by organisations such as *Grassroot Soccer, Right to Play* and *Kicking AIDS Out* for over a decade (Kaufman et al., 2012).

Yet, despite the field's international growth, evidence supporting the effectiveness of SFD approaches has been slow to develop. Reviewing the extent and types of evaluation conducted to date among 'best practice' SFD programmes, Levermore (2011) has pointed to the 'nascent level of effective evaluation' among SFD organisations, noting that evaluation is taking place but that 'the amount of publicly available, transparent results of these evaluations is minimal with less than half providing detailed information of the data' (Levermore, 2011: 351). Furthermore, much of the research conducted to date has suffered from an array of methodological and conceptual weaknesses (Coalter, 2007, 2009). UNICEF (2006: 4) has echoed the 'need to assemble proof, to go beyond what is mostly anecdotal evidence to monitor and evaluate impact of sport-in-development programme'. Why then has the evidence base of SFD been slow to develop while overall, the field has been quick to grow? We suspect that the lack of rigorous evaluation stems partly from the influx of inexperienced stakeholders to SFD – particularly from the private sector – anxious to try out a new, seemingly 'sexy' approach to development (Cameron and Haanstra, 2008). Many SFD funders – again, particularly in the private sector – seek 'results' that are often better captured in stories, integers, photos and videos, rather than rate ratios, confidence intervals and statistical tests. In fact, this holds for what the media tends to seek from SFD as well. Although vaccines or educational programmes make the news after evaluation results are published, SFD interventions typically make the news when famous sports stars or other celebrities make a guest appearance (e.g. see Lawton, 2009; Superville, 2011). Indeed, the use of celebrities in promoting SFD organisations – particularly well-known organisations with resources to attract and leverage celebrity involvement – has become rather commonplace (Darnell, 2012). Thus, it seems, the vision of a 'successful programme' in SFD has become quite different from that of parallel, non-sport-based development programmes.

The second problematic tendency is the conflation of monitoring and evaluation into a unified activity of 'M&E'. This tendency has been identified in development sectors outside of SFD (Kusek, 2011; Mavrotas, 2010), although it seems especially pronounced within SFD. While both M&E deal with the collection of data to answer questions about a programme, the simple questions answered by monitoring (e.g. How many participants were reached? Were sessions delivered according to the curriculum?) differ substantially from the more nuanced questions addressed by evaluation. Outcome evaluations respond to questions of effectiveness – the extent to which increased inputs and outputs result in increased outcomes (e.g. Is there evidence of increased self-esteem among participants from baseline to 5 months post-intervention? Did participants, on average, have fewer sexual partners over 12 months compared to a control group?). Process evaluations, meanwhile, address questions of what was delivered, what happened and why/how an intervention is or is not effective or efficient (e.g. How did participants feel about their Coach as a role model? How do participants think the intervention could have been made more effective?) (JBA, 2007).

As they pose and respond to different types of questions, it is evident that monitoring, outcome evaluation and process evaluation all require different tools, different skills, different strategies and ideally different personnel. Done well, monitoring ought to generate ongoing output and outcome data that is reviewed regularly by decision makers and tracked against key performance indicators (Bishop, 2002). Meanwhile, evaluations ought to be conducted periodically, designed and implemented scientifically and should generate data – whether quantitative or qualitative – that is analysed objectively, according to pre-set methods (Nutbeam and Baumann, 2006). Rigorous evaluation provides not only a means to address questions of effectiveness and efficiency, but also to test programmatic assumptions, gather in-depth feedback from beneficiaries and reshape programmes in order to make them more effective.

The outcome-agnostic expectations of SFD stakeholders and the tendency to conflate both M&E has resulted in a sub-optimal status quo: it is a field in which few rigorous outcome evaluations are carried out or published; in which many individuals and organisations misunderstand the concept of M&E and in which SFD interventions are held to lower standards of evidence than non-sport-based development interventions attempting to achieve similar outcomes. With this in mind, we were anxious to learn from SFD practitioners in the Caribbean about their M&E-related perceptions, best practices and challenges, in the hope that they might provide insight to assist other SFD practitioners in the complex process of creating and implementing structures, strategies and systems for monitoring and evaluating their programmes.

Programme background

A Ganar, which means 'to win' or 'to earn' in Spanish, trains youth aged 16–24 in employability and technical skills with the aim of helping them find formal employment, start their own business or return to formal schooling or training. The programme targets 'high-risk' youth who come from marginalised communities, have dropped out of secondary school, are in or are at risk of joining gangs and other vulnerable populations. *A Ganar* is led by *Partners of the Americas* and funded by United States Agency for International Development (USAID), the Multilateral Investment Fund (MIF) of the Inter-American Development Bank (IDB) and the Nike Foundation. Initiated as a pilot programme in Ecuador, Uruguay and Brazil, *A Ganar* has expanded to 15 countries in Latin America including seven countries in the Caribbean region: Dominica, the DR, Haiti, Jamaica, St. Kitts and Nevis, St. Vincent and the Grenadines, as well as Suriname.

The *A Ganar* methodology imparts six core employability skills – communication, respect, discipline, teamwork, continual self-improvement and focus on results – through dynamic sport-based activities that feature in-depth discussion and reflection on lessons learned from the field of sport and how they relate to the workplace and life. The first phase of the programme occurs over a minimum of 100 hours, half of which are conducted on the sports field and half in the classroom. On the field, youth engage in modified sports games with rules that bring them outside of their comfort zone, each day focused on one of the six core skills. For example, the participants must play football in pairs holding hands, so they are forced to work together as a team and communicate. After playing for 20 minutes, a reflection period is led by the facilitator, followed by another 20-minute period and reflection. In the classroom, facilitators lead youth through a manual that includes sport-themed mathematics, language and computer technology lessons. For example, they might read a story about a local sports hero and learn new vocabulary or do a math lesson based on tournament statistics. After this foundation in 'soft' employability skills, youth enter a second technical training phase and eventually leave the programme with an internship or 'attachment' to practice what they have learned in a local business setting. Throughout, youth are attached to a mentor and participate in a service-learning project. After about eight to ten months, it is expected that youth will have the skills and confidence necessary to become integrated or reintegrated into the formal economy or education system.

In 2010, the MIF conducted a formal evaluation of the 2005–2009 *A Ganar* pilot that they funded in Uruguay, Brazil and Ecuador, interviewing participants, coordinators and other stakeholders and assessing of changes in participants' livelihoods. The evaluation concluded that 70 per cent of the graduates of the initial pilot programme ad found employment, and that 84 per cent of the graduates felt the programme had greatly improved their ability to seek employment opportunities and be interviewed for jobs. In addition, the evaluation also concluded that the *A Ganar* programme improved the relationship between youth and their communities, amplified social networks and enhanced the ability of local implementing organisations to form institutional linkages (see Cabal, 2010). A third-party randomised controlled trial (RCT) of the programme is currently taking place in Guatemala and Honduras, but a formal evaluation has yet to take place in the Caribbean. To monitor its programmes, *A Ganar* collects basic biographic and programmatic information on participants, and tracks assessment scores throughout the three phases of implementation. They also conduct 'follow-on' in the form of alumni engagement and data collection with participants for one year after graduation to obtain information on their employment and educational status.

Deportes para la Vida (DPV, 'Sports for Life') is a HIV prevention and life skills programme run by the Dominican Republic Education and Mentoring (DREAM) Project in the DR and Mercy Corps in Haiti, using a curriculum developed by *Grassroot Soccer*. *Grassroot Soccer* uses soccer as a vehicle to educate, inspire and mobilise communities to stop the spread of HIV mostly in sub-Saharan Africa. DPV, based on *Grassroot Soccer*'s methodology, is delivered in-school and out-of-school through 'interventions' with groups of approximately 20–25 youth aged 10–18. The DPV programme has largely focused on youth in Haitian migrant communities, although it has expanded in partnership with schools to reach a broader cross section of underprivileged Dominican and Haitian youth. An intervention consists of approximately 10 hours of sport- and discussion-based activities. For example, in an activity called Risk Field (Campo de Riesgo), teams compete in a football relay race, dribbling around cones representing HIV-related risks (unprotected sex, multiple partners, older partners, drugs and alcohol). If a participant strikes a cone in the first round, he/she has to stop and perform three press-ups or jumping jacks; if he/she strikes a cone in the second round, the consequence is extended to his/her teammates and in the third round, every time a cone is struck, all participants and coaches 'suffer' the consequences of the 'risk' of one participant. Interactive discussion follows each round to name, substantiate and personalise the consequences of HIV-related risks. The entire curriculum follows this play–discuss–learn model (which is described further in Clark et al., 2006 and Peacock-Villada et al., 2007).

Recently published in AIDS Care, a quasi-experimental evaluation of DPV in the Puerto Plata province of the DR utilised structured interviews with DPV participants and non-participants in the same communities prior to, immediately after and four months post-intervention, finding very strong evidence that the intervention had positive and sustained effects on HIV-related knowledge, attitudes and communication (Kaufman, 2011). To monitor interventions, DPV collects attendance registers and conducts short pre-/post-questionnaires.

Methods

In order to better understand the challenges and best practices of monitoring and evaluating SFD programmes in the Caribbean, in-depth interviews were carried out with five programme coordinators, two with DPV and three with *A Ganar*, working in six different countries: Haiti, Jamaica, St. Kitts and Nevis, St. Vincent and the Grenadines, as well as the DR. These coordinators were responsible for overseeing the implementing organisations and the provision of data back to the head office. Interviews addressed how M&E processes were carried out, what each coordinator considered to be best practices, what challenges they encountered in carrying out processes and what they felt needed to be improved upon, what could be done to improve processes. Two 30-minute interviews with each coordinator were conducted. The first covered basic information gathering and the second dove deeper into themes that emerged during the first round. Five coordinators were interviewed in English and one in Spanish. Subsequently, each interview was transcribed to text; then, interview transcripts were reviewed by two co-authors, manually coded and analysed thematically (counting the number of times particular themes came up), with quotes pulled out to illustrate key points. An in-depth interview was also conducted with the *Trinidad & Tobago Alliance for Sport and Physical Education* (TTASPE), which has 10 years of experience in coordinating, implementing, strengthening and advocating SFD programmes in the Caribbean. TTASPE is considered the leading SFD organisation in the Caribbean and works in many different capacities throughout the region. The interview with TTASPE addressed how it builds the capacity of the implementing organisations to monitor and evaluate programmes, challenges that they have observed and contextual insights into implementing SFD programmes in the Caribbean region. In this chapter, insights from the coordinators and TTASPE have been complemented with the authors' own experiences of managing programmes, conducting evaluations, and setting up and implementing M&E systems for SFD programmes in the Caribbean.

Results

During manual coding of the interviews, five main themes surfaced. First, coordinators reiterated the need for capacity building to close gaps in skills related to monitoring programmes and collecting, managing and analysing data. Second, strains on human resources inhibited programme coordinators from dedicating sufficient time to high-quality monitoring. Third, the Caribbean presents many geographic and contextual challenges for M&E programmes. Fourth, new technology is changing how organisations manage data – many coordinators have experienced some success with online data systems but need more training in how to utilise it. Finally, the process of monitoring and evaluating SFD programmes can be motivating and inspiring, especially when field personnel interact with participants to witness personal transformations, which then allows them to produce success stories about ground-level programme impact. Interestingly, although asked broad questions about M&E, coordinators focused almost exclusively on monitoring during interviews because the programmes have yet to undergo a formal evaluation process. The topic of outcome evaluation scarcely came up, apart from DPV's very basic nine-question pre-/post-questionnaires – which they refer to as 'evaluations' – administered by coaches themselves. Examples of process evaluation were also seldom mentioned, with the exception of interviewing participants to capture success stories.

Need for capacity building

DPV coordinators linked their M&E-related successes to having personnel who specialised in data management, as well as technical advisors who provided strategy and direction. A coordinator from DPV mentioned that they have an 'expert at the NGO' who is in-charge of handling pre-/post-questionnaires: 'After collecting the evaluations, we give them to him and he puts it in the database. It's similar to how *Grassroot Soccer* does it. They sent us their forms. We just enter the data.' This expert is also a 'good manager' who provides support and is a positive influence on the organisation because he is a 'guiding light' for the less experienced staff members. Another DPV coordinator noted that someone from *Grassroot Soccer* 'works internally with us and advises us in what we do'.

The *A Ganar* coordinators, meanwhile, acknowledged shortages in field personnel and did not feel that their staff and volunteers were sufficiently skilled in entering or reviewing data. The coordinator from Jamaica reported experiencing a 'human resource challenge', and suggested having a specific person in each country to focus on monitoring the implementing organisations. According to another coordinator from St. Vincent, a major weakness of the programme is that 'the implementing organisations are involved in other [tasks related to implementing the program], so there is no one dedicated just to tracking the youth.'

A Ganar's key performance indicator is the percentage of graduates who obtain employment, return to school or start their own business after the programme. The graduates are tracked for one year after the programme ends, but this task is extremely difficult in the transient island culture where migration is common. In order to overcome the logistical challenges of tracking youth, the St. Vincent coordinator has attempted to mobilise volunteers and others involved in the programme to assist with monitoring. The challenge with volunteers – according to this coordinator – is that they lack proper training and, owing to the unpaid nature of the work, turnover rates are high and data quality is inconsistent.

Coordinators reported that regional meetings played an important role in building their monitoring capacity by providing a forum to share best practices and solve problems together. The Jamaica *A Ganar* coordinator pointed to the need for more '[workshops] on M&E and what it requires to gather specific information. We have to find a way to get this training and guidance for what M&E means [in our country].' Building the capacity of local implementers could also come from monthly meetings that provide space to share basic practices and tools. The *A Ganar* coordinator from St. Kitts felt that organisations and individuals need more exposure to, and experience with, general M&E principles and skills:

> [Implementing organisations] have the capacity to look at what they are doing – look at the impact on the youth, look at their outcomes, what is happening at the end of the program ... [with more skills] they can adapt the program to make it more efficient.

The St. Vincent *A Ganar* coordinator noted that because of the close proximity, the organisations did meet regularly to 'share information and tweak the program'.

> Every so often, we bring the 'players' together to do assessments and we make recommendations. If we find a program needs to be beefed up in a particular area, we discuss it. [Convening the implementing organisations to] discuss the positives and negatives of how the program is working has been very useful.

The desire for national or regional SFD M&E forums cut across the interviews.

Lack of sufficient time

In addition to the lack of skilled personnel, the interviewees cited the time-consuming nature of data collection, entry and analysis as a challenge, and pointed to the need for more efficient tools – both to ease the burden on personnel and to provide more effective, real-time feedback to improve programme implementation. One coordinator from DPV talked about the time-consuming nature of conducting and analysing the pre-/post-questionnaires:

> We always make a pre-evaluation for the coaches and the participants. It gives us ideas about what they know about the project and information about their environment. If we have 60 coaches in Haiti and each coach has 20 participants, then we have to make a pre-evaluation of 1200. You should analyse them . ... We have to analyse to see what we need to focus on to see what knowledge we need to share.

Analysis of the questionnaires is important to DPV because it provides information on where to focus the programmes, but the workforce required for data entry is substantial and taxing for its personnel. *Partners of the Americas* faces similar challenges with its baseline survey, which captures data on participants' economic, educational, health and family situation. While the participants have indicated that they enjoy answering the questions because the staff show an interest in their lives, many *A Ganar* coordinators commented on the survey's excessive length, suggesting that it be made more concise. For example, *Grassroot Soccer*, which runs programmes similar to DPV in Africa (see programme background), changed its pre-/post-strategy as a result of the time-cost, cutting it down to only conducting pre-/post-questionnaires with 10–20 per cent of participants. As the programme has graduated over 80,000 youth in South Africa alone over the last three years, collecting, capturing and analysing pre-/post-data for all participants became impractical, and thus the organisation decided it could get similar value with much less time and cost by sampling participants (a technique that has been used in public health for decades; see Woolsey et al., 1954).

Another tedious aspect of monitoring the *A Ganar* programme is the time needed to verify the participant information provided by local implementing organisations, such as biographical data, career choices, internship placement sites and employment status information. All of the *A Ganar* coordinators experienced challenges in relying on the data provided, and had to exert extra effort through site visits, calls and e-mails in order to optimise accuracy and on time submission of reports to the *Partners of the Americas* headquarters. While some of the implementing organisations have significant capacity and experience with major donor reporting, the grassroots organisations required additional supervision and guidance. The *A Ganar* coordinator in Jamaica noted the difference between monitoring some of the more grassroots, inner-city groups versus the rural groups; they had to step in and assist with direct monitoring of those youth in the programmes with lower resources and staff capacity and spend much more time than expected on 'follow-ups and check-ups'.

The *A Ganar* coordinator from St. Kitts recalled that she had 'just started knocking on doors of the participants to get the data'. The weakness (or non-existence) in monitoring systems of local organisations is especially apparent when the development programme ends and staff are expected to maintain contact with past participants in order to provide updates on employment or educational engagement. The same coordinator from St. Kitts said she could not rely on the individual organisations' tracking systems and thus had to go beyond her job requirements to monitor these youth through personal visits and calls.

Difficult geographies

Long distances and dangerous neighbourhoods pose additional challenges to actively monitoring some project sites. Travel is time-consuming and the mountainous landscape of some islands, like St Vincent, makes conducting consistent and frequent monitoring visits difficult and expensive. Since the Caribbean experiences natural disasters all too frequently, programme implementation and M&E activities are often disrupted by hurricanes, heavy rains, floods and power outages. Sometimes, flooding destroys programme facilities or participants' homes. In Haiti, a DPV coordinator mentioned that 'when it rains, we can't always get the kids to [the facilities to] do the [questionnaires].' For example, one implementing group in Kingston, Jamaica was cut off from the city when major floods destroyed the main connecting bridge. As a result, the coordinator had to postpone monitoring visits until the bridge was restored.

Because of the geographical proximity of small islands to one another in the Caribbean, migration is a common occurrence and represents one of the reasons that some youth do not complete the *A Ganar* programme.

For instance, some youth leave the programme to take temporary or seasonal employment on neighbouring islands. Migration not only affects retention rates but also the ability of coordinators to monitor the programme. One coordinator mentioned: 'A lot of phone numbers that we have are not connected,' making it difficult to follow up with programme graduates. The high rate of migration, the transient nature of youth and their tendency to change cell phone carriers or numbers increased the amount of time spent following up with youth, and coordinators often have to track down participants through their families or friends.

In some countries, the heterogeneity of communities in which the programmes are delivered poses a challenge to monitoring processes. As an *A Ganar* coordinator in Jamaica reported: 'We are still largely learning about the different communities and organisations, because the communities are so dynamic and diverse … There's no one specific way to monitor a particular community group, because you have a division within different community groups.' In Jamaica particularly, political tensions have created violent animosity between neighbouring communities. These 'divisions' create logistical challenges for monitoring because it is difficult to convene individuals from different groups or choose a neutral meeting place. They also create many cultural and social differences, which affect and inform the monitoring system.

In addition to the distinctive physical geography of the Caribbean, the political landscape and volatile community dynamics can negatively impact the ability of coordinators to monitor programmes. In some socially and economically challenged neighbourhoods in Haiti, noted a DPV coordinator, public demonstrations have occasionally restricted access. This is also the case for some of the *A Ganar* countries, as elections and/or political demonstrations often disrupt programme activities because roadways are blocked or violence prevents participants or facilitators from leaving their homes. In the predominantly Catholic DR, the DPV programme's HIV prevention focus has been occasionally met with resistance by religious leaders who feel that youth should not be talking about sex.

Monitoring the inner-city neighbourhoods of Kingston, Jamaica, such as Spanish Town and Whitfield Town, is very challenging because of the violence associated with local gangs. The Jamaican coordinator cannot always drive his own vehicle because of safety concerns, and thus has to arrange for private transportation in order to enter certain areas. When violence escalates, something that happens too often and unexpectedly, problem areas are impossible for outsiders to enter. Such considerations add cost and danger to the task of monitoring local organisations in Kingston, many of which require extra support due to their lack of experience in managing major donor-funded programmes and their struggles with limited safety, capacity, training and personnel.

Technology and online monitoring systems

The *A Ganar* Jamaica Coordinator pointed to the need for a 'general tool to work across different community groups' in order to monitor programme progress. It is important to note that both DPV and *A Ganar* use an online monitoring system on the Salesforce platform (a powerful online database platform that is used by hundreds of thousands of companies and organisations worldwide and offers free licenses to nonprofit organisations), allowing information on the local programmes to be entered into MS Excel and uploaded into a global database. Using Salesforce has benefited both organisations by facilitating more effective and efficient feedback loops for internal improvement and better reporting and accountability for donors. However, the system has also created the need for additional skills training, and relies on technology in a region where technology access and capacity are inconsistent. As a result, the systems have largely relied on Microsoft Excel templates that are uploaded to Salesforce. Both the power and the challenge of using online technology for programme monitoring were apparent in the interviews.

Passion for and commitment to results

A common thread across programmes was that coordinators care deeply about the impact of their work. When M&E data demonstrate the impact of the programme and the personal transformation that youth undergo, coordinators feel motivated to do their work even when human resources and time are strained.

All the coordinators interviewed expressed an interest in generating more success stories. While the quantitative data from DPV pre-/ post-questionnaires allowed them to 'see the change generated in the participant', the success stories and testimonials that they collected to complement this data provided another level of depth with regard to the programme's impact. According to an *A Ganar* coordinator from St. Vincent, success stories are the most important pieces of information to collect because they can see participants' life changes. In addition to communicating these stories externally, coordinators enjoyed this part of their job as 'the most gratifying'. The coordinator from St. Vincent mentioned that, although his work is paid for, he did not participate predominantly for the money, for 'the main reward is the change…when the participants succeed in life – that is the main reward. The transition you see [from] day one, and the transition that occurs by graduation.' We conclude that in situations with thinly stretched human resources, where coordinators are often going above and beyond the expectations of their job, it is important to recognise the inspirational role of participant success stories.

Discussion and recommendations

Upon reflection, our findings on the perceptions of SFD programme managers in the Caribbean were largely consistent with M&E challenges identified by other researchers (see Coalter, 2009; Levermore, 2011) as well as experiences of M&E activities expressed by European SFD organisations in the Network for Sport and Development, namely, the lack of sufficient time, resources and capacity (NSD, 2009). Interestingly, our interviewees were aware of the importance of ongoing assessments, and they articulated an overwhelming need for capacity strengthening in monitoring SFD programmes; for developing more efficient staffing structures and systems; for overcoming geographic and technological barriers and for providing forums for field staff to share their passions and best practices.

With quick rollout due to donor pressure, *A Ganar* – like many organisations – has not had enough opportunity to develop internal capacity for effective monitoring. Many organisations such as *A Ganar* are grass-root bodies with significant community respect and clout but low capacity for managing major donor funds. As such, they have little to no experience with the reports and accountability requirements of aid agencies. Others may have sufficient skills but lack the time and necessary human resources to deliver the high-quality, timely data expected by many donors. Although these challenges may lead us to assume a solution based on further preparation and training, organising successful workshops has been difficult because of the wide variance in skill levels among the implementing organisations. Although some have very strong capacity in monitoring and implementing, and could in fact benefit from more advanced workshop content, others need to build basic skills. With limited budgets for capacity building and workshops, it is challenging to target workshops that meet the needs of all implementing organisations.

In addition to further training and capacity building workshops, programmes such as *A Ganar* must carefully analyse staffing and organisational structure to ensure that human resources are being utilised efficiently – at both headquarters level and ground level. In particular, specialists or clerks should handle data entry, as with DPV, so that coordinators spend more time managing local organisations and creating effective feedback loops. With a powerful online data system, *A Ganar* may learn and benefit from the data that are already collected – provided it is timely and valid – in order to improve programme implementation and impact. As no formal outcome evaluation has yet taken place for *A Ganar* in the Caribbean, this represents another important step for the organisation in order to better understand its programme strengths, weaknesses and overall effectiveness.

The lack of emphasis placed on outcome evaluation in the interviews suggests that monitoring outputs and reporting to funders on time is prioritised over objectively assessing effectiveness or processes. Similar issues were previously identified by Coalter (2007) and Mavrotas (2010); our research confirms a lack of awareness, understanding and/or interest in outcome evaluations as none of the interviewees mentioned publishing or sharing results or M&E data beyond their organisation and funders. The lack of outcome evaluation, of disseminating information and of a suitable 'research culture' (TTASPE, 2012) may partly explain the pervading tendency to conflate M&E.

In order to improve M&E for SFD organisations in the Caribbean, we offer six recommendations:

1. Carefully review staff responsibilities related to monitoring, ensuring that there are sufficient and appropriate human resources dedicated to each task, particularly data entry. In other words, middle managers should not spend time entering or cleaning data; instead organisations should have entry-level staff handling these basic tasks. This has implications for budgeting and programme design – organisations should not expect programme managers to bear the full M&E burden. Given the opportunity cost of programme managers' time, hiring part-time entry-level staff to enter, clean and manage data is a smart investment.

2. Invest in building the capacity of local coordinators and implementers responsible for handling data. Efforts should focus on specific monitoring skills, including quantitative data collection techniques, processes for data entry, management, analysis and reporting and qualitative data collection techniques including focus group discussions and in-depth interviews. Depending on the data systems used, more advanced and in-depth training may be required.

Capacity building should ideally take place both within organisations, and regionally across organisations through in-person and online workshops. As this may have financial implications, organisations should consider budgeting for such capacity building initiatives when writing grant proposals or designing programmes. If budget is not available, organisations might consider reaching out to peer organisations to share best practices informally or seeking low- or no-cost online resources, such as webinars.

3. Create feedback loops. When systems are set up to only provide one-way data flows from the field to the headquarters to the funder, staff and volunteers may feel burdened and become demotivated by data entry and management tasks. Data quality may suffer if information systems do not provide staff at all levels with relevant, timely feedback. Online systems, such as those used by *A Ganar* and DPV, can improve efficiency of data collection, automate analysis and reporting and ease the burden on human resources. More importantly, they can create data feedback loops to local and international staff, which not only play an important role for transparency, accountability and results-based management, but also motivate staff and volunteers by showing them the impact of their work.

4. Collect only purposeful data. With more data collection comes more time, work and strain on programme managers. Organisations should put plans in place for exactly what they intend to do with M&E data before they design tools and certainly before they begin data collection. In the beginning stages of a project, managers should be able to answer questions such as: What two or three key performance indicators (KPIs) will be monitored? Who will receive feedback on progress against these KPIs and how often? What is *truly* necessary to know about participants? If programmes are large enough, sampling can cut down on the time-consuming nature of surveys and questionnaires while still providing meaningful and representative outcome data.

5. Seek funding and research partners to conduct rigorous outcome evaluations, such as the DPV quasi-experimental study (Kaufman et al., 2012a), the ongoing *Grassroot Soccer* RCTs in South Africa and Zimbabwe (Kaufman et al., 2012b; *Grassroot Soccer,* 2012) and the aforementioned *A Ganar* Central America RCT. In order to conduct these evaluations, as Cronin (2011) has previously suggested, organisations should consider collaborating with development economists, epidemiologists, sociologists or researchers from other development-related fields with traditionally strong evaluation backgrounds, rather

than reinventing the wheel. Where possible evaluations should mix quantitative and qualitative methods, ideally involving a control or comparison group, taking steps to minimise selection and information bias and controlling for confounding variables in analyses (see Nutbeam and Baumann, 2006; CDC, 1999 for considerations in evaluation study design). RCTs are seen by many as the 'Gold Standard' in intervention evaluation (Barahona, 2010; IES, 2003), but have been criticised by others as too expensive, time-consuming and/or complex (Clay, 2010). Indeed, RCTs yield a powerful level of evidence that most non-randomised evaluations lack, but are not always appropriate, affordable or logistically feasible. Practitioners should consult with research partners to determine an appropriate evaluation design, with the aim not of proving their programme's effectiveness but of objectively assessing it.

6. Collect and share success stories, but do not rely solely on this as an M&E approach. Individual stories play a valuable role in capturing and communicating programmatic successes (NSD, 2009), as well as inspiring staff, volunteers and donors. Success stories were previously cited as a common M&E approach by NSD organisations; 'None of the organisations, however, gathered documentation in a systematic way that can verify and demonstrate long-term impact of their projects' (NSD, 2009: 5). Indeed, case studies – whether positive, negative or neutral – present only the tip of the programmatic iceberg and thus must be substantiated with evidence of effectiveness (from rigorous evaluation) and reach (from valid – ideally auditable – monitoring data).

Finally, we would like to acknowledge that our study presented here has a number of important limitations. First, it drew from a small sample size of only six practitioners and two programmes, so it is not simply generalisable to SFD programmes across the Caribbean. Additionally, the study only looked at one point in time, limiting our ability to draw conclusions about how perceptions change over time due to varying factors. We are committed to continue our work in the SFD space and encourage others to do the same, with an attempt to minimise such limitations in the future.

With widespread enthusiasm for sport and substantial need for effective economic, educational and health promotion/development programmes, the Caribbean – like much of sub-Saharan Africa, South Asia and Latin America – is a prime environment for SFD activity. In order for SFD programmes to play a meaningful and sustainable role in improving development outcomes in the region, practitioners and funders need to move from an M&E mindset of counting, storytelling and reporting to one focused on critically assessing effectiveness and processes, ensuring data quality and routinely feeding back performance data to staff, volunteers and other stakeholders. We believe that the earlier recommendations are important steps to achieving greater impact through SFD programmes in the Caribbean and beyond.

Acknowledgements

We would like to acknowledge the coordinators who participated in interviews for this chapter as well as staff at *Partners of the Americas* and *Grassroot Soccer* for their input.

References

AUSAID (2012). *Development through Sport*. Access online at: http://www.ausaid. gov.au/aidissues/sport/Pages/default.aspx

Barahona, C. (2010). *Randomised Control Trials for the Impact Evaluation of Development Initiatives: A Statistician's Point of View*. Institutional Learning and Change (accessed online 6 January 2013). http://www.cgiar-ilac.org/files /publications/working_papers/ILAC_WorkingPaper_No13_Randomised%20 Control%20Trials.pdf

Bishop, L. (2002). *First Steps in Monitoring and Evaluation*. Charity Evaluation Services, October 2002.

Cabal, M. (2010). *Evaluación Final del Proyecto: A Ganar-Vencer: Modelo de Amplificación de Perspectivas de Empleo por Medio del Fútbol*. June 2010.

Cameron, J. and Haanstra, A. (2008). Development made sexy. *Third World Quaterly*, 29(8), 1475–1489.

CARICOM (2003). *Regional Survey of Development through Sport Programmes Implemented at the Country Level*. http://www.caricom.org/jsp/community_ organs/regionalsurvey_sportsprogrammes.jsp?menu=cob

CDC (1999). *Framework for Program Evaluation in Public Health. Centres for Disease Control and Prevention*. Atlanta, GA (accessed online 31 December 2102). ftp: //ftp.cdc.gov/pub/Publications/mmwr/rr/rr4811.pdf

Clark, T.S., Friedrich, G.K., Ndlovu, M., Neilands, T.B. and McFarland, W. (2006). An Adolescent-Targeted HIV Prevention Project Using African Professional Soccer Players as Role Models and Educators in Bulawayo, Zimbabwe. *AIDS and Behavior*, 10(4 Suppl), S775–S783.

Clay, R. (2010). The Pitfalls of Randomized Controlled Trials. *American Psychological Association*, 41(8), 52.

Coalter, F. (2007). *A Wider Social Role for Sport: Who's Keeping the Score?* New York: Routledge (Taylor and Francis).

Coalter, F. (2008) *Sport-in-Development. A Monitoring and Evaluation Manual*. University of Sterling, UK Sport. Accessed online at http://assets.sportanddev. org/downloads/10__sport_in_development__a_monitoring_and_Evaluation_ manual.pdf

Coalter, F. (2009). Sport-in-Development: Accountability or Development? In Levermore and Beacom (eds), *Sport and International Development*. (Basingstoke: Palgrave Macmillan, 55–75.

Commonwealth Games (2012). *International Development through Sport: IDS in the Caribbean.* Accessed online at: http://www.commonwealthgames.ca/ids/what-we-do/ids-caribbean/ids-caribbean.html

Cronin Ó. (2011). Comic Relief Review. *Mapping Research on the Impact of Sport and Development Interventions.* Manchester: Comic Relief.

Darnell, S. (2012). Sport for Development a Peace: A Critical Sociology. *Globalizing Sport Studies.* Accessed online at: http://www.bloomsburyacademic.com/view/Sport-for-Development-and-Peace/book-ba-9781849665896.xml

Grassroot Soccer (2012). *Bill & Melinda Gates Foundation and Doris Duke Charitable Foundation Support Innovative Grassroot Soccer Trial in Zimbabwe.* Accessed online 31/12/2012. http://www.grassrootsoccer.org/2012/10/15/mcuts/

IES (2003). *Identifying and Implementing Educational Practices Supported By Rigorous Evidence: A User Friendly Guide.* Institute for Education Sciences, December 2003. Accessed online 31/12/2012: http://ies.ed.gov/ncee/pubs/evidence_based/randomized.asp

IWG SDP (2008). *Harnessing the Power of Sport for Development and Peace: Recommendations to Governments.* International Working Group for Sport for Development and Peace, Right to Play: Toronto. Accessed online at: http://www.un.org/wcm/webdav/site/sport/shared/sport/pdfs/SDP%20IWG/Final%20SDP%20IWG%20Report.pdf

JBA (2007). *Evaluation Brief: What's the Difference? Understanding Process and Outcome Evaluation.* Arlington, VA: James Bell Associates.

Kaufman, Z.A. (2011). *M&E for the 21st Century: Harnessing New Technology and Evaluating Impact.* Presentation at Beyond Sport Summit, December 2011: Cape Town.

Kaufman, Z.A., Welsch, R., Erickson, J., Craig, S., Adams, L. and Ross D.A. (2012a). Effectiveness of a Sports-Based HIV Prevention Intervention in the Dominican Republic: a Quasi-Experimental Study. *AIDS Care*, 24(3), 377–385.

Kaufman, Z.A., Braunschweig, E., DeCelles, J., Nkosi, Z., Delany-Moretlwe, S. and Ross, D.A. (2012b). *GOAL Trial: Pilot Results of a Sport-Based HIV Prevention Intervention to Inform a Cluster-Randomized Trial in South African Schools.* Poster at XIX International AIDS Conference: Washington DC.

Kaufman, Z.A., Spencer, T.S. and Ross, D.A. (2012). Effectiveness of Sport-Based HIV Prevention Interventions: A Systematic Review of the Evidence. *AIDS and Behavior*, October 2012. Epub online: http://www.ncbi.nlm.nih.gov/pubmed/23096999

Kusek, J. (2011). Assessing Country Readiness for Results-Based Monitoring and Evaluation to Support Results Informed Budgeting. World Bank, January 2011 (accessed online 31 December 2012). http://siteresources.worldbank.org/EXTGOVANTICORR/Resources/3035863–1285601351606/GETBrief_AssessingCountryReadinessM&E_Final.pdf

Lawton, M. (2009). *Welcome Mr Posh: David Beckham Arrives in Cape Town to Revive England's Fragile 2018 World Cup Bid. Daily Mail*: 4/12/2009 (accessed online 31 December 2012). http://www.dailymail.co.uk/sport/worldcup2010/article-1233070/Welcome-Mr-Posh-David-Beckham-arrives-Cape-Town-revive-Englands-fragile-2018-World-Cup-bid.html

Levermore, R. (2008). Sport in International Development: Time to Treat It Seriously? *Brown Journal of World Affairs*, 14(2), 55–66.

Levermore, R. (2011). Evaluating Sport-for-Development Approaches and Critical Issues. *Progress in Development Studies*, 11, 339–353.

Mavrotas, G. (2010). *Foreign Aid for Development: Issues, Challenges, and the New Agenda*. Oxford Scholarship Online, May 2010.

McCree, R. (2005). *The Exclusion of Sport from Caribbean Economic Development. University of the West Indies at St. Augustine*. Accessed online at www.sta.uwi. edu/salises/workshop/csme/paper/rmccree.pdf

Nutbeam D. and Bauman A. (2006). Key Stages, Methods and Types of Evaluation. In D. Nutbeam and A. Bauman (ed), *Evaluation in a Nutshell*. Sydney: McGraw-Hill.

Peacock-Villada, P., DeCelles, J. and Banda, P.S. (2007). Grassroot Soccer Resiliency Pilot Program: Building Resiliency through Sport-Based Education in Zambia and South Africa. *New Directions for Youth Development*, Winter 2007, 116, 141–154.

Superville, D. (2011). *Michelle Obama and Desmond Tutu Do Push-Ups In Cape Town*. Associated Press: 23/6/2011 (accessed online 31 December 2012). http://www.huffingtonpost.com/2011/06/23/michelle-obama-desmond-tutu-pushups_n_883558.html

UNICEF (2006). *Monitoring and Evaluation for Sport-Based Programming for Development: Sport Recreation and Play*. Workshop Report, UNICEF, New York.

TTASPE (2012). Personal interview on 10 August 2012.

Woolsey, T.D., Cochran, W.G., Mainland, D., Martin, M.P., Moore Jr., F.E. and Patton, R.E. (1954). *American Journal of Public Health and the Nations Health*, 44 (6), 719–740.

11
Soldados Nunca Mais: Child Soldiers, Football and Social Change in Rio de Janeiro's Favelas

Elizabeth Kath and Nanko G. van Buuren

Introduction

This chapter evaluates the work of The Brazilian Institute for Innovations in Social Health (IBISS), specifically its use of sport as a vehicle for health promotion and building urban peace among youth in Rio de Janeiro. It focuses especially upon IBISS's *Soldados Nunca Mais* programme, which uses football games with a twofold aim: to break down social prejudices and to encourage child soldiers[1] to leave the drug trade. During the ten years since *Soldados Nunca Mais* was established, it has successfully supported 3,432 children to leave the drug trade, using a range of strategies among which are initiatives involving soccer. This chapter outlines the programme's successes and limitations in relation to sport, including specific strategies it has used. It also provides a general reflection upon the role of sport for social development based on these experiences. It will be shown that in IBISS's experience, football games alone do not have the power to build peace or momentous positive transformations to the lives of young people. The potential of football relies rather on the efforts of committed development workers and their ability to identify and innovate around the informal social spaces that football opens.

Methodologically, this chapter is underpinned by qualitative testimony on the part of Nanko G. van Buuren, director of IBISS, and Elizabeth Kath, a research fellow with RMIT University, Melbourne, Australia. This included a number of in depth face-to-face interviews conducted in Rio de Janeiro during periods Kath spent visiting IBISS along with subsequent follow-up conversations via e-mail correspondence. It sets out to trace the story of IBISS from the perspective of a sport-for-development practitioner with the assistance of an academic versed in Latin American Studies. This is an example of what Stake (1995) has labelled an intrinsic case study; the characteristics of an agent's context drive the research instead of the agent seeking out a context in which to investigate certain characteristics. The case is, in short, uniquely and intrinsically valuable; there is no effort nor indeed need to generalise from it (Flyvberg, 2006). A limitation of this chapter is, therefore, the reliance on expert testimony from van Buuren, although the IBISS website provides supplementary evidence in the form of documents, newsletters, photos and videos.[2] That said, some scholars put considerable weight, particularly in exploratory research, on 'the authority of the experiencer' to inform the research agent (Smith, 2005: 138). Indeed, as Campbell (1998) has put it, experience itself is a form of data that researchers can gather via interviews and endeavour to make sense of. A combination of experience and expertise is, therefore, fertile ground for qualitative interviewing (Bogner et al., 2009). This chapter is, nonetheless, a first step in terms of investigating the operation of IBISS in the favelas of Rio. Further research will be needed to investigate the many and varied experiences of those involved with the programme and challenges that the programme still faces.

The context of Rio de Janeiro

Rio de Janeiro is a paradoxical and deeply divided city. Lining its spectacular Atlantic coastlines are miles of South America's most expensive real estate; new, modern apartments that house the city's economic elite and provide luxury accommodation for tourists who flock to the city for its vibrancy, natural beauty and carnival celebrations. Clearly visible from these affluent surroundings are hillsides of impoverished shantytowns or favelas, many more of which extend across the city's North Zone (around five hundred *favelas* in total), which are home to around 40 per cent of the city's six million people (IBGE, 2012). The close geographic proximity of these contrasting worlds gives a deceiving impression that they share the same city – yet arguably more than one Rio de Janeiro exists. As one journalist has put it, 'The favelas, Rio's guilty conscience … overlook paradise but never partake … The two Rio's are on a collision course' (Thompson, 2010). It is not unusual for citizens of Rio de Janeiro (*Cariocas*) who grew up in its wealthy zones to have never set foot in a favela in their lifetime. Favelas lack basic infrastructure and services including access to (quality) health care, education and other public services[3]; they are stigmatised by intense stereotypes and prejudices, which, beyond their deep psychological impact, also have very tangible consequences, limiting opportunities for further education, vocational training, jobs and access to credit or bank loans.[4] This results from both the active stigmatisation and exclusion from opportunities, and sometimes favelados (a discriminating term for favela residents) internalise this stigmatisation wherein it becomes a self-fulfilling prophecy (*I can't get a job; why would anybody employ me if I live here?*) (Kath/van Buuren interviews, 2012-2013).

While favelas have often been depicted as marginalised communities, segregated from mainstream society, this is not entirely accurate. As Janice Perlman observes in her landmark work on marginality in Rio de Janeiro, favela residents are in fact tightly integrated into mainstream society in terms of their contributions to it, but in return are excluded from its benefits:

> Favelados or urban squatters are not *marginal* but *integrated* into the society, albeit in a manner detrimental to their own interests. They are not separate from or on the margin of the system, but are tightly bound into it in a severely radically asymmetrical form. They contribute their hard work, their high hopes, and their loyalties, but they do not benefit from the goods and the services of the system ... favela dwellers are *not economically and politically marginal but exploited and repressed, not socially and culturally marginal but stigmatized and excluded from a closed social system.* (Perlman, 1975: 131)

The state's formal role in the provision of governance and services in favela communities has historically been negligible, and so informal governance systems have filled its space. Three major illicit drug cartels control many of the city's favelas, administering their own internal system of law and governance, a situation that has been described in such terms as the 'state inside the state' or the 'shadow city' (Neuwirth, 2006; Kath/van Buuren interviews, 2012–2013). Those who live in the cartel-controlled zones identify personally with the informal system, even if they themselves are not directly involved with the drug trade, referring to themselves in such terms as *I am red command*, or *I am third command*. Rivalry between cartels and the cycle of attempts by the formal state to assert its control has ravaged favela communities with violence and fear.

In recent years, within the framework of preparing a 'safe and unarmed Rio' for the FIFA World Football Championship 2014 and the Olympic Games in 2016, the Government has elaborated a new policy to 'pacify' favelas near to the stadiums, tourist areas and highways (Barrionuevo,

2010; Zibechi, 2010). Pacification means that Police (sometimes with the help of the Army) occupy a favela 24 hours per day. The initial occupation of a favela has usually provoked a situation of extreme violence, with many victims, not only among drug soldiers and police but also among innocent favela residents who can be caught in the crossfire or hit by stray bullets (Alves and Evanson, 2011).

After the initial occupation of a favela, the Government installs UPP units (*Unidade de Policia Pacificadora*/ Pacifying Police Units) to carry out community policing in an attempt to fill the vacuum of authority and rule left after traffickers are driven out of the favelas. The responsibility of these units is to ensure that the favela remains clean of weapons and organised crime. By late 2012, around 30 favelas had been pacified under this process (Secretaria de Estado de Segurança, 2012). One of the results of this state-sanctioned process is that drug lords and drug soldiers from occupied favelas shifted territory and settled in other favela areas belonging to the same cartel. As a result, some of these favelas have become overloaded with drug lords and soldiers and turned into criminal fortresses with intensified concentrations of organised crime (Kath/van Buuren interviews, 2012–2013). This is the Rio de Janeiro in which IBISS works.

IBISS's work in Rio de Janeiro

The IBISS was established in 1989. It was created soon after van Buuren first travelled from his home country of the Netherlands to Rio de Janeiro on a mission for European funding agencies, which focused on an impact assessment of foreign aid for work with street children. His key findings were that street workers were well intentioned and had established good relationships with the street children, but had few ideas about how to support these young people and improve their social situation. Street workers regularly visited children on the streets and offered them food and blankets, but ultimately the children stayed on the streets. One of van Buuren's recommendations to the funding agencies was to set up a training centre for street workers where they could learn how to support and strengthen the children in their struggle to leave the streets and integrate into wider society. Upon his return to the Netherlands, van Buuren's employers asked him to live in Brazil for two years to establish such a training centre. In his first 18 months in Rio, van Buuren met many inspiring young street workers with interesting and innovative ideas. Yet, whenever he asked them why they did not implement these ideas, the usual response was that they were constrained by either the political or religious agendas of their Government- or Church-linked organisations. From here IBISS was born. Along with a group of 12 young street workers, van Buuren founded the organisation as a way to provide them the space and opportunities with which to experiment and produce innovative ideas. Van Buuren himself fell in love with Brazil and the people he met, and thus relocated from the Netherlands, along with his wife, to dedicate himself to the new organisation. In the early years, the group's focus was mainly on health, including AIDS/ STD prevention on the streets among street children and sex workers, as well as early detection of illnesses by community health workers.

Today, IBISS is a well-established organisation working in dozens of favela communities around Rio de Janeiro. It employs more than 300 people, over 80 per cent of whom grew up and still live in the favelas in which the organisation works. In addition to these paid employees, around ten international volunteers are employed each year. IBISS's core goal is to help address socio-economic inequality and violence and to support and empower disadvantaged groups to advocate for their human rights. In doing so, it is committed to ongoing innovation and an approach that draws principles from a number conceptual frameworks, including community engagement, reconciliation and social inclusion, in addition to reflection upon its own experiences over time. Its work focuses on communities that are socially excluded and rife with violence and health crises. It also works with specific target groups including people who are homeless, *catadores* (those who survive by collecting and reselling recyclable waste) and child soldiers – young people who are recruited to work in the drug trade. IBISS runs its programmes independently of church and government. In some cases, it receives project-based funding from government, but is autonomous in the design and implementation of projects. In these cases, the funding received comes from the Federal Government through the Ministry of Justice (Human Rights Department) and the Ministry of Health (Health Fund). In order to maintain its *Utilidade Pública Federal* status,[5] IBISS is required to report its results and impacts to these Ministries. It is also subject to a detailed audit each year.

Soldados Nunca Mais (soldiers never more)

Approximately eight-and-a-half thousand young people – some as young as eight years old – are working as child soldiers in Rio de Janeiro's drug wars (IBISS, 2012). Most children who enter the drug trade do so either

Figure 11.1   Child soldier

Notes: The two boys pictured spent part of their lives working as child soldiers in Rio de Janeiro. Both lost their lives. This article is dedicated to these boys, and every young person who has lost life in this way; and to the hope for a future where this will never again happen. Photo: Nanko G. van Buuren.

as a result of desperate poverty and/or other forms of social exclusion. Amid these very vulnerable circumstances, children can turn to the drug trade for money, or in an attempt to gain social status, identity and kinship where they otherwise have none. The outcomes of this violent and dangerous form of child labour are usually devastating; IBISS's mapping estimates that more than 80 per cent of child soldiers do not live past their twenty-first birthday (for further statistics, see also Dowdney, 2003; Jacobo Waiselsz, 2012).

The war in Rio de Janeiro

In 2010, the images of the 'War in Rio de Janeiro' shocked the world. The Police and the Army were mobilised for an intense battle against the drug mafia in Rio de Janeiro's favelas as part of the new pacification process. Dozens of 'soldados' (child soldiers recruited by the drug mafia) died, and many innocent slum inhabitants were hit by stray bullets. As a result of this violent war, over 300 'soldados' contacted IBISS saying that they wanted to leave the drug trade. Although Brazil is not typically considered a country at war, IBISS's experience has been of another reality. Many inhabitants of favelas in Rio de Janeiro live, or better said, have to survive, in a constant state of war with many casualties. Large numbers of children and adolescents involved in the drug trade and organised crime are killed in confrontation with police or rival gangs.

The phenomenon 'soldado'

Many children and adolescents are working as 'soldados' (soldiers) in the drug business. These soldados are recruited by the *Firma* (the mafia). Heavily armed with weapons such as AK-47s and AR-15s, they have to defend the 'bocas de fumo' (laboratories and selling points) against police raids and attacks from rival gangs.

From 2010, IBISS began mapping an inventory of child labour exploitation by the drug mafia. The number of soldados defending the 'bocas de fumo' was counted and the result was alarming:

• Inventoried slums	232
• Number of drug selling points	348
• Number of children and young people involved in drug trafficking, from 8 to 18 years	14,517
• Number of involved boys	11,961
• Number of involved girls	2,556
• Number of 'soldiers'	8,442
• Number of soldiers younger than 12 years	386
• Number of unarmed persons	6,075
• Number of unarmed persons younger than 12 years	919

The figures highlight that almost 8,500 children are soldiers in the drug wars in Rio de Janeiro and that more than 14,500 children and adolescents are involved in the drug trade (not only as soldiers but also as unarmed watchers, transporters, etc.).

The work of *Soldados Nunca Mais*

The main goal of IBISS's *Soldados Nunca Mais* programme is to improve the lives of child soldiers, and especially to encourage and support them to leave the drug trade. IBISS uses a wide range of initiatives towards this goal, including the following:

- street corner work with attractive activities (including football games) to reach out to soldados,

- awareness talks,
- negotiating with drug lords,
- negotiating 'conditional discharge' with the Public Prosecutor,
- trauma therapies and coping strategies,
- counselling on returning to school,
- vocational training,
- reference to the labour market,
- developing alternative jobs.

In 2010, as a result of this programme, 342 soldados left the drugs business. Since the start of the programme in 2005, over 3,400 soldados were convinced and enabled by a team of eight ex-soldados and seven ex-drug bosses to choose a new life. In the cases of very young boys and girls, this includes referral back to school (IBISS has a process for registering whether children participating in its football games are attending school). Older adolescents are referred to vocational training and the labour market. IBISS has a specific development project linked to the soldados programme, which focuses on this re-integration process. As part of this programme, a number of soldados are given work opportunities as trainees with IBISS. The rate of supporting young people to leave the drug trade and socially reintegrate not only has exceeded IBISS's initial expectations, but also presents a mixed blessing as IBISS is now faced with the task of ensuring their workers do not fall back into the trade. On the whole, the organisation's experience is that ex-soldados who are given a second chance at life go on to be highly committed and successful in both staying out of the drug trade and in their lives generally. While the programme uses all of the strategies outlined earlier, this chapter focuses on IBISS's use of sport, namely, football games, in its work with child soldiers.

The use of football games

Football is frequently described as a national obsession in Brazil; the often repeated narrative of the child born in a favela who dreams of becoming a football star is so well known that it has become entrenched in global stereotypes of the country.[6] The intense popular enthusiasm for the game extends across the deep socio-economic chasm of Brazilian society, and thus the football pitch may be one of the few spaces in which possibilities exist for Brazilians from different worlds to meet on equal footing. IBISS began to work with football as part of its child soldier programme for multiple reasons, not least because most young people, especially boys, love and will almost always show up for a game. Football matches, for this reason, presented a source and a vehicle for social development work (see Schulenkorf, 2010a). In other words, it was a blessing in the early days for IBISS health workers faced with the challenge of trying to make contact with young soldiers who were not in school and otherwise difficult to locate. The games became central to the organisation's health promotion work: it was here where large groups of children and teenagers gathered and where it was therefore possible to distribute basic health education messages, including talks on STD transmission and how to detect the early signs of serious health issues, such as leprosy and tuberculosis.

Over time, IBISS found new ways of working with and around the football games. Participation in football required a boy to first put down his gun – no weapons were allowed on the field. A precondition for playing on the team was regular school attendance. A practice was developed around 'after game evaluation circles'. Modelled on a strategy used by the national football team, evaluation circles are essentially a discussion involving the players and coach after a game to reflect upon how the team's performance on the field could be improved. IBISS appropriated the idea as a way to open a space for discussion among the young players, beginning with a reflection upon sporting performance on the field but often opening into a space for talking about and reflecting upon life off the field. The following tract provides a 'thick description' of how these conversations can unfold; using a case study approach, it relays the lived experience of one child soldier who participated in IBISS's football programme.

Juliano

Juliano[7] lived through a great deal of pain as a child, especially because his mother suffered from drug addiction. One day Juliano's mother was given a package of drugs to sell. When she used the drugs herself rather than selling them, the drug boss shot her dead. Juliano was only 14 years old. Soon after losing his mother, Juliano took up a gun and joined the drug trade, a decision which was a mystery to all who witnessed it. On occasion, Juliano, with his rifle over his shoulder, would walk past the football games IBISS was holding in the favela. The coach always encouraged him to put down his gun and come and play, but he would always shake his head and keep walking. It so happened one day that police stormed into the favela on one of their raids, and an intense shootout ensued between police and the traffickers. Amid the turmoil, the drug boss was arrested, taken away and imprisoned. The day after this shootout, Juliano put down his gun and quit the drug trade. He gave no explanation to anybody.

Onlookers found this sudden decision of Juliano's as baffling as his initial decision to take up arms.

From this point, Juliano began to participate in the IBISS football games. Typically, after each game, the previously described evaluation circle was held, a discussion in which the boys talked about any issues related to the preceding game, and what improvements can be made. The coach often guides these conversations to include discussions of the challenges the boys might be facing in life. On this particular occasion, a boy had behaved violently towards a fellow player during a game, and the discussion after the game led to the question of what strategies the boys could adopt to deal with frustration and trauma. It was then that the usually silent Juliano spoke up.

'I'll tell you a strategy I used for dealing with trauma. You know my mother died, right?'

Others in the group nodded

'When the drug boss shot my mother, I came up with a plan. I took up a gun and started working for him. My plan was that one day when there was a confrontation with police, I would stand behind the drug boss and pretend to be shooting the police, but I would shoot him in the back instead.'

Some days after this discussion took place, Juliano told IBISS staff members that some of his pain had lifted, and that his intense feelings of revenge had gone. Maybe it was the simple fact of being able to talk about what had been in his head that provided some relief (Kath/ van Buuren interviews, 2012–2013). Juliano's traumatic experiences are, it must be said, unlikely to be completely 'resolved' by participation in a football and social development programme. However, IBISS at least provided an environment in which he felt welcome and where he could share his story.

Asphalt and Favela Bridge-building: sport as a vehicle for social change

More recently, the IBISS football games have become the sites of bold initiatives intended to begin chipping away at some of Rio's deeply entrenched social barriers. Perhaps surprisingly, IBISS stages football games in favelas with the participation of visiting teams from wealthy zones of Rio (often referred to as the 'asphalt/*asphalto*'[8] by favela residents). For many of the visiting players, this provides a first time experience of entering a favela, despite living only a few hundred metres or a few kilometres away. It also provides a unique space in which young people from favelas and the 'asphalt' might meet as fellow players, and on more equal terms than might ever be possible elsewhere. For the players visiting the favela for the first time, one of the common experiences is of surprise at how well-organised favela communities can be, as opposed to common stereotypes of favelas as places of mayhem and chaos. After these football matches, some of the participants from the 'asphalt' stay in contact with the young people they met in the favelas. In the experience of IBISS, these young people appear to let go of some of the stereotypes of one another – having come face to face with the 'other', the asphalt participants are less likely to view the favela boys as dangerous criminals, while the favela residents often change their perceptions of young people from the asphalt as being arrogant playboys. IBISS has observed other outcomes of these games: some participants from favelas have been invited to play in asphalt communities, and several of the favela youth were even encouraged to attend schools in the asphalt areas. In the latter case, IBISS has noticed, the asphalt participants defended the access of the favela youth to the schools and helped to prevent them from being stigmatised by other students (Kath/van Buuren interviews, 2012–2013).

Organising games between favela and asphalt teams is not a simple process. From the outset, IBISS staff were challenged with intense

Figure 11.2   Favela painting

prejudice and social stigma towards favela players. The directors of football fields in asphalt areas are often the first to object to the initiative. Many do not like the idea of favela kids using their accommodation due to negative preconceptions that favela kids are inherently violent or will steal. Directors also worry about facing criticism from asphalt children's parents. Parents, too, can be afraid of the reputations of favelas as violent, dangerous places and will often forbid their children from going there to play a game. For IBISS, overcoming this kind of resistance has been a delicate process. The most effective approach has been aimed at integrating football directors and parents into the projects. IBISS begins by inviting wary football field directors, trainers and parents from asphalt areas to assist with the organisation of a game at a club where favela players visit and play on an asphalt football field (a club that already has a good working relationship with IBISS). By witnessing another asphalt community embracing the idea, and experiencing the exchange first hand, many of the directors, trainers and parents warm up to the idea of an intergroup exchange (Kath/van Buuren interviews, 2012–2013).

To an outside observer, it may not be immediately obvious either why a young person living in a privileged asphalt community would want to play football in a favela. Usually the interest emerges from intrigue, curiosity or challenge. Samba and football are the two arenas where favela residents are revered and often seen to be superior to those living on the asphalt. Similarities can be drawn between those from the asphalt who visit and join samba schools in favelas and those who visit favelas to play football; just as many of the greatest *sambistas* come from favelas, so too do many great football stars of Brazil. While, on the one hand, asphalt teams can be fearful of playing against favela teams, they are also aware of the high quality of players in favelas and are drawn to the challenge. IBISS has observed that the games between favela and asphalt teams also appear to have a positive effect on the self-esteem of the players from favelas, and on mitigating the self-discriminating attitudes that are commonplace. For instance, after playing competitively against asphalt teams and often winning, some 'favelados' express hopes or perceive possibilities that they might also be able to compete in other areas of life. Of course, life beyond the football pitch is far more complex and challenging than within a field of play in which equal opportunities are, in many ways, out of step with everything else in the lives of 'favelados'. Nevertheless, the external discrimination people who live in favelas suffer can often reproduce itself in people's perceptions of themselves and of their life possibilities, thereby reinforcing social exclusion. In this sense, the new ways of thinking the games can encourage are potentially powerful and transformative (Kath/van Buuren interviews, 2012–2013).

Intra-favela cartels

Some of the greatest challenges for youth are, of course, within the favelas themselves. In recognition of that complexity, IBISS has organised an ongoing series of intra-favela football matches with the goal of taking steps towards building urban peace among players by helping to address deep prejudices and hostilities between favela zones controlled by warring drug cartels. Such is the extent of segregation between favela communities controlled by enemy cartels that little movement or association between these populations is normally tolerated. Young people living in these opposing zones would never, under everyday circumstances, have the opportunity to play football together, or spend time together in any recreational or non-confrontational setting. The following interview excerpt from Dowdney's (2003: 157) case study, *Children of the Drug Trade*, provides a sense of the alienation that can develop between young soldiers from warring cartel zones. Describing the 'kill-or-be-killed' environment in which child soldiers survive, Dowdney found that some child soldiers were conditioned to believe killing to be justified where the victim was 'the enemy'. This is what 12-year-old Fogueteiro had to say:

> T: *We have to kill the police and the Terceiro Comando (Third Command) so that [people from the] Terceiro Comando die.*
> I: *Do you think it's wrong to kill people?*
> T: *Not if they're Terceiro Comando. Then we have to kill them.*[9]

In 2011, IBISS organised a game between teams of boys from a Third Command area and a Red Command area. The game, held on neutral territory, was the first of its kind and a series of similar games have since followed. To date, the games have been accompanied by a carefully designed and facilitated process. First, the facilitator/coach holds a group discussion with each team separately. During this discussion, the players (mostly around the age of 14) are asked questions, such as *What are five reasons why you are afraid to play the other team?* and *What are five reasons why the other team should be afraid to play against you? How do you think the other team 'sees' you?* These questions typically give rise to an outpouring of stereotypes and prejudices regarding the opposing team. The two teams later come together at the marked time to play each other, and through that process meet one another. As part of the game, various strategies are used to allow the boys to reflect upon their own identity and that of 'the other'. For example, those living in the 'Third Command' zone are usually forbidden from wearing red shirts in their favela. When IBISS holds its matches, it often allocates red t-shirts to the boys from the Third Command zones; in other words, they wear the clothes of 'the other' during the game, allowing a confrontation of some of the boys' most fundamental prejudices. During the breaks, the coaches encourage teams to engage and converse with one another. This can include raising the same questions that were asked in the pre-game conversations, or asking specific questions for discussion, such as why one group has a prejudice against the colour red. While sometimes reluctant at first to openly discuss their prejudices in front of the other team, the boys eventually begin to talk – usually each group has great curiosity regarding the opposing team, including wanting to find out what the other group's answers had been to the pre-game discussions (*Had they been correct in their preconceptions about the other group? And what did the other group say about them?*). Despite this curiosity, they are often initially reticent and sometimes ashamed about openly admitting their prejudices to the opposing players. After the game, a barbeque is usually held where the two teams spend some hours together and are given further opportunity to talk among themselves in a less formal environment. It is usually then that players are more likely to drop some of their prior reservations. Typically during the barbeque, players start joking, with many seeing absurdity in their previously held prejudices. Often, they set times to play each other on neutral territory again in the future (the games are facilitated by IBISS coaches) (Kath/van Buuren interviews, 2012–2013).

Although these games were first held on neutral territory, more recently IBISS has ventured further and started to hold games on the home field inside cartel zones. These games are a bold move because they often produce feelings of trepidation, excitement and nervousness among the players and their facilitators. Anecdotally, the observations of these games seem highly positive, with participants finishing the exercise with fewer negative ideas about the other and many expressing a sense that 'we were crazy'[10] for holding so many extreme prejudices and stereotypes about the other group (Kath/van Buuren interviews, 2012–2013).

As with games between favela and asphalt communities, these intra-favela, inter-cartel games are challenging to organise. The young players themselves from the different cartel teams – despite often harbouring intense fear of and hatred against one another – are nevertheless usually eager to participate in the games; the opportunity to win against another cartel is appealing. The teams also have some limited previous experience of playing against one another as part of the 'favela championships' held on neutral territory; the young players love football so much that they will usually do anything to make the games possible. On the other hand, greater effort is usually required to convince drug bosses to permit the game, especially if the game is to be held on cartel grounds. IBISS has so far negotiated by making assurances that the visiting players will not be permitted to walk through the favela and thus observe the surroundings, but instead will walk directly from the favela boundary to the football field, and return directly the same way after the post-game barbeque finishes.[11] As with all of IBISS's activities in favelas, communities (including drug lords, soldiers and presidents of resident associations) are consulted repeatedly throughout the planning process. This is vitally important to the success of projects, not least because it avoids last minute opposition and interruption (van Buuren/Kath interview 2012, 2013).

So far the discussion in this chapter has focused on male football teams; it is not immediately obvious to an outside observer how girls fit into IBISS's sport programmes. Football is a male-dominated sport and teams do not typically mix male and female players, which raises some challenges in terms of ensuring that girls are incorporated. This is no trivial consideration, particularly given that a significant proportion of Rio's child soldiers are female. IBISS's figures indicate that 17.6 per cent of children and adolescents involved in the drug mafia are girls, and of those who left the drug trade as part of IBISS's programmes, almost 20 per cent are girls. IBISS does have female football and volleyball teams, and girls are also involved in the offside[12] activities of the various football schools. However, it has not yet been possible to include girls in the inter-cartel games, mainly due to resistance from the male players. IBISS staff have observed that it is common for male and female players to be romantically involved, and that male players often seem to want to prevent their girlfriends from meeting players from opposing cartels. Further innovations are needed to find ways around this, as are strategies for girls to be included in the inter-cartel activities. Another programme that IBISS runs specifically for girls, and with high numbers of participants, is the *Sou Menina e Mãe* (I'm a Girl and a Mother) programme, designed for mothers and pregnant girls under the age of sixteen. It includes pre- and post-natal support, education and professional development, vocational training in tourism and hospitality, digital inclusion, language training (basic English and Spanish), art and craft, dance and music, sport, a child-care centre and psycho-pedagogical attention for children aged from three months to six years (Kath/van Buuren interviews, 2012–2013).

Reflections

IBISS is but one of many organisations that have used sport in disadvantaged communities for social development or peace projects. Indeed, the past two decades have seen a proliferation of such projects around the world – a movement often broadly referred to as 'sport for development and peace', often accompanied by great enthusiasm for the power of sport to bring positive changes to some of the world's most vulnerable populations (see Kidd, 2008). Reflecting upon IBISS's experience with football games, several observations can be made. On the one hand, there are qualities of sport (in this case football) that make it an ideal medium for working with child soldiers, with participation in the game (and schooling) helping to provide important, often life-changing, improvements to young people's lives. On the other hand, these social outcomes cannot be seen as the automatic or spontaneous results of sport itself (see also Schulenkorf, 2010a, 2010b; Coalter, 2010; Sugden, 2006). The positive social outcomes of the games have been realised only through very deliberate and considered efforts to develop and make use of their social potential.

Like most social practices, sport can produce all kinds of outcomes, not all of them positive. In the wrong circumstances, sport can, for example, reproduce violence, division and hostility (see Armstrong and Giulianotti, 2001; Sack and Suster, 2000). Where football's potential lies in its immense popular appeal, it is already a part of the lives of most young Brazilians. The game therefore has a special power to draw a crowd; it brings groups of young people together into the same space. Furthermore, football games offer a physical and social outlet for young people, and a moment when 'real life' is suspended. As with most team sports, football can also serve as a metaphor for ethical behaviour in life (good sportsmanship and so on), and can be a good leveller – the player leaves behind socially constructed aspects of 'self' and is judged by how he or she plays. It provides a universal language; regardless of any socio-economic, territorial or other divisions, so long as players understand the rules of the game, they can engage with one another on a more or less 'equal playing field' (see Sugden, 2006). Another dimension of football in Brazil is that it is one sphere in which it is culturally acceptable for boys to express emotion; in other spheres of life, male emotion can be treated as less acceptable. The leadership role of a socially responsible coach provides opportunity for providing young people with mentoring and support in a sport context, and this role may even extend – given the right opportunities – into a leadership role beyond the game.[13]

These are the strengths of sport that IBISS has tried to harness and make use of over the past decade in its work with child soldiers. Anecdotally, the strategies used appear to be successful: in the ten years since the *Soldados Nunca Mais* programme began, it has supported close to 3,500 children to leave the drug trade. It must be said, though, that sport is not the only medium that IBISS uses to work with child soldiers and other vulnerable groups. Indeed, many of the qualities of sport (outlined earlier) that make it a useful vehicle for working with young people are also attributable to other recreational practices with popular appeal, such as music and dance. Music, for example, also has immense popular appeal in Brazil, and provides the opportunity for suspended reality and an outlet for emotional and intellectual expression. IBISS has on many occasions run successful hip hop projects for child soldiers, providing avenues for the expression of sorrow, trauma and frustration that might not otherwise be possible in everyday settings. In IBISS's experience, what makes sport, music, dance or any other form of everyday practice valuable in relation to social development projects is the capacity of those working on the ground. What matters in achieving sustainable positive change in the lives of those IBISS works with is not so much the practice itself, but social workers who manage at minimum a combination of familiarity with local context and the dedication, imagination and innovation to adapt everyday practices to respond to the needs of their target groups. This recognition that it is the capacity of 'change agents', rather than sport itself that matters most in the development process, has also emerged from studies in entirely different social contexts. For example, Schulenkorf (2010a, 2010b) has explored sport event projects aimed at reconciliation and other social development goals involving Sinhalese, Tamil and Muslim communities in ethnically divided Sri Lanka. He found that the achievement of positive, inclusive and sustainable social outcomes relies significantly on change agents fulfilling a range of key roles and responsibilities, including being a trust builder, a networker and an agent for community empowerment.

In IBISS's case, the change agents' work often takes place behind the scenes and can easily remain unnoticed by outside observers, who might as a result attribute greater credit to football than is realistic.

Such behind the scenes work is especially important in the transition of soldiers out of the drug trade. Even if a soldier has decided to leave the drug trade, the process is rarely straightforward; he or she usually relies on a great deal of ongoing support from IBISS staff in order to achieve it. There are rules surrounding a soldier's decision to leave the drug trade: they must not have debts to the cartel; they need to talk with the drug boss about their wish to leave (which can at times be facilitated by IBISS staff); they often need to promise they will not reveal cartel secrets to anybody and that they will continue living in the favela with their family (and where the favela is taken over by another cartel, they must leave and continue to live with their original cartel). For these reasons, re-integrated ex-soldiers are often viewed with a lot of respect by favela inhabitants as 'boys and girls who made it' (Kath/van Buuren interviews, 2012–2013).

In relation to IBISS's sport projects, much work remains for further innovations and the evaluation of outcomes. It is not yet known, for example, how the social outcomes of the football matches between boys from enemy cartels will play out over the long term. In the short term, the social effects of the games appear to be positive and, for the moment, transformational. How this will unfold in relation to the young people's outlook and relationships over time is unknown and warrants more attention than has yet been possible given resource constraints. To what extent will previously held prejudices and hostilities return over time once these young people are absorbed back into the larger social and political structures in which their day to day lives take place? How will the young people cope if they come face-to-face in armed confrontation with the young people from opposing cartels whom they have previously befriended during football games? What are the best ways to follow-up on, and continue to develop, the work of these matches? Resource and staffing constraints also affect other practical possibilities for the programme's expansion. Given that success of the football programmes depends to a large extent on the capacities of the facilitator/coach, a major challenge for IBISS has been that of locating and recruiting people who have the right qualities and capacities to fit this role. The ideal facilitator/coach possesses a combination of knowledge and experience of social issues, social work and local context as well as sport, and the ability to relate to, identify with and connect with the young people that IBISS supports. At present, four football matches are being held per month involving groups from different favelas. While it is feasible to hold more, there are currently not enough game facilitators/coaches who are trained in IBISS's method.

Figure 11.3   Military in the favelas

Conclusion

Overall, IBISS's use of football games as part of its work with child soldiers in Rio de Janeiro has achieved a number of positive results. These results, however, need to be considered in the context of careful management and sustainable innovation on the part of the organisation's staff; football games alone would not have produced the positive results discussed. Participation in football games is certainly not enough to drastically improve a child soldier's circumstances or encourage him or her to leave the drug trade. What the games can provide, though, are opportunities for development workers to make contact with child soldiers in an informal, social and non-confrontational environment. Facilitators can make use of the football field (along with other spheres of everyday practice) as a place to begin conversations and share moments of reflection that can help young people to deal with trauma, question social hostilities and to imagine new life paths outside of the drug trade. Ongoing social and educational support, as well as cooperation with other social development agencies, seems necessary to support ex-child-soldiers on their way towards a sustained re-integration into society and more dignified and fulfilling life possibilities.

Notes

1. In the context of Rio de Janeiro, 'child solider' refers to a minor who has been recruited to work for drug trafficking factions. Given that Rio de Janeiro

is not usually defined as being in a state of war, the term 'child soldier' has been the subject of some debate. In his report, *Children of the Drug Trade*, Dowdney provides a detailed case supporting the appropriateness of the term 'child soldier' to describe children involved in Rio's drug factions. In doing so, he compares the experiences and circumstances of these children with those of 'child soldiers' involved in traditionally defined war situations and finds many similarities (Dowdney, 2003).

2. See, for example, http://www.ibiss-co.org.br/site/parceiros/.
3. As some of the most studied communities in the world, it is not entirely true to say that favelas are disconnected from the broader society and outside world. Indeed, it has been noted that social scientists and non-government organisations have themselves played a strong role as intermediaries between favelas and the broader society and world. That said, some favelas have attracted far more public and scholarly attention than others (typically those of the South Zone of the city) and as a result are less 'disconnected' (McCann, 2006).
4. It is often said that only once a year during carnival are the city's favelas valued, for their contribution is fundamental to the success of the annual spectacle (Kath/van Buuren interviews, 2012–2013).
5. This status gives the organisation the right to receive government funding and certain tax reductions.
6. This is the case for boys, although not girls. While girls can and do play, they are not taken as seriously as boys in sport are, and there is little prospect of a career in football (Knijnik, 2012; Votre & Mourão, 2003). IBISS has separate training sessions and teams for girls.
7. The boy's name has been changed to maintain his anonymity.
8. The '*asphalto*' (asphalt) is a slang term used by favela residents to describe the more affluent areas of the city that have sealed roads and pavements.
9. It should be noted that not all players on the favela teams are child soldiers, but nevertheless those living in cartel zones tend to adopt prejudices against residents of the opposing cartel zones.
10. While the preconceptions and stereotypes held by the boys against their peers from opposing cartels are in one sense 'crazy' in their content and usually have little grounding in reality, it is nevertheless understandable that they emerge given the structural segregation and competition between the communities.
11. This by itself speaks of the fact that the organisation's work is just a small step in the direction of breaking down social barriers, but that much remains to be done to change the broader social structures beyond the football field.
12. For example, girls sometimes help to organise and prepare the barbeques. A result of one such barbeque in which girls from different commands were involved, the participating girls organised a time to play a volleyball game together on neutral territory.
13. Aside from working with the soccer school, most of the trainers/coaches also participate in the overall programme 'Soldiers Never More/*Soldados Nunca Mais*', including the part of the programme that focuses on developing strategies for supporting traumatised children and young people. Some coaches do street work to make contacts with soldados and try to convince them to leave the drug trade; some provide 'Success for Kids' workshops in public schools to try to change attitudes towards children from favelas (Kath/van Buuren interviews 2012–2013).

214 *Elizabeth Kath and Nanko G. van Buuren*

References

Alves, M. and Evanson, P. (2011). *Living in the Crossfire: Favela Residents, Drug Dealers, and Police Violence in Rio de Janeiro.* Philadelphia, Pennsylvania: Temple University Press.

Armstrong, G. and Giulianotti, R. (2001). *Fear and Loathing in World Football.* Oxford, New York: Berg.

Barrionuevo, A. (2010) With World Watching, Rio Focuses on Security. *New York Times.* http://www.servizi-italiani.net/allegati/2010/1/18/257365_267986.pdf

Bogner, A,, Litting, B. and Menz, W. (eds) (2009). *Interviewing Experts.* Houndmills: Macmillan.

Campbell, M.L. (1998). Institutional Ethnography and Experience as Data. *Qualitative Sociology*, 21(1), 55–73.

Coalter, F. (2010). The Politics of Sport-for-Development: Limited Focus Programmes and Broad Gauge Problems? *International Review for the Sociology of Sport*, 45(3), 295–314.

Dowdney, L. (2003). *Children of the Drug Trade: A Case Study of Children in Organised Armed Violence in Rio de Janeiro.* 7Letras: Rio de Janeiro.

Flyvberg, B. (2006). Five Misunderstandings about Case-Study research. *Qualitative Inquiry*, 12(2), 219–245.

IBISS (2012). www.ibiss.info

IBGE (Instituto Brasileiro de Geografia e Estatística/ Brazilian Institute of Geography and Statistics) (2012). http://www.ibge.gov.br

Jacobo Waiselsz, J. (2012). *Mapa da Violência 2012: Crianças e Adolescentes do Brasil.* Centro Brasileiro de Estudos Latino-Americanos (CEBELA) & FLACSO Brasil. http://www.mapadaviolencia.org.br/pdf2012/MapaViolencia2012_Criancas_e_Adolescentes.pdf

Kath/van Buuren interviews (2012–2013). *Interviews on IBISS by Elizabeth Kath with Nanko G. van Buuren.* Rio de Janeiro, Brazil and Melbourne, Australia. February, November and December 2012 and January and February, 2013.

Kidd, B. (2008). A New Social Movement: Sport for Development and Peace. *Sport in Society: Cultures, Commerce, Media, Politics*, 11(4), 370–380.

Knijnik,J.(2012).VisionsofGenderJustice:UntestedFeasibilityontheFootballFields of Brazil. *Journal of Sport & Social Issues.* doi: 10.1177/0193723512455924

McCann, B. (2006). The Political Evolution of Rio de Janeiro's Favelas: Recent Works. *Latin American Research Review*, 41(3), 149–163.

Neuwirth, R. (2006). *Shadow Cities: A Billion Squatters, A New Urban World.* Taylor and Francis.

Perlman, J. (1975). Rio's Favelas and the Myth of Marginality. *Politics and Society*, 5(2), 131–160.

Sack, A. L. and Suster, Z. (2000). Soccer and Croatian Nationalism: A Prelude to War. *Journal of Sport and Social Issues, 24*(3), 305–320.

Schulenkorf, N. (2010a). Sport events and ethnic reconciliation: attempting to create social change between Sinhalese, Tamil and Muslim sportspeople in war-torn Sri Lanka. *International Review for the Sociology of Sport*, 45(3), 273–294.

Schulenkorf, N. (2010b). The Roles and Responsibilities of a Change Agent in Sport Event Development Projects. *Sport Management Review*, 13, 118–128.

Secretaria de Estado de Segurança, State Government of Rio de Janeiro (2012). http://www.rj.gov.br/web/seseg/exibeconteudo?article-id=1349728

Smith, D.E. (2005). *Institutional Ethnography: A Sociology for People*. Toronto: AltaMira Press.

Stake, R.E. (1995). *The Art of Case Study Research*. London: SAGE Publications.

Sugden, J. (2006). Teaching and Playing Sport for Conflict Resolution and Co-Existence in Israel. *International Review for the Sociology of Sport*, 41, 221.

Thompson, W. (2010). *Deadly Games*. ESPN, http://sports.espn.go.com/espn /eticket/story?page=110510/rio

Votre, S. and Mourão, L. (2003). Women's Football in Brazil: Progress and Problems. *Soccer and Society*, 4 (2–3), 254–267.

Zibechi, R. (2010). *Rio de Janeiro: Control of the Poor Seen as Crucial for the Olympics*. Americas Program, Center for International Policy, 19 March 2010.

12
Inspiring Pacific Women for Lifestyle Change: An Attempt to Halt the Spread of Chronic Diseases

Katja Siefken, Grant Schofield and Nico Schulenkorf

Introduction

> To Pacific peoples, Western individualistic pursuits may appear rude and uncultured. (Reynaud, 2006)

The Pacific region comprises 22 Pacific Island Countries and Areas (PICs), divided into the sub-regions Melanesia, Micronesia and Polynesia, each with its own cultural traditions and language variations. They cover a vast area 30,000,000 km^2 of ocean. Many Pacific nations are made up of hundreds of islands, with national populations spread across many kilometres of ocean (Griffen, 2006). To much of the world, these are remote spaces – perhaps, though, not remote enough. Over the past decades, local economies and lifestyles have been challenged by the impacts of globalisation, commercialisation and urbanisation. This involved a struggle between customary modes of agrarian production focused on localised needs versus emergent forms of manufacture and consumption under industrial and service-based capitalism. The rise to dominance of commercialisation and consumerism has had significant impact on PICs; modernisation brought lifestyle changes to the populations (Bindon and Baker, 1985; Labarthe et al., 1973; Szmedra et al., 2009), particularly in urban settings (Taylor et al., 1992). In terms of diet, physical activity (PA) and health, which are core areas of focus for this chapter, there have been two major lifestyle changes in PICs:

1. *Dietary change*: root crops were replaced by refined cereals and white sugar. Fresh fish was replaced by tinned meat and fish, the consumption of fruit and vegetables decreased, while the consumption of sugar, salt, wheat and alcohol increased (Snowdon et al., 2010; Taylor et al., 1992; Thow et al., 2011).

2. *Activity change*: physical labour on the field or sea was replaced by electronic machines. A move to urbanised areas caused an increase in sedentary occupations and motorised transport and a reduction in PA levels (Coyne, 1984; Englberger et al., 1999; WPRO and SPC, 2008).

Along with these lifestyle changes, the Pacific region experienced a major shift in disease patterns: noncommunicable diseases (NCDs) have overtaken communicable diseases and are a critical health and development issue in the region (WPRO, 2009). Diseases such as diabetes and hypertension, which were uncommon in traditional Pacific cultures, occur nowadays in many urban Pacific populations, and at rates exceeding those in the affluent industrialised countries. The frequency of coronary heart disease, alcohol abuse and cancer is rising (Coyne, 1984), while obesity contributes to the ever increasing NCD epidemic (Hodge et al., 1995: 77). In fact, the Pacific region presents the highest prevalence of NCDs globally (SEARO, 2008). Supporting the urban population by encouraging the adoption of healthy lifestyle behaviour is, therefore, of utmost importance.

This chapter intends to acquaint the reader with the challenges and recent successes of managing health promotion programmes in PICs. In particular, it reports on programme logistics, on-site issues (e.g. communication, collaboration), opportunities and challenges for health promotion programme sustainability, limitations and success stories. The research-based lifestyle change programme *Wokabaot Jalens* (Bislama language for 'walking challenge'), which was implemented in Vanuatu, serves as an example to describe our hands-on experiences; *Wokabaot Jalens* engages urban Ni-Vanuatu women in regular exercises and encourages healthy eating behaviour. Examples and experiences from neighbouring Pacific island countries are drawn upon to accentuate challenges and opportunities for health promotion programmes in this region. The presentation of this reflective praxis exercise is intended to aid future practitioners and/or researchers in programme design, management and evaluation. At the same time, it aims at enhancing collaboration with local health personnel and government authorities.

Our starting point for exploring health promotion in the Pacific is listed in Table 12.1, which summarises context-specific issues that were

Table 12.1 Barriers and facilitators for Pacific health promotion

		Pacific island context	Western country context
Individual	Attitude	Health screening is seen as a positive and encouraging action	Health screening might not be well received given that health data are treated more privately and taken by General Practitioners on a regular basis (Rosedale and Strauss, 2012; Ministry of Health New Zealand)
	Perception	Population generally welcomes new ideas from overseas	Individuals from Western countries are often overloaded with health promotion efforts and are less open to trying new ideas
	Feedback	Population is inclined to agree with researchers' efforts, critique is rare	Tendency to openly comment and critique (Tannen, 1999)
	Acceptance	Pedometers are well received	Pedometers are well received (Gardner and Campagna, 2011)
	Distribution	Participants are likely to bring message across to community/church groups. Opportunities for wider community roll out due to communal structures	Participants are less likely involved in communal activities thus less likely to distribute programmes and knowledge to community. Limited opportunities for wider programme roll out (Clary and Snyder, 2002)
Culture	Cultural structures	Strong hierarchical structures may hinder full participation	Hierarchical structures are less relevant and present no particular barrier for programme participation (Cockerham et al., 1997)
	Preferences	Culture favours communal activities	Culture favours individualistic activities (Clary and Snyder, 2002)

	Factor		
	Communication	Creation of initial contact and gaining trust from local staff takes time due to strong hierarchical structures	Communication is often easier to initiate due to less hierarchical structures (Marschan et al., 1996)
	Language	Linguistic challenges – has everybody fully understood the programme components?	Generally no linguistic challenges
	Gender equality	Husbands may not support the initiative– gender issues	Gender equality is well developed (Inglehart and Norris, 2010)
	Dress code	Dress code poses challenges for accurately wearing pedometers	Dress code seldom poses extra challenge (Gardner and Campagna, 2011)
	Data precision	Lack of data accuracy (Pacific Health Dialogue, 2012)	Data accuracy well-advanced
	Sustainability	Sustainability is often restricted due to limited capacity and expertise (Howse, 2012)	Sustainability (self-initiated actions) more feasible
External influences	Climate	Technical devices do not function accurately in humid conditions and in temperatures above 30°C	Climate is usually not an issue
	Funding	Funding for sustainable programmes is often limited (Hosey et al., 2009; WHO, 2012)	Funding for sustainability is often limited, but self-organisation more feasible
	Conduct	Conduct of health screening can be very restricted due to limited facilities	Procedure of health screening is often easier due to more advanced facilities
	Geographic location	Remoteness of PICs limits access to equipment (WPRO, 2008)	Good access to equipment

observed during a number of (pedometer-based) health promotion programmes in several PICs, including Vanuatu, Tuvalu, Kiribati and Tonga. Thematic findings are compared with issues that are typically presented in a Western context. The Western country context is provided through secondary research and by the authors extensive observations and experiences in developed world environments.[1]

Health promotion context

According to the World Health Organisation (WHO), 'Health promotion is a cornerstone of primary health care and a core function of public health' (WHO, 2007). WHO argues that health promotion is both practical and cost-effective in reducing the burden of disease and in mitigating the social and economic impact of diseases (WHO, 2007). The interrelated connections between health promotion, health status and human and economic development are widely acknowledged (WHO, 2007). Various health promotion approaches have been defined in the literature. In 1986, the Ottawa Charter for Health Promotion defined health promotion as a 'process of enabling people to increase control over, and to improve their health' (WHO, 1986). Clearly, human health behaviour is affected by various influences. Lewin (1976) proposed that human behaviour was a function of the person and his or her environment. His work led to the development of the social ecological model for understanding health behaviour (Bronfenbrenner, 1981; McLeroy et al., 1988). Social ecological models address multiple levels of behaviour influence, including individual, cultural and external influences, and lead to a more comprehensive approach to health promotion.

Over the past decades, health promotion has established itself as an accepted approach to health development in several contexts, although especially in high-income countries (Catford and Leger, 1996). However, low- and middle-income countries struggle to achieve similar outcomes, which has been explained in the literature by three key factors: (1) the flooding of health development due to multi-sectoral influences, that is, practitioners and students from a wide range of backgrounds, (2) challenges of resource allocation, legislation, policy, information and advocacy due to existing jostling for power and (3) imbalance between health promotion and health development practitioners (Nyamwaya, 1996).

Importantly, deviation in health promotion approaches for different country contexts has received little attention in the literature, and it is seldom clear how an approach that proved successful in a high-income country differs to an approach in a low- and middle-income country context. As a result of our work in several Pacific Islands, we present the first recorded overview of differences in health promotion approaches informed by cultural contexts. In doing so, we compare barriers and facilitators of Pacific and Western health promotion approaches. This information is crucial for future health promotion initiatives in the Pacific region. As a summary, Table 12.1 highlights issues that need careful consideration in health promotion planning in the Pacific region.

Undoubtedly, culturally targeted health promotion programmes are essential (Shalowitz et al., 2009; Kreuter et al., 2003). For initiatives in the Pacific region, the unique value and belief systems need particular consideration in programme design. Following Bronfenbrenner's social ecological model, the macrosystem (societal beliefs, values and attitudes) levels strongly impact on lifestyle behaviour (McCabe et al., 2011). The macrosystem is based on socio-cultural factors that have been defined as the 'structure of the society, the values in relation to the meaning of food and body size', as well as the attitudes and expectations of community members (McCabe et al., 2011). Designing health promotion interventions that are culturally centred and that build on the existing social structure may be a promising approach to create change in the region. With the *Wokabaot Jalens*, the authors have attempted to design a relevant programme to meet the needs for urban female civil servants in Vanuatu. Additional health promotion assessments conducted in Tuvalu, Kiribati and Tonga contribute to the findings and discussion of this chapter. From our experience, health promotion efforts in the Pacific region need careful planning and culturally centred approaches.

Programme context – *Wokabaot Jalens*

The following section briefly describes *Wokabaot Jalens*, a culturally centred, research-based healthy lifestyle intervention for female civil servants that was implemented in Vanuatu in 2011. Programme barriers and facilitators are identified and limitations, opportunities and recommendations are provided and management issues elicited. These are supplemented with an overview of management issues experienced during WHO consultancy work in neighbouring PICs that have influenced this work.

Vanuatu is an island nation located in the South West Pacific ocean, with a total population of 257,000 (VNSO, 2012). The nation's largest towns are the capital Port Vila, situated on Efate, and Luganville on Espiritu Santo, with 44,040 and 13,167 inhabitants, respectively. The official languages of Vanuatu are Bislama, English and French; the latter two are used as the principal languages of education (FAO, 2003). While the rural population in Vanuatu leads a predominantly subsistence living, the urban population has adopted a more Western way of life (FAO, 2003). The consumption of traditional nutrient-rich foods is lowest in urban areas, whereas imported food such as white rice, fat/oils, canned and fresh meat/fish, milk and bread is highest (Carlot-Tary et al., 2000). Research from the 1980s indicates that NCDs were not a major health problem in Vanuatu (Gani, 2009). Importantly, the rates of overweight and NCD risk factors have started to increase in certain socio-economic groups since then – particularly in urban-dwelling civil servants, politicians and professionals (Taylor, 1983; Taylor et al., 1991). In 2011, a nation-wide STEPS survey[2] in Vanuatu indicated overweight and obesity rates as high as 69.7 per cent; importantly, women (79.2 per cent) are more affected than men (59.4 per cent) (MoH Vanuatu and WPRO, 2011). This is a result of traditional gender roles that give women the task of child rearing, household management and community activities (United Nations (UN), 2005). Thus little time for female leisure activities is usually available.

Programme design

In an attempt to design a novel and culturally meaningful health intervention for Ni-Vanuatu women, we firstly set out to explore opinions, barriers and facilitators for healthy lifestyles and PA. Our formative work found that women are more likely to choose walking for leisure time PA over any other sport or recreational activity (Siefken et al., 2012c). When participants were asked for their favourite exercise, *wokabaot* was the most common answer. The Bislama term *wokabaot* translates into 'walking' in the English language. Participants further suggested they favoured a team approach over individual exercise activities. Taking these personal preferences into account the *Wokabaot Jalens* (translates into 'walking challenge') was designed in a collaborative way with female Ni-Vanuatu civil servants.

Wokabaot Jalens was externally monitored for twelve weeks by the researcher. Each step captain was required to e-mail each team member's step numbers back to the researcher on a weekly basis. The researcher set-up step overview charts and sent a weekly step update to each participant via e-mail. A minority of participants had no e-mail access. In this case, the respective step captain was asked to forward the step and health information on to her team member via hard copy.

On the basis of interviewees' thoughts and suggestions, the programme consists of four components:

1. Team-based step challenge
2. One million individual step challenge
3. Social marketing tools
4. Health education materials.

Key elements of the *Wokabaot Jalens* are now briefly described below.[3]

Team-based step challenge

Following the analysis of our formative work, a team-based step count challenge was assumed to best engage female civil servants in regular exercises with the aim of positive health outcomes. Participants were equipped with pedometers, grouped into teams of their own choice and advised to aim for 10,000 steps per day. Pedometer-based health programmes have previously shown to impact positively on a variety of health behaviours (Bravata et al., 2007; Hultquist et al., 2005) and pedometer-based PA programmes can have significant effects to increase participants' activity levels (Hill, 2006; Richardson et al., 2008; Tudor-Locke and Lutes, 2009; Kang et al., 2009). On a fun basis, groups were asked to compete against each other ('Western' approach) and to aim for the highest weekly and total team step number. The competitive element was suggested by local participants during the focus group discussions. It seems that a hybrid approach combining Western ideas and Pacific island approaches proves most successful.

One million individual step challenge

Participants were encouraged to engage in a separate but concurrent individual one million step challenge. This 'Western' approach was included, acknowledging that some participants favour Western approaches over traditional ones, particularly so the younger generation. Individuals who accumulate one million steps in 100 days achieve approximately 10,000 steps/day. The idea behind the one million step challenge was to encourage participants for extra activity and action. While this approach may be considered a 'Western notion', it is important to understand that some participants were less motivated than others. Seeking to fully engage all participants, including those individuals where other team members' motivation is low and average team performance is drained, this individual challenge served as an incentive for the more motivated team members. It further encouraged participation of individuals that favoured individual activities (due to timing difficulties) and enabled their full inclusion in the programme.

Social marketing tools

Social marketing tools play an important role as part of a sustained and coordinated multi-level strategy to change community norms towards activity, and to increase population-level PA (Wakefield et al., 2010). Strategies aim at influencing awareness, knowledge and beliefs through behaviour change approaches (Cavill and Bauman, 2004). For our study, culturally meaningful social marketing tools were designed to motivate, facilitate exchange and stimulate for action. Furthermore, a number of approaches that have proven successful in Western contexts were applied. For example, a visual walking map (A0 poster) of the islands of Vanuatu pictured walking distances and step numbers (Figure 12.1) and was given to each participating group; T-shirts were designed for step captains to create a feeling of importance, trustfulness, respect and responsibility. Each participant was further equipped with a walking log containing information regarding healthy lifestyle behaviour, programme structure and charts for daily step numbers to be recorded. A manual was provided to each step captain with additional information regarding team motivation, programme adherence and health advice and posters with health information were distributed as hard-copies and electronically. Further, a website was designed to collect information from the teams' activities and to provide easy access to all participants (http://wokabaot.blogspot.com/). Finally, healthy lifestyle information was communicated on a weekly basis to all participants via e-mail. Recipients were encouraged to share information with colleagues, families and communities.

Health education

Various health information approaches were applied in order to inform participants about lifestyle choices. After consultation with staff from the Ministry of Health, local food consumption (locally grown fruits and vegetables, fish and other seafood) and locally attractive activities were promoted to stimulate action. Health seminars informed participants about the relevance of healthy lifestyles, NCD prevention, PA and healthy eating behaviour in the local context. Participants received weekly tailored health messages from

Figure 12.1   Wokabaot Jalens: visual walking map

the researchers during the first eight weeks per e-mail. Step captains reminded and encouraged group members to achieve their daily step goals and to eat healthily. Group sessions were conducted fortnightly in order to enable sharing of experience, thoughts and challenges.

After programme termination, participants were repeatedly encouraged to continue monitoring their step numbers and to maintain the lifestyle change.

Programme logistics

The *Wokabaot Jalens* was administered by the lead researcher, based in New Zealand. All materials were designed, purchased and printed in New Zealand and brought to Vanuatu upon programme implementation. Well-functioning e-mail communication with NCD key focal persons in the Ministry of Health was essential for the planning and implementation of this intervention.

During the programme preparation phase, the researcher collected all female civil servants' e-mail addresses by contacting the different ministries since no official list could be provided. In a lengthy effort, approximately 300 e-mail addresses were finally gathered and individuals were invited to partake in the opening of the *Wokabaot Jalens*. The programme was finally implemented in Port Vila, Vanuatu in March 2011. Ethics approval was received by the AUT University Ethics Committee The official opening was initiated by the Director of Public Health, the NCD team from the Ministry of Health and the lead researcher. TV Vanuatu and Radio Vanuatu recorded a short video and interview about the activities. Following the opening, 207 participants enrolled. Before the official start of the Walkabout Jalens, participants were equipped with a Yamax SW200 pedometer, an Actical waist-band (details, see later) and a log book. They formed teams of two to eight participants to their liking. Eventually, 39 teams were formed.

Baseline and follow-up health screenings were managed by the lead researcher and were carried out in collaboration with the Ministry of Health personnel. Screening set-up was based on the WHO STEP survey instrument,[4] but was a minimised version for the community setting. Two identical health screening sessions were conducted measuring PA levels (step numbers), anthropometric measures, blood pressure and blood samples for the determination of fasting serum glucose and blood lipid parameters. The NCD team was previously consulted and trained by the researcher; questionnaires were explained, the taking of health measurements demonstrated and room for questions and discussion was provided. Overall, the NCD team felt familiar and comfortable with the processes and was motivated to conduct the health screenings within the subsequent four days.

Programme impacts and outcomes

The *Wokabaot Jalens* was successful in increasing participants' PA levels. There was an objective daily mean step increase of 2510 ± 6922 steps in all participants during the time of programme implementation (Figure 12.2). A more in-depth analysis can be found in the outcome evaluation (Siefken et al., 2012c).

While the *Wokabaot Jalens* was considered a great success for participants and their groups, programme sustainability has been identified as both an opportunity and a challenge. Clearly, sustainability is dependent on (1) management capacities and (2) individuals that aim to create lasting lifestyle changes. The most committed individuals demonstrated sustained actions trough the participation in a subsequent international online pedometer challenge which was arranged by the Australian Government and free of charge – an ideal example that sustained actions are feasible. Several women formed new walking teams and signed up to participate in the challenge. Participants demonstrated autonomy and were able to compete with 1800 individuals from Australia. Some participants even aimed for 30,000 steps a day which resulted in self-reported weight loss, better sleep, feeling better and increased well-being. Importantly, to accumulate 30,000 steps in a walking pace, three to four hours of walking is required.

As a further challenge for sustainability, local expertise and finances in programme management appeared lacking. While capacity building for programme managers is generally seen as essential for sustained

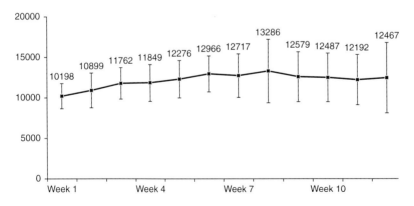

Figure 12.2 Mean steps, weeks 1–12

programme success (Siefken et al., 2012b), significant staff turnover and the loss of key supporters in the Ministry of Health Vanuatu brought the *Wokabaot Jalens* spirit to an end. Regrettably, to the researcher's knowledge, no future plans to re-activate the programme are currently in place despite the great amount of informal and formal requests from both civil servants and the private sector. Fourteen months after programme termination, some participants reported to repeatedly participate in a global online pedometer challenge. Furthermore, the researcher randomly met some participants 15 months after programme termination: the continuous use of pedometers was recorded. While these individual actions indicate success in sustained effects in some individuals, the programme is limited in effective means of prolonged actions. The assumption that the Ministry of Health would continue the programme after tailored capacity building proved wrong for the reasons provided earlier.

Individual feedback often illustrates the perceived success of programmes such as the Wokabaot Jalens.[5] We would, therefore, like to share some of the feedback and comments provided by programme participants. For example, one hypertensive and diabetic participant reported that after 15 years of seeking doctors' advices without positive results, *Wokabaot Jalens* was the single best prescription she had received. This programme improved her quality of life to the extent that she was able to sense her limbs and see long distances. She reports that regular exercise is the best medication she has received and the pedometer assists her in monitoring her activity levels. Upon programme termination, she was able to actively play with her children, which had been impossible for her previously.

Another participant commented:

> Thank you to help us Ni-Vanuatu women and to encourage us to do the *Wokabaot Jalens*. It is a very important programme for our health and I am very glad and proud that we, Ni-Vanuatu women, finally come to realise that we can do our best for our own health. There are lots of women left to be part but no more pedometers. Is there any chance to get more of them? The message is going around mouth to mouth to other women who are not working for government but for the private sector. They are interested in participating in the programme and are asking when will the next round be starting? Many thanks again and our male colleagues also told me they want to do this too. When?

Comments like these suggest that both parties – local women and researchers – have greatly benefitted from their co-operation during the *Wokabaot Jalens* experience: participants learned how to make healthy choices in their everyday lives and reduce NCD risk factors, whereas the researchers were able to enhance their understanding of the local state of knowledge around healthy lifestyle behaviour and the cultural particularities regarding programme design and implementation.

Overall, the *Wokabaot Jalens* suggests that a community participation approach can result in meaningful health programmes. It also suggests that in a low- and middle-income world context, communities are often dependent on some form of external support when realising their development efforts. However, such approach to development requires reciprocal engagement and participation. Looking at the *Wokabaot Jalens*, the reciprocal learning experiences of local communities and external researchers are a great example: while locals received expert advice with regard to planning, implementing and managing a health programme, the researchers learned about the significance of walking as the preferred type of exercise for Ni-Vanuatu women and other perceived barriers and facilitators. It can be said that if the co-operation between locals and researchers is one of engagement and respect, the ability of the target population to build their own future programmes and skills can be strengthened, so that they are better able to define their objectives and achieve their targets of conducting, sustaining, growing and leveraging future health projects.

Challenges encountered and ideas for programme improvement

Reflecting on the *Wokabaot Jalens*, a number of challenges have been identified. Clearly, challenges should not hinder future programme implementation, but should be considered as thought stimulating and lead to continuous programme improvement.

The official languages of Vanuatu are English, French and Bislama. Bislama is the first language of many urban Ni-Vanuatu. For the urban population, the majority speak Bislama and French or Bislama and English. Prior to programme design, the researchers were informed that all civil servants were fluent in the English language and all materials were designed in English. However, upon programme implementation, a small number of participants requested documents to be translated into French, since both English and French are principal working languages. Regrettably, this request was received after the official opening when all materials had been printed in New Zealand. Subsequently, it was agreed that participants consult with the researcher in person should there be any questions or concerns. Nevertheless, for future programme design, it is suggested to have all brochures and programme instructions in all three official languages available for best programme outcomes.

Following this experience, the researchers questioned whether all participants had understood all programme elements in full detail, given that the opening discussion and programme explanation was conducted in the English language. A detailed visual instruction of wearing the pedometer accurately aimed at avoiding step miscalculations. Furthermore, team captains were continuously encouraged to explain all programme elements to team members accurately in respective languages. While there was no incident in which a participant indicated that she did not know or understand programme elements in the process evaluation, questions remain if this outcome is related to the cultural tendency to agree, as Pacific individuals have been found to frequently assent with external ideas (Siefken et al., 2012d).

Our initial formative work revealed that husbands may not support the *Wokabaot Jalens* since it was directed at women only (Siefken et al., 2012c). Their cultural expectations were often cited to be the major hindrance for women to engage in regular exercise programmes. Women are 'supposed to stay back home and look after the children' instead of exercising outdoors. Future research may aim at discovering how men perceive healthy lifestyle behaviour in women, which may be an important way to design appropriate interventions that involve men, women and the family as a whole.

Lessons learnt – running Pacific health promotion interventions

The Pacific region is a multinational region with a large variety of cultures, languages and customs. Clearly, it is challenging and complex – if not impossible – to report on the management of *Pacific* health programmes. However, on the basis of our personal experiences an overall idea of how Pacific attitudes can affect programme management issues is meant to be provided, so that future programme development can be enhanced.

Table 12.1 opposed findings from a Pacific island context with a Western context and outlines important differences which are crucial for future Pacific programme design and management. On the basis of Bronfenbrenner's (1981) social ecological model, we categorised findings into individual, cultural and external influences that impact health promotion activities. Each category is now discussed in greater detail later.

Individual

On the individual level, personal and social values play an important role for programme management. Attitudes, perceptions and the social connectivity that shape Pacific individuals need consideration in programme management. In Table 12.1, we identified *attitudes* as potential facilitators for health screenings, as we experienced the turnout for health screenings that measure weight, Body Mass Index, blood pressure and blood glucose levels to be particularly high in PICs. For example, in our research sites, we experienced response rates of nearly 100 per cent. People in PICs seem to handle health data differently, and it is of little concern if, for example, colleagues know each other's blood pressure or other data. Rather, participants would exclaim 'oh, [I've got] high sugar, and you?' This action differs significantly to dealing with health data in a more Western context where it is handled more privately. Accordingly, health screening response rates in Western countries are significantly lower. For example, New Zealand's health target for 2012 is to increase response rates to 60 per cent (Ministry of Health New Zealand). Such high response rates in PICs are an important finding. Stakeholders, interested in surveillance mechanisms, may allocate financial resources accordingly.

Table 12.1 lists *perception* as a potential facilitator for Pacific health promotion. Overall, open-mindedness towards new ideas and suggestions for programme design were experienced in various PICs. This is important for future programmes and should be valued. For example, the use of pedometers was very well received by Ni-Vanuatu women, despite women generally wearing dresses which complicate the actual use of pedometers. Participants showed an open attitude towards using an extra elastic waist-band underneath their dresses that allows the pedometer to function accurately, albeit this being potentially uncomfortable for some. The use of pedometers is generally also well received in participants of a more Western context but is also more appropriate due to dominant dress codes in PICs.

The provision of individual feedback was identified as a potential barrier in Pacific health promotion, as listed in Table 12.1 under *feedback*. An important side-observation from our evaluation efforts is that Pacific people are frequently inclined to assent with external ideas and suggestions, while critique towards the researchers' efforts is rare. For this reason, it can be difficult to know whether ideas from the researcher's/programme implementer's side are actually well received or whether agreements are culturally related. We suggest including open-ended questions (in initial and evaluation work) and open discussion sessions to uncover true ideas and opinions on the planned programme. These can focus on individual suggestions of what works best; previous experiences of what did and did not work; individual experiences, such as likes, dislikes and challenges and suggestions for programme improvement. In a Western context, critique to programme elements is often readily available which may assist in continuous programme improvement.

A sharp difference has been identified in communal *distribution* of new information. Table 12.1 lists this health promotion facilitator as a distributor. Because of the existing communal structures in the PICs and the 'sharing and caring' attitude (Griffen, 2006), Pacific people are more likely to bring health messages across to communities and churches. For instance, some participants from the *Wokabaot Jalens* distributed all health information materials further to their churches and social groups to engage the community in healthy lifestyle behaviour. This proactive communication approach is an important finding as the Church plays a vital role in Pacific lifestyles: it is the central meeting point of many communities where knowledge and experiences are shared. With Pacific lifestyles being more centred on communal activities, opportunities for wider community roll out are stronger than in a more individualistic Western lifestyle. We conclude that using the church setting for health promotion initiatives in the Pacific region can prove highly effective due to the high church attendance rates and influential roles church leaders can have (Campbell et al., 2007).

Culture

Cross-cultural collaboration may pose management challenges due to varying expectations and ideas and extra linguistic obstacles. A number of cultural issues for health programme management were defined and should be taken into consideration for any Pacific programme development intention.

Table 12.1 lists *cultural structure* as a potential barrier for health promotion initiatives. The communal nature of Pacific people produces a series of typical values and behaviours, despite varying traditions among Polynesian, Melanesian and Micronesian communities. However, certain generalisations can be made: one important associated core value that has been identified is the obedience to authority (Reynaud,

2006). For Polynesian countries, traditional leadership has been defined as based on hereditary rank in a context of social hierarchy and for Melanesian countries based on achieved status in a context of competition (Douglas, 1979). Irrespective of regional affiliation, leadership and authority strongly impact every day behaviour and attitude in Pacific cultures (Reynaud, 2006). This system can pose remarkable difficulties when running health promotion programmes, both in the development and in the implementation phase. For example, programme leaders may rank officially lower than some participants, which may cause tension and discomfort in both parties during programme activities and in usual office work hours. The system can further lead to reluctance towards communicating with individuals that do not form part of the communal system (e.g. researcher). Hence, we conclude that formative research prior to programme design may assist in the development of culturally centred approaches that are supported by all contestants involved.

In a region where authority systems prevail strongly, a first hurdle may be the creation of initial contact with respective local staff (Reynaud, 2006). Table 12.1 highlights this as *communication* issues. Distinct reluctance was felt towards the researchers' effort in some countries in an attempt to initiate communication with local health professionals, particularly in Polynesian countries. This reluctance is culturally rooted and can be explained with the particular authority system. However, this first obstacle can be overcome through continual culturally targeted communication efforts. A change in attitude was felt once researchers were in direct face to face contact with local staff. This insight is crucial for future programme planners: for an effective collaboration with local Pacific health professionals, it is of utmost importance to collaborate face to face wherever possible and to understand the existing authority system. While e-mailing is common in the region, it has not reached the plausible standards it has in some higher income countries. Moreover, expectations differ in terms of timing and the need for immediate responses and e-mail replies.

Gender inequalities are strong in the Pacific region (Griffen, 2006). Among the major gender issues in the region are high rates of gender-based violence of men against women, low proportions of women in all levels of decision making, significant under-representation of women in the normal economy, and inequitable access to clean water and sanitation (SPC, 2010). As discussed, our formative work in the region found that men may not support Pacific women to engage in regular exercises due to child rearing and household expectations (Siefken et al., 2012c).

A particular challenge in running pedometer-based health promotion programmes in the Pacific region is the *dress code* of women (and, in fact, sometimes men). Traditional dress codes of women are expected in different Pacific countries and the particular style often defines national or regional origin. Clearly, the use of pedometers becomes challenging when wearing dresses that are generally loose, not tight. In some Melanesian countries, particularly so in Fiji, male counterparts wear *sulus* which resemble skirts and pose similar challenges to wearing the pedometer and attaining accurate step count results. Pedometers track the number of steps a person takes throughout the course of the day and is clipped to a belt. Clearly, for women who wear long dresses without waistlines (such as in Vanuatu), different solutions are needed. From our experience, elastic belts that are worn underneath the dresses have proven effective and were well received by participants. A side-observation during the implementation phase was the need for accurate explanation of how to wear the pedometer. While being common sense for Westeners, detailed explanation, including dos and don'ts are essential for a target audience that is not familiar with the devices.

During the conduct of health screenings, differences in data measurement *precision* were observed among the researchers and the local staff team. While the researchers intended to explain the exact use of tape measurements and height scales prior to health screening commencement, our colleagues from the Ministry of Health (mainly nurses) indicated the accurate procedure was known and no further instruction was needed. However, during the health screenings, we observed that data accuracy varies widely and attitudes towards precise measurements did not always prevail. For example, it was observed that a second blood pressure reading was not considered relevant because 'He's my friend, I know he is healthy.' This issue, though culturally delicate, was raised instantly to avoid data imprecision. The necessity of data precision was explained in detail.

In relation to *sustainability*, we encountered another challenge when conducting research work in the Pacific. While we were informed by WHO that all relevant Ministry of Health offices are equipped with well-functioning health screening devices, we experienced a different scenario. Where devices existed, they were often not functioning –due to broken batteries, insufficient knowledge of operating the devices or maintenance issues such as expired blood testing strips. Clearly, this hinders health screenings to be run efficiently by the respective local offices and it clarifies the request for continuous external support with health screenings.

External influences

The *climate* may pose challenges to data collection in the Pacific region. Where temperatures exceed 30°C, inaccurate readings of health data may occur. Given that air-conditioned facilities are rare, health screenings commonly occur in open-air community houses. Technical devices are generally defined to be well-functioning to up to 30°C only. Whenever possible, it is therefore recommended to arrange health screening in air-conditioned rooms to allow accurate functioning of devices and to make the health screening procedure more enjoyable for all. Fans may be used were air-condition is not feasible. In remote region, where electricity is limited, it is suggested to conduct data collection in the very early morning hours when temperatures are generally below 30°C.

The large majority, if not all, of PICs strongly rely on external aid such as WHO, the Secretariat of the Pacific Community (SPC) and the Australian Government Overseas Aid Programme (AUSAID). Clearly, countries that are largely dependent on foreign aid require thorough capacity building approaches in order to achieve sustained programme outcomes. A major problem related to donor-supported health projects in LMICs is their lack of sustainability once external assistance has ceased: Often, there is a significant lack of long-term approaches which means that upon programme termination and usage of project grants, the local staff – often highly motivated – is left without adequate resources for programme continuation. We suggest that a re-thinking of the funding models with a more sustained approach towards health promotion management and delivery is one of the most important issues for international donor organisations to be resolved.

A further logistical challenge is the remoteness of the Pacific islands, listed in Table 12.1. Researchers have previously described the detrimental effects of geographical distance and the linked dependency on imports from overseas (Hughes and Lawrence, 2005; Hughes and Marks, 2009; Coyne, 1984). The unfavourable effects are indeed obvious and can be seen particularly in many urban areas in the Pacific region. Regarding technical PA equipment we experienced the heavy dependency on imports first hand. While myriad requests were made in Vanuatu to provide the public with opportunities to purchase pedometers at their own cost, no action has been taken. This same issue was further found to be of importance in Tuvalu, Tonga and Kiribati where local health staff had wished they could provide the population with these simple-to-use and relatively affordable PA monitor tools. During planning and implementation, this issue can become significant when equipment brought from overseas stops functioning properly and needs to be renewed. We do not call for more technological devices to be on the market in the respective countries, but we recommend being stocked up with more equipment than actually needed to be able to replace devices whenever needed. Disappointment has been felt in *Wokabaot Jalens* participants when pedometers went missing or were broken and could not be replaced.

Further research is needed to investigate whether long-term lifestyle change has occurred and been maintained. While the Vanuatu Ministry of Health and relevant stakeholders (donors) were repeatedly encouraged to initiate a 12-month follow-up health screening with all participants, this has not taken place by the time of writing (December 2012). From a practical perspective, the Ministry of Health Vanuatu has been prepared to run and monitor this programme independently for long-term life-style changes. Staff turnover and work overload in the health personnel, however, was reported to hinder continuation. A formal commitment to long-term planning prior to programme implementation on the sides of the donor and targeted organisation and the creation of a formal job description for the person running the programme was suggested to aid in programme maintenance.

The researchers strongly recommended the Ministry of Health personnel supporting participants with their lifestyle change throughout the subsequent year and beyond. While this has happened informally via face to face conversations of health personnel and participants, no systematic approach was taken. Besides, it was suggested to expand the programme beyond the workplace focus (communities, churches and schools), as this can impact both the external environment and the participants. As such, opportunities of leveraging health initiatives for wider community benefit should be sought. Regrettably, to the researchers' knowledge, no action has been taken since programme termination.

To conclude, a successful health promotion programme was developed and implemented. Lifestyle behaviour was changes, albeit evidence is available for a short period of time only. Alas, the depletion of funds and the loss of key supporters in the Ministry of Health eaHcaused programme discontinuation and prevented us from experiencing and evaluating lasting change. While long-term plans were included in programme planning by the researchers, no sustainable funding and support on the part of the donor were intended. This illustrates the complexity of donor–implementer–recipient relation: while the programme proved successful and the target audience was highly motivated to create change, sustained success eventually depends on both the donor's actions and the key supporters' drive. We assume that donors funding is an essential piece for sustained programme continuation; moreover, the loss of key drivers and the loss of support from the Government play an even larger role for programme sustainability. The lesson learnt is that capacity building, local training and transfer of responsibilities does not necessarily suffice to generate sustained programme success. Ultimately, the donor, the targeted community and supporting organisation are required to commit to long-term intentions prior to programme commencement.

Summary and future paths in Pacific health programme planning

It is widely accepted that the most serious problem facing Pacific nations today is the rapid growth of NCDs. Clearly, there is a need to encourage Pacific urban adults to adapt healthier lifestyles. This chapter highlighted challenges and opportunities for Pacific health promotion programmes. When investigating the management challenges in detail, three phenomena are apparent. First, we found that cultural issues pose notable challenges to programme success and community involvement is of utmost importance during the design, implementation and evaluation phase. Second, there is a lack of local capacity available to secure the monitoring and evaluation of programmes. Third sustaining the projects beyond the time of international funding is particularly difficult.

Interestingly, health promotion interventions are usually directed towards increasing an individual's control over their health (WHO, 1986). However, according to WHO's Ottawa Charter, directing action towards changing social, environmental and economic conditions can help individuals 'to achieve their fullest health potential' ... 'by taking control of those things which determine their health'. Community participation was first adopted as a health promotion strategy by the WHO(1978) and has been described as a social process in which groups with shared needs living in a 'certain geographical area' actively identify needs, make decisions, and set-up mechanisms to achieve solutions (Bichmann et al., 1989). Evidence suggests that, specifically, health interventions that incorporate cultural contextualisation are more effective than those that do not (Campbell et al., 2007). As a consequence, for Pacific health professionals to design culturally meaningful health programmes, community-based participatory approaches are essential.

Throughout this chapter, we have provided examples from the PICs that highlight the importance of co-operation between health experts and the local community. In an attempt to achieve culturally centred health outcomes, we support Stokols' (1996) recommendation to shift from a person-focused approach to a community-oriented health promotion approach to foster socially supportive norms and community participation in health promotion programmes. For example, we found that team-based pedometer-based health programmes with additional nutrition education components can be effective approaches in improving population health. Importantly, programme components and materials must be acceptable to participants and must build on the existing cultural structures. Sustained actions are likely to result in health benefits, or as Aristotle phrased it: 'We are what we repeatedly do. Excellence then, is not an act, but a habit.'

Against this background, a systematic approach for structuring, implementing, monitoring and evaluating programmes both internally and externally is indispensable for sustained programme success and underpinning all this, finances that make sustained programme (and thus sustainable impacts) possible. While a large number of health and physical activity programmes prevail in a variety of settings in the Pacific region, the majority of these programmes are not embedded in regular evaluation, let alone ongoing monitoring mechanisms or evaluations of programme effectiveness (Siefken et al., 2012a; Snowdon, 2011). We argue that best-practice programme planning can only be achieved through the use of formative research, inclusive process evaluation and cooperative outcome evaluation because the success or failure of a programme can only be understood through evaluation work conducted with the support and/or leadership of those who are the intended beneficiaries of health interventions (Suchman, 1967).

Notes

1. Two of the authors are of German background, and one is from New Zealand.
2. STEPS survey: The WHO STEPwise approach to Surveillance (STEPS) is a simple, standardised method for collecting, analysing and disseminating data in WHO member countries WHO (2013).
3. Further details can be found in the report *Wokabaot Jalens – Waes woman wokabaot blong laef – Evry dei 10,000 steps!* Siefken and Schofield (2011).
4. STEPS survey: The WHO STEPS is a simple, standardised method for collecting, analysing and disseminating data in WHO member countries WHO (2013).
5. An abundance of individual feedback e-mails was received by the researcher from participants. A selection is available at the *Wokabaot Jalens* website (http://wokabaot.blogspot.co.nz/).

References

Bichmann, W., Rifkin, S. and Shrestha, M. (1989). Towards the Measurement of Community Participation. *World Health Forum*, 10(3–4), 467–472.

Bindon, J.R. and Baker, P.T. (1985). Modernization, Migration and Obesity Among Samoan Adults. *Annals of Human Biology*, 12, 67–76.

Bravata, D.M., Smith-Spangler, C., Sundaram, V., Gienger, A., Lin, N.D., Lewis, R., Stave, C.D., Olkin, I. and Sirard, J.R. (2007). Using Pedometers to Increase Physical Activity and Improve Health. a Systematic Review. *Journal of the American Medical Association*, 298(19), 2296–2304.

Bronfenbrenner, U. (1981). *The Ecology of Human Development: Experiments by Nature and Design*. London, UK: Harvard University Press.

Campbell, M., Hudson, M., Resnicow, K., Blakeney, N., Paxton, A. and Baskin, M. (2007). Church-Based Health Promotion Interventions: Evidence and Lessons Learned. *Annual Review of Public Health*, 28, 213–234.

Carlot-Tary, M., Hughes, R. and Hughes, M.C. (2000). *1998 Vanuatu Non-Communicable Disease Survey Report*, Health Department, Government of the Republic of Vanuatu, Port Vila, Vanuatu.

Catford, J. and Leger, L. (1996). Moving into the Next Decade – and a New Dimension? *Health Promotion International*, 11(1), 1–3.

Cavill, N. and Bauman, A. (2004). Changing the Way People Think about Health-Enhancing Physical Activity: Do Mass Media Campaigns Have a Role? *Journal of Sports Sciences*, 22(8), 771–790.

Clary, E. and Snyder, M. (2002). Community Involvement: Opportunities and Challenges in Socializing Adults to Participate in Society. *Journal of Social Issues*, 58(3), 581–591.

Cockerham, W., Rütten, A. and Abel, T. (1997). Conceptualizing Contemporary Health Lifestyles: Moving beyond Weber. *The Sociological Quarterly*, 38(2), 321–342.

Coyne, T. (1984). *The Effect of Urbanisation and Western Diet on the Health of Pacific Island Populations*, South Pacific Commission. New Caledonia: Noumea.

Douglas, B. (1979). Rank, Power, Authority: A Reassessment of Traditional Leadership in South Pacific Societies. *The Journal of Pacific History*, 14(1).

Englberger, L., Halavatau, V., Yasuda, Y. and Yamazaki, R. (1999). The Tonga Healthy Weight Loss Program 1995–1997. *Asia Pacific Journal for Clinical Nutrition*, 8(2), 142–148.

FAO (2003). *Nutrition Country Profiles Vanuatu*, Nutrition Country Profiles (NCP), Rome.

Gani, A. (2009). Some Aspects of Communicable and Non-Communicable Diseases in Pacific Island Countries. *Social Indices Resources*, 91, 171–187.

Gardner, P.J. and Campagna, P.D. (2011). Pedometers as Measurement Tools and Motivational Devices: New Insights for Researchers and Practitioners. *Health Promotion Practice*, 12(1), 55–62.

Griffen, V. (2006). Gender Relations in Pacific Cultures and Their Impact on the Growth and Development of Children. Paper Prepared for a Seminar on 'Children's Rights and Culture in the Pacific'. *United Nations Children Fund (UNICEF)*.

Hill, J.O. (2006). Understanding and Addressing the Epidemic of Obesity: An Energy Balance Perspective. *Endocrine Reviews*, 27(7), 750–761.

Hodge, A.M., Dowse, G.K., Zimmet, P.Z. and Collins, V.R. (1995). Prevalence in Obesity in Pacific and Indian Ocean Island Population. *Obesity Research*, 3(2), 77–87.

Hosey, G., Aitaoto, N., Satterfield, D., Kelly, J., Apaisam, C.J., Belyeu-Camacho, T., deBrum, I., Solidum Luces, P., Rengiil, A. and Turituri, P. (2009). The Culture, Community, and Science of Type 2 Diabetes Prevention in the US Associated

240   Katja Siefken, Grant Schofield and Nico Schulenkorf

Pacific Islands. *Preventing Chronic Disease: Public Health Research, Practice and Policy*, 6(3), 1–10.

Howse, G. (2012). Elements of Pacific Public Health Laws: An Analysis of the Public Health Acts of Papua New Guinea, Vanuatu, the Solomon Islands, and Fiji. *Asia-Pacific Journal of Public Health*, 24(5), 860–866.

Hughes, R.G. and Marks, G.C. (2009). Against the Tide of Change: Diet and Health in the Pacific Islands. *Journal of the American Dietetic Association*, 109(10), 1700–1703.

Hughes, R.J. and Lawrence, A. (2005). Globalisation, Food and Health in Pacific Island Countries. *Asia Pacific Journal for Clinical Nutrition*, 14(4), 298–306.

Hultquist, C.N., Albright, C. and Thompson, D.L. (2005). Comparison of Walking Recommendations in Previously Inactive Women. *Medicine and Science in Sport and Exercise*, 37(4), 676–683.

Inglehart, R. and Norris, P. (2010). *Rising Tide: Gender Equality and Cultural Change Around the World*, Cambridge: Cambridge University Press.

Kang, M., Marshall, S.J., Barreira, T.V. and Lee, J.O. (2009). Effect of Pedometer-Based Physical Activity Interventions: A Meta-Analysis. *Research Quarterly for Exercise and Sport*, 80(3), 648–655.

Kreuter, M., Lukwago, S., Bucholtz, D., Clark, E. and Sanders-Thompson, V. (2003). Achieving Cultural Appropriateness in Health Promotion Programs: Targeted and Tailored Approaches. *Health Education & Behavior*, 30(2), 133–146.

Labarthe, D., Reed, D., Brody, J. and Stallones, R. (1973). Health Effects of Modernization in Palau. *American Journal of Epidemiology*, 8(3), 161–174.

Lewin, K. (1976). *Field Theory in Social Science: Selected Theoretical Papers*.

Marschan, R., Welch, D. and Welch, L. (1996). Control in Less-Hierarchical Multinationals: The Role of Personal Networks and Informal Communication. *International Business Review*, 5(2), 137–150.

McCabe, M.P., Mavoa, H., Ricciardelli, L.A., Schultz, J.T., Waqa, G. and Fotu, K.F. (2011). Socio-Cultural Agents and Their Impact on Body Image and Body Change Strategies Among Adolescents in Fiji, Tonga, Tongans in New Zealand and Australia. *Obesity Reviews*, 12, 61–67.

McLeroy, K.R., Bibeau, D., Steckler, A. and Glanz, K. (1988). An Ecological Perspective on Health Promotion Programs. *Health Education Quarterly*, 15(4), 351–377.

Ministry of Health New Zealand, New Zealand Health System – The 2011/12 Health Targets. available at: http://www.health.govt.nz/new-zealand-health-system/health-targets/2011–12-health-targets.

MoH Vanuatu and WPRO (2011). *Vanuatu STEPS Survey 2011: Factsheet*, Suva, Fiji.

Nyamwaya, D. (1996). Impediments to Health Promotion in Developing Countries: The Way Forward. *Health Promotion International*, 11(3), 175–176.

Pacific Health Dialogue (2012). Special Edition: Health Information System in the Pacific. *Pacific Health Dialog*, 18(1).

Reynaud, D. (2006). South Pacific Cultures and the Concept and Practice of History. *Arts Papers and Journal Articles*, 1.

Richardson, C.R., Newton, T.L., Abraham, J.J., Sen, A., Jimbo, M. and Swartz, A.N. (2008). A Meta-Analysis of Pedometer-Based Walking Interventions and Weight Loss. *Annals of Family Medicine*, 6, 69–77.

Rosedale, M.T. and Strauss, S.M. (2012). Diabetes Screening at the Periodontal Visit: Patient and Provider Experiences with Two Screening Approaches. *International Journal of Dental Hygiene*, 10(4), 250–258.

SEARO (2008). *Health in Asia and the Pacific: Chapter 8: Priority Noncommunicable Diseases and Conditions*, Manila.

Shalowitz, M., Isacco, A., Barquin, N., Clark-Kauffman, E., Delger, P., Nelson, D., Quinn, A. and Wagenaar, K. (2009). Community-Based Participatory Research: A Review of the Literature with Strategies for Community Engagement. *Journal of Developmental and Behavioral Paediatrics*, 30(4), 350–361.

Siefken, K. and Schofield, G. (2011). *Wokabaot Jalens: A Workplace Healthy Lifestyle Intervention for Female Civil Servants in Port Vila, Vanuatu, 2011*. Report for the World Health Organization, Auckland, New Zealand.

Siefken, K., Macniven, R., Schofield, G., Bauman, A. and Waqanivalu, T. (2012a). A Stocktake of Physical Activity Programs in the Pacific Islands. *Health Promotion International*, 27(2), 197–207.

Siefken, K., Schofield, G. and Malcata, R. (in submission). Engaging Urban Pacific Women in Healthy Lifestyle Behaviour. An Outcome Evaluation of a Workplace-Based Physical Activity Intervention in Vanuatu. *Journal of Sport for Development*.

Siefken, K., Schofield, G. and Schulenkorf, N. (2012b). *Formative Assessments of Healthy Workplace Initiatives in Tuvalu, Tonga and Kiribati: May 2011–February 2012*. Report prepared for WHO Western Pacific Regional Office.

Siefken, K., Schofield, G. and Schulenkorf, N. (2012c). Laefstael Jenses: An Investigation of Barriers and Facilitators for Healthy Lifestyles of Women in an Urban Pacific Island Context. Accepted for publication by the *Journal of Physical Activity and Health*.

Siefken, K., Schofield, G. and Schulenkorf, N. (2012d). Novel Techniques to Visualize Evaluation Data and to Communicate Health Promotion Programme Successes and Challenges – A Strategy to Engage Health Practitioners in the South Pacific. Unpublished.

Snowdon, W. (2011). Challenges of Noncommunicable Diseases in the Pacific Islands: The Need for Evidence and Data. *Asia-Pacific Journal of Public Health*, 23(1), 110–111.

Snowdon, W., Lawrence, M., Schultz, J., Vivili, P. and Swinburn, B.A. (2010). Evidence-Informed Process to Identify Policies That Will Promote a Healthy Food Environment in the Pacific Islands. *Publice Health Nutrition*, 13(6), 886–892.

SPC (2010). *Beijing + 15: Review of Progress in Implementing the Beijing Platform for Action in Pacific Island Countries and Territories*, Noumea.

Stokols, D. (1996). Translating Social Ecological Theory into Guidelines for Community Health Promotion. *American Journal of Health Promotion*, 10(4), 282–298.

Suchman, E. (1967). *Evaluative Research: Principles and Practice in Public Service and Social Action Programs*. New York: Russell Sage Foundation.

Szmedra, P., Sharma, K.L. and Rozmus, C.L. (2009). Health Promoting Behavior Among Chronically Ill Pacificans Living with Non-Communicable Disease in Fiji, Nauru, and Kiribati. *Pacific Health Dialog*, 15(2).

Tannen, D. (1999). *The Argument Culture: Stopping America's War of Words*. New York: Ballantine Books.

Taylor, R. (1983). Prevention and control of non-communicable diseases in Pacific Island nations. Prospects and constraints. *The Medical Journal of Australia*, 2(8), 389–394.

Taylor, R., Badcock, J., King, H., Pargeter, K., Zimmet, P., Fred, T., Lund, M., Ringrose, H., Bach, F., Wang, R. and Sladden, T. (1992). Dietary Intake, Exercise, Obesity and Noncommunicable Disease in Rural and Urban Populations of Three Pacific Island Countries. *Journal of the American College of Nutrition*, 11(3).

Taylor, R., Jalaludin, B., Levy, S., Montaville, B., Gee, K. and Sladden, T. (1991). Prevalence of Diabetes, Hypertension and Obesity at Different Levels of Urbanisation in Vanuatu. *The Medical Journal of Australia*, 155(2), 86–90.

Thow, A.M., Heywood, P., Schultz, J., Quested, C., Jan, S. and Colagiuri, S. (2011). Trade and the Nutrition Transition: Strengthening Policy for Health in the Pacific. *Ecology of Food and Nutrition*, 50(1), 18–42.

Tudor-Locke, C. and Lutes, L. (2009). Why Do Pedometers Work? a Reflection upon the Factors Related to Successfully Increasing Physical Activity. *Sports Medicine (Auckland, N.Z.)*, 39(12), 981–993.

United Nations (UN) (2005). *Convention on the Elimination of All Forms of Discrimination against Women: CEDAW country report Vanuatu.*

VNSO (2012). Ministry of Finance and Economic Management. available at: http://www.vnso.gov.vu/index.php?option=com_content&view=article&id=9&Itemid=4.

Wakefield, M.A., Loken, B. and Hornik, R.C. (2010). Use of Mass Media Campaigns to Change Health Behaviour. *The Lancet*, 376, 1261–1271.

WHO (1978). *Declaration of Alma-Ata.*

WHO (1986). *Ottawa Charter on Health Promotion: International Conference on Health Promotion.* Geneva: World Health Organization (WHO).

WHO (2007). *Health Promotion in a Globalized World: Report by the Secretariat.* Geneva.

WHO (2012). Health Financing for Universal Coverage. available at: http://www.who.int/health_financing/strategy/revenue_collecton/en/.

WHO (2013). STEPwise Approach to Surveillance (STEPS). the WHO STEPwise Approach to Chronic Disease Risk Factor Surveillance (STEPS). available at: http://www.who.int/chp/steps/en/ (accessed 22 February 2010).

WPRO (2008). Health Sector Development. available at: http://www2.wpro.who.int/southpacific/sites/hsd/.

WPRO (2009). *Western Pacific Regional Action Plan for Noncommunicable Diseases: A Region Free of Avoidable NCD Deaths and Disability*, Manila.

WPRO and SPC (2008). *Pacific Physical Activity Guidelines for Adults: Framework for Accelerating the Communication of Physical Activity Guidelines*, Manila.

Part IV
Conclusions

13
Global Sport-for-Development in Theory and Praxis: Reflections

Daryl Adair and Nico Schulenkorf

This chapter reflects on what the combination of essays in this book has revealed about the nuances of theory and praxis in sport-for-development (S4D). This is done against a background where each of the chapters under 'Framework', while focused primarily on conceptual concerns, has also drawn upon experiences from field work. Similarly, each of the chapters under the 'From the Field' section, while focused primarily on programme delivery issues, has been informed by theoretical assumptions. Therefore, the final chapter allows for commentary within these two sections. In the process, it dwells upon opportunities and challenges for the S4D genre, including emerging trends with respect to critical engagement and reforms to practice.

Framing and critiquing S4D

The 'Framework' section of the book featured thoughtful and provocative scene-setting essays. John Sugden, ever the practitioner-scholar, summarised much of his life's work: a commitment to using sport in targeted and sophisticated ways as a vehicle by which to facilitate inter-community dialogue between antagonistic groups in societies under extreme conflict. Sugden evinced a combination of pragmatism about the present and imagination about how it might be improved: he is thus both a sociological realist and an idealist. Neither despairing nor naive, Sugden is well aware about the limits of S4D, as well as its benefits to small numbers of people and communities when conceived and operationalised appropriately. According to Fred Coalter, though, Sugden's sense of perspective and vast experience in S4D is all too rare. He lamented that many S4D practitioners and their financial supporters are too often imbued with fanciful assumptions about what can be achieved by outside interventions and externally conceived programmes. Coalter railed against ad hoc, rather than systematic approaches to S4D, particularly given that development projects are typically located in societies with major conflicts or disadvantaged communities – both are extremely complex and context-specific environments in which to engage locals.

Coalter's concerns about methodology, scope and scale were shared by Giulianotti and Armstrong, who endeavoured to map what has become a vast S4D genre into organisational categories and project types. They concluded that S4D has become overly routinised, this limiting creativity in environments where flexible approaches are needed. The authors also dwelt upon the purposes of development; they concluded that global S4D projects ought to actively engage locals in civil society, and (if so) it is therefore possible for glocalisation to be an enabler of positive change. This view assumes, of course, that S4D programmes actually empower locals, something that Darnell and Hayhurst were sceptical about. Like Giulianotti and Armstrong, they were conscious about the global, international and transnational nature of S4D, which include such a diversity of governments, NGOs, charitable organisations and so on. Both groups of authors favoured critically informed S4D projects: in this view, both practitioners and providers do not simply saunter to the 'rescue' of those deemed less fortunate. Instead there was a progressive or radical awareness among them that S4D ought to be more than remedial; it should be transformative. From the perspective of Darnell and Hayhurst, this meant a robust critique of the neo-liberal ideology underpinning so much institutional and philanthropic backing for S4D. Funding or donating to development programmes is, from that view, more about the political agenda of providers and their commitment to stabilising a neo-liberal global order. Overall, the 'Framework' section provided readers with insights into the researchers' longstanding experience within the S4D genre, critiques of its scope, scale and function, as well as criticisms of the purposes and motivations of development funders and implementers. This provided a basis for interpreting the case studies to follow in the 'From the Field' section of the book.

Delivering and monitoring S4D

The seven chapters in 'From the Field' provided perspectives from a range of geographical, political and socio-cultural environments. They were each different, but there was a range of challenges and concerns with S4D programmes that were common to most, if not all, of the cases under investigation. First, the perennial problem of securing funding for projects was compounded by a lack of follow-up resources. As Katja Siefken, Grant Schofield and Nico Schulenkorf revealed, the *Wokabaot Jalens* programme, which was introduced to assist women in Vanuatu to exercise regularly in groups, was stymied by a national government decision not to renew funding – despite the project having been welcomed by participants as a significant boost to their health. Second, the issue of programme co-ordination. This was especially difficult in the Caribbean, where Zak Kaufman, Brooke Rosenbauer and Gabriela Moore observed that S4D project leaders faced the challenge of delivering a programme across different islands. They also had difficulty keeping track of participants – many of whom were mobile and transient, moving from one island to another.

Third, the need for monitoring and evaluation. This could be something of a dilemma for programme co-ordinators: on the one hand, they are expected to deliver a project on what is often a very limited budget; on the other hand, they are typically required to provide funding bodies with 'proof' that resources have been allocated propitiously and, moreover, that there have been positive outcomes for locals that are measurable. All that said, Justin Richards and Charlie Foster, as well as James Wallis and John Lambert, made strong cases for why M&E ought to be embedded into the structure and funding of S4D projects at the planning stage. Their messages seem to be that unless donor providers are prepared to adequately resource M&E, both in terms of funding and personnel, then it will never be delivered fulsomely. And that has major implications for what we know about the efficacy (or otherwise) of S4D programmes.

Fourth, the gender dynamics of contexts in which S4D is delivered. In some communities, such as in the Middle East, there are very different expectations about whether sport is appropriate for boys and girls. Even if dominant cultural norms can be negotiated, there are then complexities about dress codes that, once again, can be very different according to gender and context. The *Football for Peace* programme, discussed by Wallis and Lambert, has extensive experience in the nuances of gender and culture in inter-faith and cross-community settings in Israel. Meanwhile, for Ruth Jeanes and Jonathon Magee, gender was at the forefront of their focus on the experiences of Zambian females who were involved in a health promotion campaign that included participation in women's football. The authors were especially interested in whether these females had the opportunity, by virtue of their engagement in a S4D programme, to feel empowered as women and subsequently to achieve a greater sense of gender equity in their lives. The results, as we saw, were mixed. The participants relished their involvement in the project and especially their opportunity to play sport, but this appears to have had little impact on the gender dynamics within their families or communities. In fact, some of the women were required to work longer hours at home in order to 'compensate' for time spent playing football.

Fifth, the political and cultural complexities of particular S4D settings. The Middle East, mentioned previously, is an obvious example of the extraordinarily difficult task any 'outsider' has in terms of even contemplating setting up a development programme. Even with local advisers – Arab, Jew, Muslim, Christian (among others) – the learning curve is immense. Even more significantly, Elizabeth Kath and Nanko van Buuren, in their discussion about the role of The Brazilian Institute for Innovations in Social Health (IBISS) in Rio de Janeiro's favelas, took the reader into what might be described as a society exhibiting civil war – specifically in terms of illicit drugs and firearms. Van Buuren, a man of Dutch background, spent many years in Brazil in order to understand the politics and culture of the favelas and the concomitant exploitation of child soldiers. It would not be feasible for a S4D practitioner to enter that domain without the type of local knowledge that van Buuren acquired over a long time. In fact, it would be reckless for a novice to attempt it.

Of course, not all political and cultural complexities involve open conflict. As Oscar Mwaanga and Kabanda Mwansa demonstrated, a key challenge for S4D advocates in Zambia is the need to understand indigenous philosophy and its cultural nuances. Ubuntu, as they showed, is a cornerstone of Zambian social relations, and so to misunderstand this guiding principle is to misjudge the wider community and its needs and aspirations. Intriguingly, while Ubuntu is widely described as focused on groups rather than individuals, thereby providing a sense of 'freedom to be together in a way that enhances everyone's capability to transform themselves in their society', it is also strongly patriarchal (Mwewa, 2011), which helps to explain why Jeanes and Magee observed resistance to the empowerment of women in their Zambian study. There was, none the less, subtle evidence of hybridity in Mwaanga and Mwansa's chapter: the EduSport Foundation they were studying was influenced by both Ubuntu and Christian philosophies, suggesting that there may be prospects for inter-cultural and inter-faith engagements in particular S4D settings.

The 'From the field' section of the book provided important insights into seven S4D cases in a diverse array of places and contexts. For some readers, the practicalities of delivering programmes are their core focus; for others it is the theoretical rigour underpinning such projects. Our quest, in producing this book, was to encourage everyone with an interest in S4D to examine both sides of the development window and, thus, to engage in two-eyed seeing.

We certainly hope that this edited volume will be useful for practitioners and academics in the field of S4D. It has been conceived as an alternative to mythopoeic S4D literature that presents naively optimistic and simplistic 'solutions' to complex social and situational problems. We are hopeful that the book will alert development agencies, funding bodies, sport managers and policymakers to many of the challenges, opportunities and limitations underpinning social development objectives through sport.

Reference

Mwewa, C. (2011). Ubuntu and the Zambian Culture, http://www.izambia. co.zm/news/inews/item/1254-ubuntu-and-the-zambian-culture.html (accessed 2 April 2013).

Index

Printed and bound in Great Britain by
CPI Group (UK) Ltd, Croydon, CR0 4YY